WITHDRAWN
UTSA LIBRARIES

Doing Narrative Research

Doing Narrative Research

Edited by
Molly Andrews, Corinne Squire
and Maria Tamboukou

Los Angeles • London • New Delhi • Singapore

First published 2008

SAGE Publications Ltd
1 Oliver's Yard
55 City Road
London EC1Y 1SP

SAGE Publications Inc.
2455 Teller Road
Thousand Oaks, California 91320

SAGE Publications India Pvt Ltd
B 1/I 1 Mohan Cooperative Industrial Area
Mathura Road, Post Bag 7
New Delhi 110 044

SAGE Publications Asia-Pacific Pte Ltd
33 Pekin Street #02-01
Far East Square
Singapore 048763

Library of Congress Control Number 2007937581

British Library Cataloguing in Publication data

A catalogue record for this book is available from the British Library

ISBN 978-1-4129-1196-2
ISBN 978-1-4129-1197-9 (pbk)

Typeset by CEPHA Imaging Pvt. Ltd., Bangalore, India
Printed in Great Britain by TJ International Ltd., Padstow, Cornwall
Printed on paper from sustainable resources

In memory of Phil Salmon

Wendy Patterson, is a freelance researcher and writer with a particular interest in narrative and sociolinguistics. She is also an editor of academic texts. Her publications include *Strategic Narrative: New Perspectives on the Power of Personal and Cultural Stories* (Lexington Books, 2002).

Ann Phoenix is Professor and Co-Director of the Thomas Coram Research Unit at the Institute of Education, University of London. Her research interests centre on social identities, including those of race, ethnicity, gender and motherhood. Her publications include *Black, White or Mixed Race?* (with Barbara Tizard, 2nd edn, 2002) (Routledge); *Young Masculinities* with Stephen Frosh and Rob Pattman (Palgrave, 2002); and a special issue of the *European Journal of Women's Studies on Intersectionality* (with Pamela Pattynama, 2006).

Catherine Kohler Riessman is Research Professor in the Department of Sociology, Boston College and *Emerita* Professor at Boston University. Her research examines interrupted lives, specifically the narrative accounts women and men develop to make sense of biographical disruptions, such as chronic illness, divorce, and infertility. She teaches frequently in the European Union and Australia as a specialist in qualitative research methods. She has published articles and book chapters; books include *Divorce Talk: Women and Men Make Sense of Personal Relationships* (Rutgers University Press, 1990); *Narrative Analysis* (Sage, 1993); *Qualitative Studies in Social Work Research* (Sage, 1994); and *Narrative Methods for the Human Sciences* (Sage, 2007).

Phillida Salmon was an early advocate of the narrative approach in psychology and the social sciences – a commitment that developed from her central involvement in Personal Construct Theory. Many of her publications illuminate how and why the life story method provides insights and understandings of what it means to be human. She worked for 11 years in the NHS, but taught in universities for most of her career – at Brunel, Surrey and the Institute of Education. After her retirement she worked as a tutor for the Open University, gave courses on narrative and identity at Birkbeck College Centre for Continuing Education and worked as a psychotherapist at the Medical Foundation for the Victims of Torture. One of her major contributions to academic life was her distinctive approach to supervising her numerous PhD students. Her most renowned books are *Living in Time* (Dent, 1985); *Achieving a PhD: Ten Students' Experiences* (Trentham, 1992); *Psychology in the Classroom* (Cassell, 1995); and *Life at School: Education and Psychology* (Constable, 1998). She died of cancer in 2005.

Margareta Hydén is a Professor of Social Work at Linköping University, Sweden. Her areas of interest include domestic violence, narrative and gender studies. Her work has appeared in *Discource & Society, Narrative Inquiry, Feminism & Psychology* and *Child and Family Social Work.* Her recent work focuses on children's narratives of witnessing violence in the family.

Paul Gready is Director of the Centre for Applied Human Rights at the University of York. His most recent publications are *Reinventing Development? Translating Rights-based Approaches from Theory into Practice* (co-edited with Jon Ensor) (Zed books, 2005); and the *No-nonsense Guide to Human Rights* (with Olivia Ball) (New Internationalist, 2006).

What is narrative research?

Corinne Squire, Molly Andrews and Maria Tamboukou

I live in terror of not being misunderstood (Oscar Wilde, 'The Critics as Artist')

In the last two decades, narrative has acquired an increasingly high profile in social research. It often seems as if all social researchers are doing narrative research in one way or another. Yet narrative research, although it is popular and engaging, is difficult; how to go about it is much discussed. People working in this field are frequently approached by students and colleagues, in and outside academia, asking questions like, 'Should I request respondents to tell stories or not?'; 'What happens if my respondents don't produce any narratives?'; 'What *is* a narrative, anyway?' and, most regularly, 'What do I do with the stories now I've got them?' Narrative data can easily seem overwhelming: susceptible to endless interpretation, by turns inconsequential and deeply meaningful.

Unlike many qualitative frameworks, narrative research offers no automatic starting or finishing points. Since the definition of 'narrative' itself is in dispute, there are no self-evident categories on which to focus as there are with content-based thematic approaches, or with analyses of specific elements of language. Clear accounts of how to analyse the data, as found for instance in grounded theory and in Interpretive Phenomenological Analysis, are rare. There are few well-defined debates on conflicting approaches within the field and how to balance them, as there are, for example in the highly epistemologically-contested field of discourse analysis. In addition, unlike other qualitative research perspectives, narrative research offers no overall rules about suitable materials or modes of investigation, or the best level at which to study stories. It does not tell us whether to look for stories in recorded everyday speech, interviews, diaries, tv programmes or newspaper articles; whether to aim for objectivity or researcher and participant involvement; whether to analyse stories' particularity or generality; or what epistemological significance to attach to narratives.

Despite these difficulties, many of us who work with narratives want to continue and develop this work. Most often, perhaps, we frame our research in terms of narrative because we believe that by doing so we are able to see different and sometimes contradictory layers of meaning, to bring them into useful dialogue with each other, and to understand more about individual and social change. By focusing on narrative, we are able to investigate not just how stories are structured and the ways in which they work, but also who produces them and by what means; the mechanisms by which they are consumed; and how narratives are silenced, contested or accepted. All these areas of enquiry can help us describe, understand and even explain important aspects of the world. It is our hope that this book will contribute to this multilevel, dialogic potential of narrative research.

In the rest of this Introduction, we explore further the popularity of narrative research, its diverse histories and its theoretical contradictions, in an effort to describe both its complexity and the possibilities for working productively within that complexity.

Narrative research: popularity and diversity

Narrative is a popular portmanteau term in contemporary western social research. The crowd of much-used summary and outline texts about narrative research (Clandinin and Connelly, 2004; Elliot, 2005; Freeman, 1993; Holstein and Gubrium, 1999; Langellier and Peterson, 2004; Mishler, 1986; Ochs and Capps, 2001; Personal Narratives Group, 1989; Plummer, 2001; Polkinghorne, 1988; Riessman, 1993a, 2008; Roberts, 2001; Sarbin, 1986; Wengraf, 1999) exemplifies its popularity. So does the recent burst of empirically-based texts focused on specific studies, (Andrews, 2007; Emerson and Frosh, 2004; McAdams, 2006; Mishler, 1999; Squire, 2007; Tamboukou, 2003), the rich crop of narratively-themed collections of essays (Andrews et al., 2004; Bamberg and Andrews, 2004; Brockmeier and Carbaugh, 2001; Chamberlayne et al., 2000; Clandinin, 2006; Patterson, 2002; Rosenwald and Ochberg, 1992) and the increasing number of books addressing narrative in specific domains such as development, health, sexuality and social work (Daiute and Lightfoot, 2004; Greenhalgh and Hurwitz, 1998; Hall, 1997; Mattingley, 1988; Plummer, 1995; Riessman, 1993b).

Aside from this current ubiquity within social research, 'narrative' is also a term frequently heard in popular discourse. Often, these popular uses of the term work to connote a particularly acute understanding. Politicians or policymakers suggest they are doing their jobs well because they pay close attention to people's everyday 'narratives', or because they themselves have a joined-up 'narrative' of what they are doing. Journalists claim a good understanding of events by spelling out for their audiences the underlying 'narrative'. Citizens are urged to achieve better comprehension of difficult circumstances by reading or hearing the 'stories' of those affected – for example, the World Health Organisation portrays the HIV pandemic to us through individual 'Stories of Tragedy and Hope' (http://www.who.int/features/2003/09/en/). Sometimes, though, public 'narratives' are treated with suspicion, as obfuscators of the 'realities' they gloss and hide. In addition, the term 'narrative' is used descriptively in popular discourse, as it is in academic humanities disciplines, to indicate the line of thematic and causal progression in cultural form such as in a film or a novel. Here again, 'narrative' may be a good thing – exciting, compelling, insightful – but it may also be criticized – as over-complex, over-simple, too long, too conventional.

Both in popular culture and in social research, then, 'narrative' is strikingly diverse in the way it is understood. In popular culture, it may suggest insight into – or concealment of – important biographical patterns or social structures – or, simply, good or less good forms of representational sequence. In social research, 'narrative' also refers to a diversity – of topics of study, methods of investigation and analysis, and theoretical orientations. It displays different definitions within different fields, and the topics of hot debate around these definitions shift from year to year.

On account of this prolixity, many accounts of narrative research begin by exploring the field's different contemporary forms. This Introduction is no exception, but it approaches the task a little differently. It sets out two overlapping fields within which narrative research's diversity appears: those of narrative research's history, and its theory. For, we shall argue, narrative research's incoherence derives partly from its divergent beginnings, and partly from the theoretical fault lines that traverse it.

Where does narrative research come from? Historical contradictions

The antecedents of contemporary narrative social research are commonly located in two parallel academic moves (Andrews et al., 2004; Rustin, 2000).[1] The first is the post-war rise of humanist approaches within western sociology and psychology. These approaches posed holistic, person-centred approaches, often including attention to individual case studies, biographies and life histories, against positivist empiricism (Bertaux, 1981; Bruner, 1990; Polkinghorne, 1988; Sarbin, 1986). The second academic antecedent to contemporary narrative social research is Russian structuralist and, later, French poststructuralist (Barthes, 1977; Culler, 2002; Genette, 1979; Todorov, 1990), postmodern (Foucault, 1972; Lyotard, 1984), psychoanalytic (Lacan, 1977) and deconstructionist (Derrida, 1977) approaches to narrative within the humanities. These approaches had effects on social research in the English-speaking world from the late 1970s, initially through the work of Althusser, Lacan and Foucault, film and literary critics and feminist and socialist theorists, as it appeared in translations; and in journals such as *Ideology and Consciousness* and *mf*, and in books like *Changing the Subject* (Henrique et al., 1984) and later, in the US, Gergen's (1991) and Sampson's (1993) work.[2] Such work was often interested in story structure and content. But unlike the humanist narrative move within social research, it was concerned with narrative fluidity and contradiction, with unconscious as well as conscious meanings, and with the power relations within which narratives become possible (Parker, 2003; Tamboukou, this volume). It assumed that multiple, disunified subjectivities were involved in the production and under-standing of narratives, rather than singular, agentic storytellers and hearers, and it was preoccupied with the social formations shaping language and subjectivity. In this tradition, the storyteller does not tell the story, so much as she/he is told by it.

Despite the theoretical differences, there are many convergences between these humanist and poststructuralist traditions within current narrative research. Most researchers are affected by both conceptual histories. For example, Wendy Hollway and Tony Jefferson use what they have called 'free association narrative interviewing' (2000) to map individuals' biographical accounts of crime in the community. They also apply psychoanalytic understandings of fractured subjects to these individual biographies, and draw on poststructural formulations of the uncertainties of language.[3] Similarly, Mark Freeman (2004) traces the life histories of individual artists, but at the same time he positions these life histories within the modern western narratives of art that 'write' these lives, and he also pays attention to the unconscious structures of meaning that traverse life stories.

More generally, humanist and the poststructuralist traditions of narrative research are brought together by their shared tendency to treat narratives as modes of resistance to existing structures of power. This tendency may involve, for instance, collecting the oral histories of working class communities. It may mean investigating the (auto)biographical expression of women's subject positions: how women write within the contexts of their lives; and how other women read their texts within the conditions of their own lived, subjective place within power relations (Hydén, this volume; Stanley, 1992; Tamboukou, 2003). It may stimulate a linguistic study of the storytelling sophistication of African–American adolescents (Labov, 1972). Some narrative researchers use extensive life histories in order to understand how personal lives traverse social change (Andrews, 2007; Chamberlayne et al., 2002). Others deploy narratives to try to change people's relations to their social circumstances. This is the terrain of narrative therapy and other therapies that use storied material, as well as of some community research that enables collective storytelling (Sliep et al., 2004). Still other researchers analyse the conditions and effectiveness of community and 'public' narratives (Gready, this volume; Plummer, 1995, 2001).

Politics thus seems at times to bring the two historical trends in narrative research together (Squire, 2005). Nevertheless, their theoretical assumptions about subjectivity, language, the social and narrative itself remain in contradiction. Current syntheses of the two often involve, for instance, maintenance of a humanist conception of a singular, unified subject, at the same time as the promotion of an idea of narrative as always multiple, socially constructed and constructing, reinterpreted and reinterpretable. These contradictions do not go unnoticed. But many researchers think it more important to do useful and innovative work across the contradictions, rather than trying to resolve conflicting positions that are historically and disciplinarily distinct, as well as logically incommensurable.

Theoretical divisions in narrative research

The historically-produced theoretical bricolage in narrative research is largely responsible for the current wide variability in how researchers conceptualize what is narrative, how to study it and why it is important – as material, method, or route to understanding psychological or social phenomena, or all of these.

The following section of the Introduction sketches some obvious and some less obvious theoretical division in contemporary narrative research.

One of the most well-rehearsed differences is between research focused on the spoken recounting of particular past *events* that happened to the narrator, the person telling the story – classically described in Labov's (Labov and Waletsky, 1967; see also Patterson, this volume) work on event narratives – and *experience-centred* work (see Squire, this volume), exploring stories that range in length from segments of interviews, to many hours of life histories, and that may be about general or imagined phenomena, things that happened to the narrator or distant matters they've only heard about. This second kind of narrative research encompasses varying media, too: not just speech, but also writing – scraps of letters, laundry lists, extensive multi-volume diaries – visual materials – photo albums, video diaries – and narratives inhering in objects and actions – the arrangement of objects on mantelpieces, the everyday activities of shopping, cooking and eating (Seale, 2004). Such expansion of narrative data seems to some to give the term 'narrative' a meaning so broad as to rob it of descriptive, let alone explanatory power (Craib, 2004). Yet throughout this second field of work, the life experiences that infuse the data constitute the primary topic, the true 'narrative' (Bruner, 1990).

What is shared across both event- and experience-centred narrative research, is that there are assumed to be individual, internal representations of phenomena – events, thoughts and feelings – to which narrative gives external *expression*. Event-centred work assumes that these internal and individual representations are more or less constant. Experience-centred research stresses that such representations vary drastically over time, and across the circumstances within which one lives, so that a single phenomenon may produce very different stories, even from the same person.

A third form of narrative research, which addresses the co-constructed narratives that develop, for instance in conversations between people or email exchanges, does not fit into either of these two initial fields of event- and experience-oriented narrative research. This third field *may* operate with the assumption that its more 'social,' co-constructed, stories are expressions of internal cognitive or affective states. However, most often, it views narratives as forms of social code, addressing stories as dialogically constructed (Bakhtin, 1981) and not as expressions of internal states. Researchers in this field are interested, rather, in the social patterns and functioning of stories, whether the 'stories' are short, disjointed sequences of conversation or much more extensive representations that exemplify broad cultural narratives (Abell et al., 2004; Bamberg, 2006; Georgakopoulou, 2007; Plummer, 2001; Squire, 2007).

Narrative research's divergences over whether stories are representing internal individual states or external social circumstances, relate to another dichotomy. Are narratives shaped by the *audiences* to whom they are delivered, and if so, to what extent? For some narrative researchers, the most interesting features of personal narratives lie in what they tell us about individual thinking or feeling, whether the narratives themselves are about events or experiences (Chamberlayne et al., 2002; Hollway and Jefferson, 2000; Labov, 1997). Other researchers are more concerned with the social production of narratives by their audiences: in how personal stories get built up through the conversational sequences in people's talk (Bamberg, 2006; Georgakopoulou, 2007); or how they are tied up with the performance and negotiation of social identities in a common space of meaning (Phoenix, this volume; Riessman, 1993a, 2008; Salmon and Riessman, this volume).[4] Some narrative researchers are occupied more widely with how narratives follow, are constrained by, or resist, larger social patterns of social and cultural storytelling (Gready, this volume; Malson, 2004; Plummer, 2001). Narrative researchers may also be interested in how researchers' own 'stories' vary, depending on the social and historical places from which they 'listen' to their data (Andrews, this volume; Riessman, 2002). These primarily social research interests are seen in some narrative researchers who think of stories themselves as expressions of personal states, as well as in those who treat stories as manifestations of social or cultural patterns, though they are commonest among the latter.

Of course, researchers who are mainly interested in what seems like the simplest kind of stories, event narratives told by individuals, also acknowledge that stories are shaped by their listeners. But for them, these social factors are not the defining or most interesting aspects of personal narratives. Similarly, most biographical and life history researchers accept that social formations shape personal stories. Indeed, they often work with this interaction, tracing the impact of social factors on individual stories and 'reading' the significance of social change in those stories. However, some biographical researchers often claim an irreducible personal bedrock for personal narratives, based in the fundamentals of human experience, which are often unconscious, and therefore not fully reachable by social analysis. Such researchers are not, generally, too interested in the narrative 'performance' of identities in social contexts, the interpersonal construction or 'co-construction' of narratives at the level of sequences of utterances or across an interview, or the shaping of personal narratives by larger social and cultural narratives or metanarratives.

This division between socially- and individually-oriented narrative research relates to yet another theoretical divergence: that between narrative researchers who are interested in the *agency* of narratives and narrators, and those who are either uninterested, or who argue that agency is not linked to narrative. Researchers who are interested in narratives as individualized accounts of experience tend to be the most convinced of the significance of stories as ways of expressing and building personal identity and agency (Bruner, 1990; see also Squire, this volume). Work that addresses event narratives, or stories co-constructed in talk-in-interaction, tends to be least interested in issues of agency, most aware of the varied and 'troubled' subject positions occupied by narrators (see Georgakopoulou, 2007; Labov, 1997; Phoenix, this volume). Narrative research that is interested in unconscious elements of experience is also sceptical about the possibility of individual 'agency', let alone its operation in and through narrative (Craib, 2004). Whether or not such narrative research – event-focused, interested in co-construction and positioning, or psychoanalytically-inflected – operates with a conception of an agentive subject, it does not tie that concept to an assumption that narrative 'makes sense of' and enables action within lives. This assumption of a necessary link between narrative and agency is found most strongly in approaches to narrative that focus on personal experience.

However, many researchers who are concerned with the social and cultural place of narrative, are also interested in the socially effective 'agency' of personal stories. Sometimes they pursue this interest by offering a broadly humanist assertion of individuals' and collectives' potential to make changes, alongside a loosely poststructural account of shifting systems of representation and representations' interactive relations with material realities. Alternatively, the concept of performance is often applied in narrative work, lifted from Goffmanian accounts of social roles, and from Butler's (1993) post-Goffman performativity,[5] in order to retain a potential for agency within a theoretical framework that puts it in question. This is a good example of contemporary narrative research's finessing of theoretical incommensurabilities, in this case by ignoring the different concepts of the subject in play around 'performance' or – at best – hoping to resolve them by what has become known as 'strategic essentialism,' that is, the assumption of agentive subjects where politically expedient.[6]

These kinds of lived-with contradictions in narrative research refer us back to the way in which narrative research's emancipatory aims often bring together historically and theoretically distinct traditions of narrative work. Certainly, some researchers' concern with whether narratives – and their work on them – 'make a difference' may lead them to adopt an optimistic position on narrative agency that seems at odds with their theoretical commitments to, for instance, the socially constructing powers of language, and that can be too simple really to address the involved and politically intractable situations within which personal narratives appear and are studied (see Gready, this volume).

A recent articulation of the divisions within narrative research has taken the form of posing 'small' against 'big' stories (Bamberg, 2006; Freeman, 2006; Georgakopoulou, 2007). Those on the side of 'small' narratives argue that we need to pay more attention to the micro-linguistic and social structure of the everyday, small narrative phenomena that occur 'naturally' between people. These 'small stories' may concern unfolding, anticipated, imaginary, habitual and indefinite events and states, as well as past, singular 'events'; they may also, for some, involve repeated content or themes spread out across representations (see Phoenix, this volume). They occur in spoken language, but also in writing – text messages, for example – paralanguage and perhaps even in action. This emphasis on 'small stories' brings together the Labovian commitment to research on 'naturally'-occurring stories, and conversation-analytic as well as some discourse-analytic commitments to studying 'natural' language, and applies them to a wider and more social range of narrative phenomena than has previously been addressed in this way, including interactions of the kind previously investigated mostly by conversation and discourse analysts (Bamberg, 2006; Georgakopoulou, 2007). The emphasis on 'small stories' tends to prioritize 'event' over experience, and socially-oriented over individually-oriented narrative research; but it formulates 'event' in a broadened way, and pays attention to the 'social' in its most microsocial versions, as well as in its wider, cultural variants.

Against such 'small story' arguments, Freeman (2006), Wengraf (1999) and other biographical and life story researchers defend the experiential richness, reflectiveness and validity of big stories. However, writers on the small story side of the debate do recognize the separate value of big story research, and big story researchers often pay attention to the small aspects of their data. For many, the big/small division may not be too significant. Moreover, Freeman (2006) points out the parallel tendencies in some 'small story' research to claim it is the 'real thing', and in some 'big story' research to claim an immanent validating identity behind its narratives. These claims can return proponents on both sides of the argument to the unproblematically expressivist approach to narrative described earlier in this Introduction.

The 'small' versus 'big' story argument overlaps with another contemporary debate over the *tyranny of the transcript*. Some narrative researchers – for instance those who work with 'small' narratives, or with visual materials – criticize the hegemony, in the narrative field, of interview-obtained transcripts of people talking, usually one at a time, often reflexively, about their life experiences; and the large, content-based, biographical and social interpretations that narrative researchers derive from such materials. The criticisms thus address both the restricted narrative material privileged by transcripts – mostly speech, rarely paralinguistic material, other media, interpersonal interactions or other social context – and the content-based analysis that is consequently prioritized. However, the polarity between transcript-based and other forms of narrative research can be overstated. Approaches that are primarily concerned with narrative structure and context (including 'small story' ones), also unavoidably address content. Thematic approaches are, increasingly, explicitly interested in context, and in any case *have* to address structure and context, at least implicitly, since the meanings in which they deal are embedded in these. As with the similar and long-running debate about levels of discourse analysis, a dialogic approach that advocates doing both kinds of research at the same time is a conceivable and helpful solution (Wetherell, 1998).

A more interesting aspect of the alleged conflict between structural, content and context-based approaches is that it draws attention to two other important, though largely implicit, divisions within narrative research. The first of these relates to the status of *language* in contemporary narrative research. Paradoxically, a cursory or non-existent attention to language characterizes the narrative social research field. Narrative is always defined first of all as a kind of language. Yet research that focuses on narrative as an expression of individual experience, or as a mirror of social realities, tends to bypass the language of stories in order to focus on their meanings, or the social positionings they produce or reflect. Approaches that focus on event narratives or narratives in conversation tend to be interested in underlying cognitive structures, or in the social functionings of narrative, 'what narrative does'. For many researchers, narrative language is again therefore secondary. It is the transparent window onto narrative's universal human, possibly even biological, significance in individual and social life, its involvement in all patterns of interaction, ethics and 'living in time' (Salmon, 1985; see also Bruner, 1990; MacIntyre, 1984; Seale, 2004). This narrative transcendentalism is very rarely defended; it is assumed to be a self-evident truth. The 'small story' argument, as well as other work that emphasizes the sociality of narrative and its separateness from agency, tends to undo this certainty about narrative's universality and redemptiveness. But the rapid passing-over of narrative language to get to narrative 'meaning' or 'function,' is a broad trend in current narrative research, affecting small and large story study alike. A fetishization of narrative language in social research would not be a happy remedy. However, a slower and more attentive reading of narrative language might be (Derrida, 1985).

Another theoretical division related to the place of language in narrative research is that between researchers who assume that their data will contain relatively stable and unified narratives of experience, identity and the social world, at least in a particular time and social context; and those who are less convinced that such narratives can be accessed by them, or even that they are produced. The degree to which narrative researchers adopt this second, *postmodern* take on narrative, relates strongly to their engagement with language's complexity and non-transparency.[7] A postmodern approach is commonly argued to compromise the political engagement which many narrative researchers seek. However, narrative research that engages thoroughly with postmodernism does not necessarily exhibit such compromises. Some narrative researchers operate with an extended version of postmodern or poststructuralist critiques of 'narrative', formulating narrative research as a poststructural enterprise, aware of narratives' social positioning as discourses and of the problematics of subjectivity and story 'meaning' (Burman, 2003; Edley, 2002; Parker, 2003, 2004; Tamboukou, 2003). Such thoroughgoing poststructural takes on narrative are relatively infrequent, but they are important reminders of where many narrative researchers' theoretical concerns with language, subjectivity, discourse and power relations might lead, if they followed them more thoroughly.

One area of poststructuralist theoretical interest has given rise to an extensive debate within the narrative field. This is psychoanalysis, particularly those forms of it that are inflected by Lacanian and postlacanian concerns with the psyche as a form of language, even a 'narrative', in itself. In these accounts, narratives represent unconscious emotions, as well as conscious cognitions and feelings. Consequently, narratives are rarely straightforward. Often, they work as forms of dissembling or 'telling stories' (Craib, 2004). Sometimes, you won't get the 'whole story'; and all stories will be incomplete, since experience and subjectivity cannot fully make their way into language.

Psychoanalytic takes on narrative research try to address aspects of experience or subjectivity such as anxiety, or desire, that fall *outside narrative* – that seem difficult or impossible to represent in narrative, or to understand from a straightforward approach to story structure or content (Burman, 2003; Chamberlayne et al., 2002; Frosh, 2002; Hollway and Jefferson, 2000; Sclater, 2003).[8] Debate between these positions relates both to their different theoretical formulations of the unconscious, and to the varied extent to which psychoanalytically-influenced narrative researchers claim interpretive authority. Some psychoanalytic work on narrative interprets research materials 'as if' they were materials from an analytic session. More cautiously, other psychoanalytic researchers treat their narrative data as representations of more generally found individual or social structures of feeling. Outside this psychoanalytically-inflected work, questions about the interpretive authority of even the more cautious psychoanalytically-inflected work are frequent, and are often accompanied by queries about the explanatory value of the 'unconscious' as a concept. Many narrative researchers reject psychoanalytic frameworks on the grounds that detailed analyses of story form and content can generate equally rich and nuanced understandings, without needing to assume the existence of an untestable 'unconscious' entity and set of processes (Wetherell, 2005).

But the problems of what is 'in' narrative that is not straightforwardly said or written, and what cannot even be brought into it, remain. They are crucial for many narrative researchers, working in widely divergent theoretical frameworks. Sometimes, these difficulties are formulated in terms of storytellers and story hearers cognitively, emotionally and socially divergent narrative worlds, that may or may not be brought into a workable convergence (Hydén, this volume; Ricoeur, 1984; Salmon and Riessman, this volume;). These problems have also given rise to considerable current interest in how to analyse elements of paralanguage in narrative – tone of voice, pauses, laughter – as well as visual elements such as eye movements, facial expression, body posture and gestures, and more broadly, aspects of emotionality and embodiment within narratives. Theoretically, these elements are difficult to incorporate within existing models of narratives. Moreover, they are hard to define and measure, and, just as much as language structure and content, they vary across social and cultural situations. They may prove just as contentious for narrative research as 'the unconscious'. Contemporary interest in them indicates, though, the continuing and growing division between researchers who are prepared to settle for relatively straightforward spoken, written, visual, object or action sequences as their materials, and those who are concerned that this specificity about what constitutes the 'language' of narratives, is inadequate.

Finally the problem of what may lie 'outside' narrative raises another issue which implicitly divides narrative researchers, but which is often understood as uniting them. Narrative is almost always said to be about *time* – not just succession in time, but change through time (Brockmeier, 1993; Bruner, 1990; Ricoeur, 1984). Time, psychically processed, is thought to make us into subjects through its articulation in narrative. Transformation – meaning, not always, but frequently, improvement – is also assumed to be integral to narrative: in the story itself; in the lives of those telling it; even in researchers' own understandings of it.

Through this emphasis, representations of simple contingencies – events that follow each other but that have no necessary relation to each other – are taken 'out' of the narrative category. Representations of causal but not chronological or experiential succession are also seen as theoretical, not 'narrative', in nature. Yet from a psychoanalytic perspective, temporally separate events, and events whose relations are not fully describable, may lie next to each other in the archaeological narrative of the unconscious, without any personally meaningful succession being available to us.[9] And researchers trying to build social or psychological theory certainly see a large difference between their models and theories, and the highly particular 'theoretical' causal sequences that characterize personal narratives.

For researchers who are interested in non-verbal aspects of narrative, such as paralinguistic characteristics, moving and still images and objects, narrative chronology also has temporal and semantic patterns that are difficult to assimilate into the conventional view of narrative 'time'. Even film, which itself tells stories in time, involves image successions whose semantic relationships are more complex than those in a verbally told story. Increasingly, even narrative researchers dealing with fairly 'conventional' personal interview data that represent temporal succession and that themselves unfold in time, are reappraising assumptions about progression and transformation in narrative time. When we revisit data, for instance, it is too simple to say that time has sequentially or experientially 'moved on'. We are different people, and the pasts of the data, and our own present reading situation, are as much 'another country' as are materials gathered in situations unfamiliar to us (Andrews, this volume). Describing these complexities temporally, as the co-presence of past and future in the present, for example, does not necessarily capture their multilayered quality better than a spatialized or historical description, unless we assume autobiographical time's priority for narrative research.

Thus, a focus on chronological or experienced 'time' may close off information about unconscious realities and material causalities, both of which may order stories outside time: about non-verbal narrative sequences; and about other, for instance, spatialized and sociohistorical, ways of understanding succession (Clark, 2003; Frosh, 2002; Harrison, 2004; Hollway and Jefferson, 2000; Mishler, 1999; Riessman, 2002; Tamboukou, 2003). Narrative social research has some catching up to do here with literary and cultural studies and social theory, particularly those developed by feminists, which have long adopted more nuanced approaches towards narrative sequencing. This work recognizes, for instance, the co-presence of futurity and past in the present, the reconstruction of the past by new 'presents', and the projection of the present into future imaginings, in ways that do not give an implicit priority to personally experienced time (Mulvey, 1991; Stanley, 1992; Steedman, 1987).

A number of narrative social researchers are now putting into question the use of 'time' as a narrative-defining trope. Psychoanalytically-influenced narrative researchers have been among those most ready to address alternative temporalities – those of the unconscious as well as of lived realities – in their interpretations. Moreover, in a kind of translation of Freud's idea of *nachträglichkeit* (deferred action) into social research, narrative researchers more generally are becoming increasingly interested in the complex effects of temporal gaps and reinterpretations on our approaches to narrative data (Andrews, this volume; Riessman, 2002; Salmon and Riessman, this volume). At times, *state, social, historical* or *spatial* succession and change are taken as alternative or additional narrative criteria. (see Andrews, this volume; Langellier and Peterson, 1992; Patterson, this volume, on Polanyi, 1985; also, Clark, 2003; Tamboukou, 2003 and this volume).

The broadening of the concept of narrative to include sequences whose ordering occurs in dimensions other than those of chronologically, verbally and experientially-ordered time could again seem to some to give narrative research a generality that trivializes it (Craib, 2004). However, narrative remains defined in all this work by sequences with a specific order, temporal or otherwise, which takes it beyond description; and by a particularity that distinguishes it from theoretical representations.

This sense of 'narrative' as the ordering of particularities fits well with some rather underacknowledged aspects of the term's meanings. Narrative's Latin etymology lies in knowing, not telling. Without overextending its remit, or treating personal narratives as universal theories, research on narratives as ordered representations can indeed claim to be mapping forms of *local* knowledge or 'theory'. Narrative research thus converges across its differences, not so much in its political interests, but in the possibility of having microsocial and micropolitical effects through the local knowledges that it produces. These knowledges may be particular, but they can enter into dialogue with each other and produce, as happens across the chapters in this volume, larger and more general, though still situated, narrative knowledges.

Narrative research is a multilevel, interdisciplinary field and any attempt to simplify its complexity would not do justice to the richness of approaches, theoretical understandings and unexpected findings that it has offered. We have thus imagined this book as a compass for navigating the rough seas of narrative research; a hands-on resource that can suggest paths to take, but that also allows for diversions and excursions.

Organization of the book

The idea for this book came from a series of narrative symposia which we have run, and continue to run, at our Centre for Narrative Research, based at the University of East London. In the opening paragraph of this Introduction, we described the kinds of questions that we have often heard from those who wish to use narrative in their research, but are not exactly sure how to go about it. In response to questions like these, through the years we have invited narrative researchers from a wide range of fields (for instance education, politics, health) to spend a day talking about the nuts and bolts of their work. Those who came to talk about their work were asked to address a problem or set of problems which they have encountered, to provide a concrete demonstration of how they analyse their data, and finally, to provide an annotated bibliography for participants. Invariably, the days were long, intense and very rewarding. In this book, we have tried as much as possible to replicate the framework of the symposia, specifically the concrete demonstration of how to work with narrative methods. The key challenge we faced in the collective creation of this book was to capture the dynamism which had characterized the symposia. We asked our contributors (all of whom had participated in one or another of the symposia) not to present their research findings, but rather to give readers a sense of how they used narrative methods in their scholarly pursuits.

The book begins by setting out some of the key paradigms within narrative research, moves to addressing issues of positionality, reflexivity and power which lie at the heart of narrative research, and closes with chapters which illustrate how narrative can be used to investigate real social problems, and considers some of the ethical dilemmas which researchers confront in their scholarly pursuits.

In Chapter 1 Wendy Patterson introduces narrative analysis by describing the classic and highly influential Labovian account of the structure or 'syntax' of the personal experience narrative – the story of a single event that happened to the narrator in the past. Patterson uses a short extract from her own work on personal narrative of the experience of trauma as a model for analysis, and through it some limitations of the Labovian approach are highlighted. This leads to a consideration of event-centric versus experiential approaches to narrative analysis, and an exposition of the more interpretive experiential perspective.

Chapter 2, by Corinne Squire, examines two large and interrelated narrative research perspectives. It starts by describing the assumptions underlying the experience-centred approach with which Chapter 1 leaves us, an extremely powerful take on narrative as integral to people's lives and sense of themselves, which addresses the semantics rather than the syntax of narrative. The chapter moves on to sketch out that approach's modes of material collection and analysis. Examining the difficulties associated with this approach's potentially over-strong interpretive claims, over-psychological framework and simplifying assumptions about subjects and time, it explores attempts that have been made to develop such experience-centred models within more context-rich frameworks that pay attention to social discourses and practices, and cultural genres. The chapter enumerates the continuing contradictions and continuing difficulties associated with these moves. The chapter returns to many of the narrative examples used by Patterson, but adds a number from Squire's own research, involving stories that HIV positive South Africans tell about living with the virus.

In Chapter 3 Ann Phoenix analyses smaller-scale, interpersonal aspects of 'context', in particular, the interpersonal relations between interviewer and interviewee within which narratives are produced. The chapter analyses the ways in which narratives are co-constructed within such interpersonal contexts. The aim is to demonstrate the complexities of understanding that can be achieved through different levels of analysis of narrative context. The chapter examines how, in interviews, people both demonstrate awareness of what 'society' thinks of them, and also justify their individual positioning, moving in and out of 'troubled subject positions'. Such social and emotional contexts also change over time. To demonstrate this approach, the chapter uses extracts from a study of social identities, drawn from an interview with a white mother of a child of mixed-race parentage. In contexts such as these, narrative analysis provides a means to consider the multilayered ways in which research participants understand their situations.

Chapter 4 is an exchange between Phillida ('Phil') Salmon and Cathy Riessman, two very senior narrative scholars, and reflects Bakhtin's sentiment: 'To live means to participate in dialogue …'. Here, the reader must confront the 'messiness' which characterizes narrative practice, and some of the clarity offered by the previous chapters begins to fall away. The authors were originally asked to co-write a chapter on narrative analysis, but they responded by suggesting that instead, they contribute a written exchange of ideas between them. We accepted this, regarding it as fitting that their writing about dialogic narrative would take the form of a dialogue.

Sadly, however, Phil Salmon died before the dialogue could be completed, but we have included it in this collection as we feel that it represents the dynamic and contested nature of narrative enquiry. 'Narratives are, in a fundamental sense, co-constructed' Phil Salmon writes, and Cathy Riessman develops this point further: 'The speaker's intent is always met with the analyst's interpretation, which in turn, is situated in discourses, history, politics and culture. It is never ending, always open to re-interpretation'. The meaning of words is never constant, neither for speakers nor listeners. Narrative research which is based on conversations between people is invariably a process of ongoing negotiation of meaning. People answer the questions which they think we are asking them, and we respond to the answers with which we think they have provided us.

Our understanding of their words is always contingent upon our ability to imagine the worlds they are trying to convey. This capacity to see other than what we know changes in time, appearing both to diminish and to grow: sometimes we can no longer find the feelings and dreams which were once ours, and at other times, having seen more of our own life appears to give us greater access to understanding parts of the lives of others which had once evaded us. And so the meaning we discern in the narratives we collect and help to create is always in the process of transformation, is always a becoming.

In Chapter 5, Molly Andrews explores some of the implications of this for narrative research; in Rosaldo's words 'all interpretations are provisional' (Rosaldo, 1989: 8). There is no 'view from nowhere' (Nagel, 1986), and neither is our positioning constant. Rather, in the course of our lives passions shift; those things which we thought we knew well become strange to us; the objects of our affection grow closer to us, or further away. All of this affects us as people, and as researchers. And when we return to our data, our new and altered selves often see things differently from before. There has been an increasing tendency among narrative researchers to revisit former research projects, and this chapter reports on some of those journeys. Central to this discussion is a consideration of what constitutes an 'adequate interpretation'. Does someone have special analytic insights simply because they gathered the original data? What right, if any, do we have to challenge the interpretations which researchers make about their work? Is there ever an end-point to narrative analysis, or is it always, and only, 'provisional'? The chapter considers the ongoing relationship between power, history and biography, and how shifting circumstances both of the individual and of society, cause us to understand ourselves and the world which surrounds us in forever changing ways.

In Chapter 6, Maria Tamboukou picks up the threads of the relationship between power, discourse and history, and offers a Foucauldian approach for using narratives to re-imagine history, investigating the interrelationships between narrative, subjectivity and power. The chapter is divided into three sub-sections, namely, (a) genealogical problematics, a section discussing the particular problems that Foucault's theories raise in narrative research; (b) questions of method, a section where the 'how' of a Foucauldian approach to narrative analysis is under scrutiny; (c) emerging themes, a section where the author draws on her own research to demonstrate some of the research effects of a Foucauldian approach to narrative analysis. Tamboukou argues that rather than being considered as representing realitiy/ies, narratives should be seen as productive: narratives do things, they constitute realities, shaping the social rather than being determined by it. Indeed narrative research informed by Foucauldian insights is particularly concerned with the processes, procedures and apparatuses, whereby truth, power knowledge and desire are interrelated in the production of narratives and in their effects. But are narrative researchers or practitioners and professionals who draw on narrative methods always aware of the effects of what they do? '... [Narrative researchers] ... know what they do. They frequently know why they do what they do; but what they don't know is what what they do does' (paraphrasing Foucault, cited in Dreyfus and Rabinow, 1982: 187). The importance of this question is dramatically illustrated in the chapter which follows.

In Chapter 7, Margaretta Hydén takes up the theme of narrating sensitive topics by problematizing the very concept of the sensitive topic itself and showing how it is relationally and culturally defined, as well as embedded in power/knowledge relations. Making a useful distinction between sensitive events and sensitive topics, Hydén focuses on methodological strategies in the process of researching sensitive issues in contested areas. She argues that narrative analysis is particularly well-suited for this task, since it gives informants the possibility to develop their points of view uninterrupted and the researcher the opportunity to analyse their stories as emerging in the interviews, in their entirety. The context of the interview thus becomes a central site for the analysis of the chapter, which draws on Hydén's experiences as a social worker and as an academic, particularly focusing on her work with battered women. In this light Hydén addresses the problem of power relations between the interviewer and the interviewee, showing that imbalances and hierarchies are not always well-defined and/or established, Foucault's model of power becoming the theoretical underpinning of such an approach. She further discusses the issue of victimization of the interviewee's experience and finally points to the risks of the circulation of narratives on sensitive points beyond the control of the narrator and indeed the researcher, a problem that is further developed in the final chapter which follows.

In Chapter 8, Paul Gready reflects on the public life of narratives, considering the effects of narrative research once its results reach the public realm, and how the possibility of such effects must be factored into the research. Gready particularly deals with the methodological problem of whether researchers need to anticipate the public life of narratives, and if so in what contexts, why and how. In particular, the chapter focuses on oral testimony narratives, which are an increasingly common focus of interest and research. Evidence from a range of sources – advocacy networks, truth and reconciliation processes, Holocaust testimonial video archives – suggests both the arbitrariness of testimonial uptake and circulation in the public sphere, and challenges to testifiers' sense of control and ownership when their testimony takes on an unanticipated public life. The main argument made here is that research on public narratives, without an understanding of the public sphere, of the unsafe spaces surrounding the (sometimes) safe spaces of delivery, can become a violation of trust. With voice comes power; the lack of control over representation in human rights reports, the courtroom, the media or elsewhere, marks a return to powerlessness. In this context, to speak is not a one-off event, but a process, spanning various narrations and interpretations. Using case studies, the chapter outlines the methodological challenges posed by the increasingly public life of personal narratives, suggests ways of addressing these problems methodologically and details how individuals and organizations are reclaiming control and ownership over their own life stories, thus outlining a methodological ethics and politics for contemporary testimonial research.

We have ordered the chapters in this way because for us this sequencing was most compelling, developing as it does from basic models of narrative practice to the less concrete and ethically pregnant questions of what happens to our work after it is released it into the public world. We are of course aware that readers may choose to dip in and out of the collection in a different sequence, depending upon their interests and preoccupations, and thus we would also like to suggest a few alternative ways of clustering the chapters.

A number of chapters deal with what is referred to as 'sensitive issues'. Although Gready and Hydén deal with this topic most explicitly, there are a number of other chapters which also explore some of the difficulties which come with this territory. Sometimes sensitive topics reveal themselves not in what is said, but in what cannot be said, or cannot be expressed coherently. Phil Salmon's piece opens with an attempted suicide, and immediately conveys the cost of telling stories that are missing their connective tissue. Percy's suicide attempt makes no sense to us because it does not appear to be endowed with meaning by Percy. His story doesn't 'work' because he does not offer his listener an account of his actions which can render them 'socially and culturally comprehensible'. It is perhaps this very aspect of narrative deficiency that has contributed to his attempt to end his life. Ann Phoenix, in her chapter on 'mixed-race' children, discusses how individuals establish 'an entitlement to talk about racism'. Clare, who is white, describes herself as one who has experienced racism, and indeed feels that in some situations she has experienced more 'prejudice' than her black husband. Key to this discussion are issues relating to what is considered 'sensitive', who can claim to have insight into this, and how issues of power and positionality enter into the interview situation. In Squire's chapter on South African HIV stories we see how individuals meet the challenge to narrate experiences which are both everyday and life-threatening.

Issues of power and narratability run throughout many of the chapters. Maria Tamboukou adopts a Foucauldian analysis to her work with autobiographical narratives of women artists, highlighting the potential of genealogical work to uncover 'new questions to interrogating truths of our world'. One of the benefits of adopting such a lens is that it recognizes the forever changing circumstances of our lives, and of our world. This theme is demonstrated in the exchange between Phil Salmon and Cathy Riessman, both in terms of the issues which they raise, and also in Phil Salmon's unforeseen death, which renders the communication with a different layer of meaning than it would have otherwise contained. Molly Andrews also explores the theme of the changing questions that guide our research, and the dynamic nature not only of our interpretations, but of our data themselves.

Wendy Patterson's opening chapter of the book helps us to think carefully about what constitutes a narrative, and she demonstrates what can be lost if one focuses exclusively on a linear model of narrative structure. The story of Percy, referred to above, demonstrates the importance we attach to apparent coherence and meaning of narratives. His tale doesn't work because it is not offered in a cultural framework which is recognizable, and hence he is abandoned by others, and even by us, his potential audience. Context cannot be stripped away, nor can it be separated from questions of meaning. Squire's chapter draws our attention to the need for sensitivity towards cultural genres, and Gready's chapter points to the importance of context, not only in terms of understanding the narrative, but also in terms of the interpretive community. When we are conducting our research, what is the context in which it will be read, and how should this feed into decisions about what to write, and what to leave out?

The question of how we hear, and often fail to hear, aspects of the narratives we encounter, and how we decipher their meaning, is an issue which is addressed from a number of different angles throughout the book. We as narrative researchers are crucially a part of the data we collect; our presence is imprinted upon all that we do. It is left to us then to determine how we account for ourselves in the work that we do, to consider the impact of our own positioning and that of others – that is, those whose lives lie at the centre of our research – on our scholarship. All of the contributors to this volume stand somewhere in relation to the topics which we are exploring, and reflexivity upon this positioning is a part of each of the chapters.

There are yet many other pathways through these chapters; we have attempted to outline but a few. It is our hope that the chapters in this book will provide the readers with much food for thought, and that in the tradition of good narrative research, that they will raise at least as many questions as they answer.

Notes

1 For a take on the interactions of these traditions through some specific texts, see Hyvarinen (2006).
2 We are not considering here the much larger field of journals and books within the humanities and philosophy that were 'cross-read' by social researchers – journals such as *Radical Philosophy, Screen* and *Signs* and books by Coward, Heath, Jameson, Eagleton, Rose.
3 This form of argument is apparent in for instance Hollway's earlier work in *Changing the Subject* (Henriques et al., 1984).
4 Ricoeur's (1984) work has had perhaps the greatest effect in promoting this understanding of narrative .
5 The more agentic versions and interpretations of Butler's work are mostly relevant here.
6 Spivak (1993) has famously objected to this overuse of strategic essentialism in situations of theoretical and political difficulty.
7 Some 'small story' researchers associate themselves with this postmodern perspective. However, the association is not generally accompanied by any theorization of linguistic or subject indeterminacy, or of the larger place of discourses, to support it. The 'small stories' position does not, then, seem to be necessarily a poststructural or postmodern one.
8 To a limited extent, psychoanalytic understandings of such emotionality allows that signs of it appear within narratives, as do other contemporary but determinedly non-psychoanalytic frameworks for understanding desire (Deleuze and Guattari, 1980).
9 The chronological and semantic spaces which such unconscious proximities span,depend on the psychoanalytic framework with which the researcher works.

References

Abell, J., Stokoe, E. and Billig, M. (2004) Narrative and the discursive (re)construction of events. In M. Andrews, S. D. Sclater, C. Squire and A. Treacher (eds) *Uses of Narrative*. New Jersey: Transition.

Andrews, M. (2007) *Shaping History*. Cambridge: Cambridge University Press.

Andrews, M., Day Sclater, S., Rustin, M., Squire, C. and Treacher, A. (2004) Introduction. In M. Andrews, S. Day Sclater, C. Squire and A. Treacher (eds) *Uses of Narrative*. New Brunswick, NJ: Transition.

Bakhtin, M. (1981) *The Dialogic Imagination* ed. by M. Holquist, Austin: University of Texas Press.

Bamberg, M. (2006) Stories: Big or small. Why do we care? *Narrative Inquiry* 16(1): 139–47.

Bamberg, M. and Andrews, M. (2004) *Considering Counter-Narratives*. Amsterdam: John Benjamins.

Barthes, R. (1977) *Image Music Text*. New York: Hill and Wang.

Bertaux, D. (1981) *Biography and Society*. Beverly Hills, CA: Sage Publications.

Brockmeier, J. (1993) Translating temporality? Collegium Budapest Discussion Paper Series No. 4, December. http://www.colbud.hu/main_old/PubArchive/DP/DP04-Brockmeier.pdf. [Accessed 16 December 2007].

Brockmeier, J. and Carbaugh, D. (2001) *Narrative and Identity: Studies in Autobiography, Self and Culture*. Amsterdam: John Benjamins.

Bruner, J. (1990) *Acts of Meaning*. Cambridge, MA: Harvard University Press.

Burman, E. (2003) Narratives of 'experience' and pedagogical practices. *Narrative Inquiry* 13(2): 269–86.

Butler, J. (1993) *Bodies That Matter*. London: Routledge.

Chamberlayne, P., Bornat, J. and Wengraf, T. (eds) (2000) *The Turn to Biographical Methods in Social Science*. London: Routledge.

Chamberlayne, P., Rustin, M. and Wengraf, T. (eds) (2002) *Biography and Social Exclusion in Europe: Experiences and Life Journey*. Bristol: Policy Press.

Clandinin, D. (2006) *Handbook of Narrative Inquiry*. Newbery, CA: Sage.

Clandinin, D. and Connelly, F. (2004) *Narrative Inquiry: Experience and Story in Qualitative Research*. New York: Jossey-Bass.

Clark, J. (2003) Urban culture: Representation and experiences in/of urban space and culture. *Agenda* 57: 3–10.

Craib, I. (2004) Narratives as bad faith. In M. Andrews, S. D. Sclater, C. Squire and A. Treacher (eds) *Uses of Narrative*. New Jersey: Transition.

Culler, J. (2002) *The Pursuit of Signs*. Ithaca, NY: Cornell University Press.

Daiute, C. and Lightfoot, C. (2004) *Narrative Analysis: Studying the Development of Individuals in Society*. Oxford: Oxford University Press.

Deleuze, G. and Guattari, F. (1980) *Mille Plateaux*. Paris: Minuit.

Derrida, J. (1977) *Of Grammatology*. Baltimore: Johns Hopkins University Press.

Derrida, J. (1985) *The Ear of the Other*. New York: Schocken Books.

Dreyfus, R. and Rabinow, P. (1982) *Michel Foucault: Beyond Structuralism and Hermeneutics*. Chicago: Chicago University Press

Edley, N. (2002) The loner, the walk and the beast within: Narrative fragments in the construction of masculinity. In W. Patterson (ed.) *Strategic Narrative: New Perspectives on the Power of Stories*. Oxford: Lexington.

Elliot, J. (2005) *Using Narrative in Social Research: Qualitative and Quantitative Approaches.* London: Sage.

Emerson, P. and Frosh, S. (2004) *Critical Narrative Analysis in Psychology.* London: Palgrave.

Foucault, M. (1972) *The Archaeology of Knowledge.* London: Routledge.

Freeman, M. (1993) *Rewriting the self. History, Memory, Narrative.* London: Routledge.

Freeman, M. (2004) When the story's over: Narrative foreclosure and the possibility of renewal. In M. Andrews, S. D. Sclater, C. Squire and A. Treacher (eds) *Uses of Narrative.* New Jersey: Transition.

Freeman, M. (2006) Life on 'holiday'? In defense of big stories. *Narrative Inquiry* 16(1): 131–8.

Frosh, S. (2002) *After Words.* London: Palgrave.

Genette, G. (1979) *Narrative Discourse: An Essay in Method.* Ithaca, NY: Cornell University Press.

Georgakopolou, A. (2007) *Small Stories, Interaction and Identities.* Amsterdam: John Benjamins.

Gergen, K. (1991) *The Saturated Self.* New York: Basic Books.

Greenhalgh, T. and Hurwitz, B. (1998) *Narrative Based Medicine.* London: BMJ Books.

Hall, C. (1997) *Social Work as Narrative: Storytelling and Persuasion in Professional Texts.* Aldershot: Ashgate.

Harrison, B. (2004) Photographic visions and narrative inquiry. In M. Bamberg and M. Andrews (eds) *Considering Counter-Narratives.* Amsterdam: John Benjamins.

Henriques, J., Hollway, W., Urwin, C., Venn, C. and Walkerdine, V. (1984) *Changing the Subject.* London: Methuen.

Hollway, W. and Jefferson, T. (2000) *Doing Qualitative Research Differently: Free Association, Narrative and the Interview Method.* London: Sage.

Holstein, J. and Gubrium, J. (1999) *The Self We Live by: Narrative Identity in a Postmodern World.* New York: Oxford University Press.

Hyvarinen, M. (2006) Towards a conceptual history of narrative. In M. Hyvärinen, A. Korhonen and J. Mykkänen (eds) *The Travelling concept of Narrative.* Helsinki: Collegium.

Labov, W. (1972) *Language in the Inner City: Studies in the Black English Vernacular.* Oxford: Basil Blackwell.

Labov, W. (1997) Some further steps in narrative analysis. *Journal of Narrative and Life History* 7(1–4): 395–415.

Labov, W. and Waletsky, J. (1967) Narrative analysis: Oral versions of personal experience. In J. Helms (ed.) *Essays in the Verbal and Visual Arts.* Seattle: University of Washington.

Lacan, J. (1977) *Ecrits.* New York: Norton.

Langellier, K. and Peterson, E. (1992) Spinstorying: An analysis of women storytelling. In E. C. Fine and J. H. Speer (eds) *Performance, Culture and Identity*, Westport, CT: Praeger.

Langellier, K. and Peterson, E. (2004) *Storytelling in Everyday Life.* Philadelphia, PA: Temple University Press.

Lyotard, J.-F. (1984) *The Postmodern Condition.* Manchester: Manchester University Press.

McAdams, D.P. (2006) *The Redemptive Self: Stories Americans Live By.* Oxford University Press.

MacIntyre, A. (1984) Fictional(ising) identity ontological assumptions and method-
    ological productions of 'anorexic' subjectivities. *After Virtue*. Bloomington, IN:
    University of Notre Dame Press.
Malson, H. (2004) In M.Andrews, S.D.Sclater, C.Squire and A.Treacher (eds) *Uses of
    Narrative*. New Brunswick, NJ: Transaction.
Mattingley, C. (1998) *Healing Dramas and Clinical Plots*. Cambridge: Cambridge
    University Press.
Mishler, E. (1986) *Research Interviewing: Context and Narrative*. Cambridge, MA:
    Harvard University Press.
Mishler, E. (1999) *Storylines: Craftartists' Narratives of Identity*. Cambridge, MA: Harvard
    University Press.
Mulvey, L. (1991) A Phantasmagoria of the female body: the work of Cindy Sherman.
    New Left Review 188: 136–50.
Nagel, T. (1986) *The View from Nowhere*. Oxford: Oxford University Press.
Ochs, Elinor and Capps, Lisa (2001) *Living Narrative: Creating Lives in Everyday
    Storytelling*. Cambridge, MA: Harvard University Press.
Parker, I. (2003) Psychoanalytic narratives: Writing the self into contemporary cultural
    phenomena. *Narrative Inquiry* 13(2): 301–15.
Parker, I. (2004) *Qualitative Psychology*. Milton Keynes: Open University Press.
Patterson, W. (ed.) (2002) *Strategic Narrative: New Perspectives on the Power of Stories*.
    Oxford: Lexington.
Personal Narrative Group (1989) *Interpreting Women's Lives: Feminist Theory and Personal
    Narratives*. Bloomington and Indianapolis: Indiana University Press.
Plummer, K. (1995) *Telling Sexual Stories*. London: Routledge.
Plummer, K. (2001) *Documents of Life 2*. London: Sage.
Polanyi, L. (1985) Conversational storytelling. In T.A. van Dijk (ed.), *Discourse
    and Dialogue, volume 3 of Handbook of Discourse Analysis 4*. London: Academic
    Press.
Polkinghorne, Donald E. (1988) *Narrative Knowing and the Human Sciences*. Albany,
    NY: State University of New York Press.
Ricoeur, P. (1984) *Time and Narrative*. Chicago: University of Chicago Press.
Riessman, C. (1993a) *Narrative Analysis. Qualitative Research Methods* Vol 30. Newbury
    Park, CA: Sage.
Riessman, C. (1993b) *Qualitative Studies in Social Work Research*. Newbury Park, CA:
    Sage.
Riessman, C. (2002) Analysis of personal narratives. In J.Gubrium and J.Holstein (eds)
    Handbook of Interview Research. Thousand Oaks, CA: Sage.
Riessman, C. (2008) *Narrative Methods in the Human Sciences*. New York, Sage.
Roberts, B. (2001) *Biographical Research*. Milton Keynes: Open University Press.
Rosaldo, R. (1989) *Culture and Truth: The Remaking of Social Analysis*. London:
    Routledge.
Rosenwald, G. and Ochberg, R. (1992) *Storied Lives. The Cultural Politics of Self-
    Understanding*. New Haven: Yale University Press.
Rustin, M. (2000) Reflections on the biographical turn in the social sciences.
    In P. Chamberlayne, J. Bornat and T. Wengraf (eds) *The Turn to Biographical Methods
    in Social Science*. London: Routledge.
Salmon, P. (1985) *Living in Time: A New Look at Personal Development*. London: Dent.
Sampson, E. (1993) *Celebrating the Other*. New York: Oxford University Press.

Sarbin, T. (1986) *Narrative Psychology. The Storied Nature of Human Conduct*. New York: Praeger.

Sclater, Day S. (2003) What is the subject? *Narrative Inquiry*, 13(2): 317–30.

Seale, C. (2004) Resurrective practice and narrative. In M. Andrews, S. D. Sclater, C. Squire and A. Treacher (eds) *Doing Narrative Research*. New Brunswick, NJ: Transaction.

Sliep, Y., Weingarten, K. and Gilbert, A. (2004) Narrative Theatre as an interactive community approach to mobilizing collective action in Northern Uganda. *Families, Systems and Health*, 22(3): 306–20.

Spivak, G. (1993) Interview Sara Danius and Stefan Jonsson. *Boundary 2*(20): 24–50.

Squire, C. (2005) Reading narratives. *Group Analysis* 38(1): 91–107.

Squire, C. (2007) *HIV in South Africa: Talking about the Big Thing*. London: Routledge.

Stanley, L. (1992) *The Auto/Biographical I: Theory and Practice of Feminist Auto/Biography*. Manchester University Press.

Steedman, C. (1987) *Landscape for a Good Woman*. New Brunswick, NJ: Rutgers University Press.

Tamboukou, M. (2003) *Women, Education, the Self: a Foucauldian perspective*. Basingstoke: Palgrave Macmillan.

Todorov, T. (1990) *Genres in Discourse*. Cambridge: Cambridge University Press.

Wengraf, T. (1999) *Biographical Methods in Social Sciences*. London: Routledge.

Wetherell, M. (1998) Positioning and interpretative repertoires: Conversation analysis and post-structuralism in dialogue. *Discourse & Society* 9: 387–412.

Wetherell, M. (2005) Unconscious conflict or everyday accountability? *British Journal of Social Psychology* 44(2): 169–73.

Chapter 1

Narratives of events: Labovian narrative analysis and its limitations

Wendy Patterson

This chapter introduces the seminal work on personal experience narratives by sociolinguists William Labov and Joshua Waletzky. In the first part of the chapter, Labov's model of the structure of the personal experience narrative is presented, his method of analysis is described and its advantages explored. In the second part, some limitations of the Labovian approach are identified and discussed.

The Labovian approach

Now nearly 40 years old, the influential work of Labov (1972) and Labov and Waletsky (1967) has become paradigmatic in the field of personal narrative research. Labov's model of the structure of the personal experience narrative has provided the starting point for a wide range of studies that utilize narrative, and the merits and limitations of the model continue to be debated.[1]

Labov's work on narrative is but a small part of his highly influential sociolinguistic work on the varieties of English. In his book *Language in the Inner City* (1972), Labov presented a developed version of his model of the structure of the personal narrative. However, the most important aspect of the book was not this model, but rather Labov's groundbreaking scholarship which argued that black English vernacular (BEV) should be recognized as a language in its own right, rather than as an incorrect or stunted version of standard English. His defence of BEV was fully supported by his analysis of BEV speech data, which showed that BEV speakers were just as skilful, expressive and effective in their use of language as any other speech community. As part of the data analyses, Labov focused on stories told by young, male BEV speakers, and it was from this data that he formulated his model of the personal experience narrative.

Labov and his colleagues provided us with a method that produces *structural analyses of specific oral personal experience narratives*. Within Langellier's (1989) classification of different approaches to the personal narrative, the Labovian approach is part of the category that treats personal narrative as story text, as distinct from approaches which understand personal narrative as storytelling performance, conversational interaction, social process or political praxis. In Mishler's (1995) typology of narrative-analytic models, the Labovian model is a subclass of the general category focused on reference and temporal order, as distinct from those focused on textual coherence and structure, or narrative functions. Mishler also presents Labov's model as the exemplar of approaches that see narrative as 'recapitulating the told in the telling' (1995: 92), rather than as 'reconstructing the told in the telling' or 'making a telling from the told'.

These two contextualizations of the Labovian approach within the field of personal narrative research highlight its fundamental premise and key characteristic. It understands the personal narrative primarily as a text, and that text's function is to represent past events in the form of a story, as expressed in Labov's description of the oral personal experience narrative:

> one method of recapitulating past experience by matching a verbal sequence of clauses to the sequence of events which (it is inferred) actually occurred.

(Labov, 1972: 359)

We can see, therefore, that the Labovian approach is *event-centred*, in that it defines narrative in terms of the representation of events. It is also *text-centred*, in that it embodies an understanding of the personal experience narrative as a text and takes little account of context.

This focus on events, and the premise that narrative's primary function is the recapitulation of events, is very widespread in definitions of narrative from different academic fields. Consider, for example, Genette's characterization, in linguistics, of an:

> oral or written narrative statement that undertakes to tell of an event or events.

(Genette, 1980: 25)

Onega and Landa's definition, within literary criticism, is that:

> a narrative is the semiotic representation of a series of events meaningfully connected in a temporal and causal way.

(Onega and Landa, 1996: 3)

Within narratology, Toolan's account of narrative is of:

> a perceived sequence of non-randomly connected events.

(Toolan, 1988: 7)

Later in this chapter I will discuss how approaching oral personal experience narratives as though they are primarily about events, rather than *experience*, gives rise to a range of theoretical, methodological and interpretational problems.

Analysing transcripts using the Labovian approach

Using Labov's criterion for what constitutes a minimal narrative, 'a sequence of two clauses which are temporally ordered' (Labov 1972: 360), and his analytic method, narratives can be extracted from other language data, and parsed into numbered clauses. Each clause can then be assigned to one element of Labov's six-part model: abstract (A), orientation (O), complicating action (CA), result (R), evaluation (E), coda (C). The following 'Lift Story' example of a personal experience narrative is presented and analysed according to the Labovian method. This story is an 'ideal type'; while the experience happened, the transcript is not taken from a spoken narrative but rather acts as a demonstration text for Labov's method.

The Lift Story

1.	Did I ever tell you	A
2.	about the time I was stuck in a lift?	A
3.	Well, it was about five years ago	O
4.	when I was working in London	O
5.	I was the last one to leave the office late on a Friday night	CA
6.	and the lift just stopped between the eighth and seventh floors	CA
7.	I was terrified, terrified	E
8.	I mean I really panicked	E
9.	I thought there was no one else in the building	E
10.	and I would be stuck there until Monday morning	E
11.	It really was the most awful feeling	E
12.	anyway I frantically pushed the alarm button for about ten minutes	CA
13.	which seemed like hours	E
14.	Then I heard someone calling	CA
15.	and then suddenly the lift started moving down	CA
16.	and vibrating and rattling and sort of juddering	CA
17.	I screamed 'GET ME OUT OF HERE'	CA/E
18.	I thought the lift was going to plunge down into the basement	E
19.	and then suddenly the doors opened in between two floors	CA
20.	and the caretaker was there	CA
21.	and he helped me climb out	CA
22.	I was free at last!	R
23.	I burst into tears	CA/E
24.	I was so relieved	E
25.	there is no way	C
26.	I ever get into a lift on my own now	C

27. so that's why   C
28. I've just climbed ten floors   C
29. to get to your flat   C

Labov recommends the 'question method' for the categorization of clauses. This is based on the idea that a narrative can be understood as a series of answers to the underlying questions that all narratives address. The clauses within a narrative thus function to answer different questions:

1. Abstract – what is the story about?
2. Orientation – who, when, where?
3. Complicating action – then what happened?
4. Evaluation – so what?
5. Result – what finally happened?

The sixth element, the Coda, functions to sign off the narrative as it returns to the present time of the telling, to hand the 'floor' over to the hearer(s). Rather than answering a question, it '*puts off* a question', signalling that questions 3 and 4 are no longer relevant' (Labov, 1972: 370, emphasis in the original).

Abstract

This is optional; depending on the context in which the story is told, narrators may or may not provide a summary of the story to come. For example, the question 'Did I ever tell you about the time I got stuck in a lift?' (lines 1–2), provides a summary of the story to come and is also a bid for an extended speaking turn. It provides a clear indication to the listener that if they give a negative response to the question, they are implicitly agreeing to listen to a story. In an interview situation, where an interviewer asks a question in order to elicit a narrative, the question itself may be seen to constitute the abstract, negating the need for the narrator to produce one. For example, Labov and his researchers used the question, 'Have you ever been in danger of death?' to elicit personal experience narratives from young, black American males; the resultant narratives made up the primary data-corpus used by Labov and Waletsky to develop their model. In response to the question, an interviewee might respond 'Yes, this kid once tried to stab me' (Abstract) or might go straight into the story 'Yes, it was about five years ago when I was at a party and …' (Orientation). The abstract, if it is present, will be at, or very near, the beginning because its main functions are to introduce the story and, depending on the context, to make a bid for the floor.

Orientation

Orientation clauses, in a personal experience narrative, function to answer the questions 'who is the story about?', 'when did it happen?', 'where did it happen?' thereby providing a setting in which the events of the story will be told. For example, 'Well, it was about five years ago when I was working in London' (lines 3–4). Although orientation clauses usually occur early in the narrative text, it is not uncommon for narrators to insert extra background information' at later points.

Complicating action

Sometimes referred to as the 'skeleton plot' (Mishler, 1986: 237) or the 'spine' of the narrative (Linde, 1993: 68), the complicating action clauses relate the events of the story and typically follow a 'then, and then' structure which gives a linear representation of time and permits an open-ended series of events to be related. The series can be added to, indefinitely, as if in response to 'and then what happened?' as long as the events are related in chronological order. For example, 'and then suddenly the doors opened in between two floors and the caretaker was there and he helped me climb out' (lines 19–21). Any deviation from chronological order must be accompanied by explanatory clauses which clearly indicate the actual order of events, for example, 'But before that happened …'

Evaluation

Labov describes evaluation as 'perhaps the most important element in addition to the basic narrative clause' and one which has been neglected by other accounts of narrative (1972: 366). It is evaluation that, in Labov's terms, mediates the crucial 'point' of the story, thereby justifying its telling, and it reveals the narrator's perspective on the events being told. The 'so what?' question, with which a story without a point could be dismissed as not worthy of telling, is pre-emptively answered by the inclusion of evaluation clauses that tell the listener what the point is by conveying the narrator's experience of the events at the time they took place and his or her feelings about the experience at the time of the telling.

Labov (1972) identifies three main types of evaluation: external, embedded and evaluative action:

> **External evaluation** is overt. The narrator stops the complicating action, stands outside the story and tells the listener what the point is, for example 'It really was the most awful feeling' (line 11).
> **Embedded evaluation** preserves the dramatic continuity of the story as the narrator tells how she/he felt at the time, for example, 'I was terrified, terrified' (line 7) and 'I was so relieved' (line 24).
> **Evaluative action** stays firmly within the story by reporting actions that reveal emotions without the use of speech, for example 'I burst into tears' (line 23).

Labov further categorizes the evaluative elements in a narrative text into different types of devices. These include:

> **Intensifiers,** which include expressive phonology [I screamed 'GET ME OUT OF HERE' (line 17)]; quantifiers [the *most* awful feeling (line 11); and repetition (I was terrified, terrified (line 7)].

Comparators, which compare what did occur to what did not, but might have done. For example, 'I thought there was no one else in the building and I would be stuck there until Monday morning' (lines 9– 10) and 'I thought the lift was going to plunge down into the basement' (line 18).

Explicatives, which often involve causality and explain why something happened. For example, 'I burst into tears [because] I was so relieved' (lines 23–24).

In Labov's and Waletzky's original (1967) model, evaluation was regarded as a discrete element occurring at one place in the narrative text. In Labov's later (1972) model, evaluation is described as spreading like a wave through the narrative and as having the ability to permeate all the other elements. Here, the status of evaluation was elevated from an element to a 'secondary structure which is concentrated in the evaluation section but may be found in various forms throughout the narrative' (Labov, 1972: 369). Riessman (1993: 21) refers to evaluation as 'the soul of the narrative', expressing both the point of the story and, crucially, how the narrator wants to be understood.

Result

The result, or resolution, tells the listener how the story ends. For example, 'I was free at last!' (line 22).

Coda

If present, the coda occurs at the end of the narrative when the narrator returns to the present time of the narration, clearly indicating that the story is over. For example, 'there is no way I ever get into a lift on my own now so that's why I've just climbed ten floors to get to your flat' (lines 25–29). The coda links the past world of the story to the present world of the storytelling and functions to 'sign off' the narrative and offer the floor to the listener.

Researchers who present their data following Labov's method and model typically extract narratives from the full transcript of an interview, number and categorize each clause according to elements of the model, and then present a 'core narrative' which leaves out evaluation and anything else that does not fit into the categories of Abstract, Orientation, Complicating action and Resolution – for example, interactions between teller and listener, descriptions and asides.

Mishler (1986: 237) provides a good example of the presentation of data according to a conventional Labovian approach whereby a 'core narrative' is presented which has been extracted from the complete transcript of a narrative produced in an interview. In Mishler's example, the core narrative is entitled 'Yet we always *did* what we had to do some*how* we did it' which is the analyst's interpretation of the main point of the story. Mishler explains that this is a radically reduced version of the full transcript and only consists of key sections of the Orientation, the Abstract, the Complicating Action and the Resolution. This 'skeleton plot' is understood to be referential, rather than evaluative, that is, it represents 'what happened' without any of the narrator's evaluation.

The evaluation clauses which mediate the 'point' of the narrative are excluded from 'the core narrative' and then re-introduced into the analysis in order to examine the narrator's perspective on the 'bare bones' of what actually happened. In this way, a clear distinction is maintained between the referential and the evaluative functions of the narrative.

Advantages of the Labovian approach

The Labovian approach utilizes a detailed and rigorous method for the analysis of personal experience narratives, and can provide an excellent starting point for analysing transcripts of talk produced in a variety of different contexts. First, Labov's definitional criteria can be used to identify some important narratives within the transcript. Second, the application of the model reveals the specific structure of individual narratives and allows comparison. Third, a Labovian analysis of the linguistic features that encode various types of evaluation enables the analyst to examine the perspective of the narrator on the events recounted. Fourth, the approach is particularly suited to some specific forms of data and research.

Identifying and understanding event narratives

While event narratives are not always told, and some speakers produce them rather rarely, they can be very prominent parts of interview material, particularly, as Labov mentions, around situations of 'sex, death and moral injury'. The Labovian approach facilitates the identification and analysis of event narratives, which are often very striking aspects of narrative data. But in so doing, it rules out of its field of interest many other kinds of talk which might be commonly classified by both speakers and hearers as 'stories' – stories about events that did not happen directly to the speaker, that happened more than once, that may happen in the future or that might have happened, for instance – and that use imperfect or conditional tenses that do not fit with Labov's focus on past tense narrative clauses. I shall return to this problem later.

Comparing narratives

Labov's systematic approach to the identification and interpretation of evaluation in personal experience narratives also provides researchers with the means to produce detailed comparative analyses of evaluation across a sample of narratives. Such analyses might compare: the amount of evaluation; the type of evaluation; different narrators' evaluations of the same event; changes in event narratives within a single interview as the interview progresses or as different events are addressed (Bell, 1988); changes in evaluation over time in narratives of the same experience produced by the same narrator; differences in evaluation in narratives of the same event told by people at different times or in different circumstances; evaluation in narratives of the same experience told to different people. For example, Ferrara (1994) uses a Labovian analysis of narratives produced in a therapeutic context to show that two narratives produced by one narrator at different times can be categorized as 'retellings' because although they relate different *events*, they include the same type of evaluation and therefore convey the same type of *experience* and function in the same way within the narrator's life story.

The narrator's perspective

As is now widely recognized by narrative researchers across many different disciplines, whatever else a personal narrative is – oral history, dinner party anecdote, legal testimony, response to an interview question – the list of possibilities is endless – it is also and *always* a narration of the self. In personal narration, a particular personal, social, cultural, political identity is claimed by narrators and, as Mishler (1986: 243) says, 'everything said functions to express, confirm and validate the claimed identity'. Indeed, many identity theorists now conceptualize personal identity as the accumulation of stories we tell about ourselves, and dialogic approaches to the self and to narrative are brought together in many different ways in order to theorize their complex interrelationship.[2]

Labov's work on evaluation provides analysts with useful, and useable, tools for undertaking a systematic textual analysis that can generate an interpretation of the perspective, and the claimed identity, of a narrator. We can appreciate, therefore, that although the Labovian approach is text-centred, or 'surface-oriented' (Gülich & Quasthoff, 1987: 174), the concepts and analytic tools it provides can take the analyst below the surface of the text, as long as the link between the linguistic description and the interpretation is strictly maintained.

Finding or eliciting personal narratives

Finally, the Labovian approach to the analysis of personal experience narratives has significant implications for the way in which data is produced. Labov focuses on the personal narrative as a monologue that straightforwardly represents past events in a story. He isolates it from its surrounding text and pays little attention to the context of the narration. The 'ideal' data for a Labovian analysis are therefore most likely to be produced by recording stories produced 'naturally', in non-research situations, without the story-eliciting and constructing context of an interview; or at the least, by interviews within which the interviewer has a minimal role, the variables of the interview context are in some way controlled and the narrator 'sticks to the point' (a rare occurrence, in my experience). Yet clearly, this might not be the first, or most appropriate, choice of data production for many research projects.

Some theoretical and methodological problems have started to emerge from this consideration of the benefits of the Labovian approach, indicating that its usefulness may be more limited than its widespread application would suggest. Researchers have discussed the problems with the approach over decades. A useful compendium of papers that both appreciate and criticize the approach was published in 1997 in Volume 7 the *Journal of Narrative and Life History* (now *Narrative Inquiry),* including contributions from Labov (1997) himself, Mishler and Riessman. The next two sections discuss the problems of the Labovian approach as they affect narrative research generally.

Some theoretical problems with the Labovian approach

Looking again at the example from Mishler (1986: 237) as described above, it quickly becomes clear that it is the Labovian method and model that has determined what the 'core narrative' is. This narrative is then taken to be a representation of 'what actually happened': an objective reality is being assumed when this 'reality' has been constructed by the method. Mishler (1995: 94–5) discusses the way in which Labov later moved away from the definition of narrative as 'the construction of an objective event sequence' (Labov, 1982: 232) and focused on sequences of speech acts and actions which mediate social status relationships between speakers within the narrative. But as Mishler notes, this later version of the Labovian approach still relies on 'an assumed correspondence between the temporal orderings of speech acts and the sequence of social moves in the negotiation of status relationships' (Mishler, 1995: 95).

Within a strictly Labovian analysis, there is no allowance made for the inevitably *partial and constructed* nature of any account of personal experience. This has significant implications for the distinction Labov makes between referential (narrative) clauses, which report the sequence of events, and evaluative clauses, which tell how the narrator feels about what happened and mediate the point of the story. For many narrative analysts, this distinction is hard to maintain.

The attempt to match narrative clauses to events and to maintain a strict distinction between referential clauses and evaluative clauses is often problematic. As Culler (1981) points out, any clause may be present because it fulfils the evaluative rather than the referential function. In other words, a clause that appears to be a simple narrative clause referring to an event is not necessarily present in the text just because it is what happened – for all narration is highly selective – but may have been selected for inclusion because it supports the point of the narrative. Its primary function may, therefore, be evaluative rather than referential. Labov himself notes that the evaluative function may well override the referential function: 'the narratives themselves may serve only as a framework for the evaluation' (Labov, 1972: 371). What this means is that the narrator's *experience* of the event, their perspective on what happened, determines how the story is told and which events are selected for inclusion (see Patterson's (2002) analysis and discussion of 'liminal zone' stories for evidence that personal experience narratives are primarily about experience rather than events). An event-centric approach, which assumes the primacy of events, fails, therefore, to appreciate the essential creativity of the act of telling a story of personal experience, which involves *reconstructing* the past for the purposes of the present telling. This touches on a deep philosophical issue concerning the relationship between life and story, and readers who wish to delve into this further can take up the suggestions for further reading provided at the end of the chapter.

For now, it is interesting to note the way in which this issue comes to the fore in Mishler's (1986) discussion of his interpretation of the 'yet we always did what we had to do' narrative. In the light of a narrative produced by the interviewee's wife, in which she talks about her husband's alcoholism, erratic job history and their marital conflict, Mishler had to modify his interpretation of the story the interviewee had told him, within which all these issues were entirely absent. Here we see that the 'yet we always did what we had to do' story tells us far more about the narrator's claimed identity in this interview context than it tells us about past events in the narrator's life – and the same would have to be said of the wife's narrative. As the Personal Narratives Group (1989) explain, narratives do not 'reveal the past', neither are they 'open to proof' but through interpretation they *do* reveal truths about narrators' experiences and how they want to be understood. This is a very valuable insight into the nature of the personal experience narrative and an important reason to promote an experiential rather than an event-centric understanding of personal narration.

Other critiques of the theoretical premises of the Labovian approach have highlighted its specificity in terms of culture and gender. As previously discussed, a Labovian approach extracts narrative sequences from the rest of the talk by means of definitional criteria, which determines what constitutes a minimal narrative, 'a sequence of two clauses which are *temporally ordered*' (Labov, 1972: 360). These will be past tense clauses because narrative is defined as 'one method of recapitulating past experience by matching a verbal sequence of clauses to the sequence of events which (it is inferred) actually occurred' (Labov, 1972: 359). Polanyi (1979: 208) points out that this is a culturally-specific conceptualization of narrative, noting that non-Indo–European stories may be structured so that later actions, states or events precede earlier ones. In addition, some narrative traditions organize stories around place, or around the hierarchy of ranks of the characters or their relationship to the speaker, rather than around time.

A further, and very disturbing, claim by critics of Labov's model, is that, due to the inferred correlation of *competence* with fully-formed evaluative narrative syntax and because of the success of the model, it 'has functioned normatively to set the standard against which other personal narratives are measured' (Langellier, 1989: 248–9). According to this argument, a 'good' narrative is one that fits neatly into Labov's model, and it may be inferred that those that do not fit have been produced by less than competent storytellers. In fact, this is far too simplistic an interpretation of Labov's work and his notion of competency. He did not promote any generalized judgement about 'good' or 'bad' narratives but rather presented a detailed, sociolinguistic account of the differences he observed in narrative production between people of different classes and ethnicities. He also specifically argued against equations of 'competence' with large amounts of evaluation, especially external evaluation. 'Competence', in this context, refers to the ability to command the attention of an audience. Labov stated that middle-class speakers tend to overuse external evaluation and syntactic elaboration, which is detrimental to audience interest, whereas embedded evaluation successfully dramatizes personal narration. He concluded, therefore, that stories told by working-class speakers demonstrated a higher level of competence than those of middle-class speakers (Labov, 1972: 396). In addition, Labov firmly refuted the idea, prevalent at the time, that black speakers were linguistically, and intellectually, undeveloped, 'behind or backward', and claimed that they may be more competent storytellers than white speakers of the same age and class. Labov was not simply correlating syntactic complexity with competence, therefore, but these kinds of interpretations have been an occasional, and regrettable, outcome of the widespread application of the model.

Langellier and Peterson (1992) also criticize the Labovian approach on the grounds of its specificity in terms of gender. Their research, and that of others they review, shows that there are significant differences between stories told by men and stories told by women. For this reason, they claim that the approach developed by Labov, which was based on the study of men's narration, fails adequately to address the subtle interactional intricacy of women's personal narratives. Langellier and Peterson (1992: 173) coin the term 'spinstorying' in order to convey the way in which 'stories are tellable because they are drawn from the fiber of women's experiences', and to suggest a spiralling interaction between conversation and story and story and conversation, as women collaboratively weave stories of a shared reality. These stories do not prioritize the telling of discrete events or centre on a 'point' that exists before or outside of the interaction, but neither are they 'pointless'. The 'point' of the telling develops dynamically in interaction as 'when women act as audience, they speak [...] and, when women speak, they act as audience' (Langellier and Peterson, 1992: 174). Consequently, to define narrative in terms of the recounting of specific past time events would be to miss the point that what matters to some narrators, the 'point' of their narrative, is to share their experiences with others, not to impart information about some historical event. Langellier and Peterson are particularly interested in women sharing their stories in groups but many of their observations are relevant to the research interview context. An important methodological question about the role of the researcher arises from their observation that only by entering 'the realm of spinstorying as collaborators' can researchers adequately understand women's storytelling (1992: 177).

To summarize the points I have made in this section, there is much to be gained by the judicious use of a Labovian approach, but if one takes a strictly Labovian approach to some types of data then much will be lost. Focusing solely on chronologically ordered past tense clauses, analyzing them in isolation from the rest of the transcript, and taking no account of the context in which the narrative was produced, can only produce an overly simplistic, reductive analysis and interpretation. If used in isolation, therefore, a standard, linear model of narrative structure, confining itself to the relationships between clauses in sections of text which conform to a restrictive event–centric definition of narrative, will count as 'non-narrative' much that is fundamental to personal narration, perhaps especially women's personal narration, and may also serve to perpetuate an inadequate theory and an inflexible approach.[3]

Some methodological problems with the Labovian approach

One of the first problems I encountered when trying to use the Labovian method and model to analyse transcripts of interviews with people talking about their traumatic experiences, was that my data did not seem to conform to the structure that the model was designed to analyse. What was even more disturbing was that, according to Labov's definition of a minimal narrative 'a sequence of two clauses which are *temporally ordered*' (Labov, 1972: 360), the vast majority of the transcripts were not narrative. For example, here is Janice talking about herself in the immediate aftermath of the death of her teenage daughter in a car accident:

1. and of course I wasn't sleeping I was just you know in this
2. manic rush I don't know I was writing stuff down and going
3. through pictures I don't know I just I was just trying to make
4. sense of it I just couldn't sleep and erm as I suppose looking
5. back on it probably being like that I was trying to just block it
6. out ...

(Janice, 17: 881–9)[4]

The clauses which make up this extract are not chronologically ordered and do not correspond to discrete events. Therefore they do not count as narrative according to Labov's definition of narrative. There is no doubt, however, that Janice *was* telling me about her personal experience. Given that the main aim of my research was to investigate the relationship between the narration of the personal experience of trauma and the process of coping, or not coping, with that experience, it was crucial for me to be able to include this type of text in my narrative analysis.

Polanyi (1985) came up against the same methodological problem when using the Labovian approach to try to locate narratives within the full text of an interview. She describes this as 'a seemingly insurmountable problem for analysts' (1985: 183). In Polanyi's 'The Robbery' story, containing over 300 clauses, she could only identify eight narrative clauses, in Labov's terms. The problem is, then, how narrative is defined. Polanyi concludes that while Labov's model is:

> successful in part because ... [it indicates] *the classical development of the plot in conversational stories* ... [it is not] *ultimately very helpful* ... [as] *the clauses that one finds in the transcripts of taped stories hardly ever correspond to this ordering.*

(Polanyi, 1985: 193–4)

Polanyi develops Labov's work in interesting ways. She extends his limited 'narrative clause = event' formulation to include *state clauses* in conversational narratives which represent states of affairs that persist over time, in contrast to *event clauses* which represent one unique, discrete happening (Polanyi, 1985: 191).[5]

Extending the range of the types of clauses that 'counted' as narrative meant that many more sections of my transcripts could now be classified as narrative, including the extract from the interview with Janice, above, where states of 'not sleeping' and 'writing stuff down' are narrated using past participle verb inflections to encode experiences that persisted over time.

The limitations of Labov's definitional criteria were also recognized by Riessman (1993: 44) when she encountered a transcript of a personal narrative that 'felt' like a narrative but resisted analysis in terms of his model. She found, as I did, that Labov's theory and model is inadequate for 'subjective experiences, events that extend over time and even extend into the present ... [as such narratives are] as much about affective "actions", things the narrator feels and says to herself as ... about "what happened" in a more objective sense' (Riessman, 1993: 51–2). Riessman found that using Gee's (1991) poetic structural approach to narrative and analysing this text in terms of stanzas and themes was far more appropriate and rewarding.

Riessman (1993) offers a reconceptualization of narrative which allows for the inclusion of the narration of ongoing or enduring states of being, or of present, future or hypothetical experience, by using the term 'narrative' in two ways. First, the entire response of the interviewee is a narrative if it has sequential, thematic and structural coherence, according to Gee's (1991) approach. Second, embedded in this 'overarching narrative' there may be narrative segments which meet Labov's more limited criteria.

Using this approach, Riessman was able to identify a tension in the structure of the particular narrative she was analysing 'between the real and the wished for, the story and the dream' which, Riessman believes, enabled her to 'come close to seeing into [the narrator's] subjective experience – what life "means" to her at the moment of telling' (Riessman, 1993: 52). This insight was achieved through the identification of a contradiction between two narrative segments in the transcript, one representing reality and one representing a dream of how the narrator would like life to be. These are embedded in a series of stanzas that convey the ongoing conditions of the narrator's life and the way she experiences, and endures, them (Riessman, 1993: 45–52).

This notion of imagined experience, and its juxtaposition in a narrative with past and present experience, was crucial to the development of my understanding of the relationship between narration and coping in the aftermath of trauma. My data contained past, present, future and hypothetical narratives, densely interwoven. Through my analyses of imaginary, or hypothetical, narratives of what the traumatic event might have been ('comparators', in Labov's terms, which may offer worse, better or just different outcomes) I came to understand that these 'narrative imaginings' were as crucial an aspect of the process of narration and coping, as were the narratives of the actual past events (Patterson, 2002).

In addition, the realm of the imaginary is an important aspect of the interactive context in which traumatic experience is narrated. At the very moment when a narrator says 'you cannot imagine what it is like' or 'you can never know what it feels like', the listener is *invited to imagine*, to enter into a realm of experience which is not their own but neither is it any longer only the speaker's. Such invitations to imagine often herald a 'narrative proper', in Labov's terms, as the speaker provides a specific example from their past experience in order to help the listener to imagine what it would be like to share the narrator's subjective experience. Gail's 'shabby man' story is a good example of such a narrative and this is analysed in the next section in order to highlight a further methodological problem with the Labovian approach.

This problem relates to the inherent tendency in the Labovian approach to decontextualize narratives by treating them as self-contained monologues which have an autonomous existence. The talk surrounding them, their textual context and the interactional context within which they are produced, are disregarded or treated as secondary, 'add-on' features. In order to illustrate the problems of such an approach, let us see what a basic Labovian analysis can reveal about Gail's 'shabby man' story. This story is told by Gail to a psychotherapist in the context of a one hour interview within which Gail talks about her experiences in the aftermath of being seriously sexually and physically assaulted by an intruder in her home:

The shabby man story

1.	there was an incident actually a few weeks ago	A/O
2.	I was with my mother-in-law and my daughter and the little girl from next door (.)	O
3.	we were walking the dog	O
4.	and there was a man	O
5.	who was sitting (.) erm (.)	O
6.	drinking a bottle of wine or sherry or something	O
7.	looking very er (.) well down (.) dirty and shabby	O
8.	but he had that look (.)	O
9.	and he watched (.)	CA
10.	as we passed very intensely (.)	CA
11.	now if I hadn't been with my mother-in-law	E
12.	I would have been absolutely (.) scared out of my mind	E
13.	but because she was there you know	E
14.	I felt OK (.) just about (.)	R
15.	she was worried …	R

(Gail, 16: 813–23)

Underlining – emphasis
(.) – clearly discernible pause

Although the 'plot' here is minimal, 'and he watched as we passed' (lines 9–10) this *is* a narrative, according to Labov's definitional criteria for identifying a minimal narrative, 'a sequence of two clauses which are temporally ordered' (1972: 360).

The evaluation in this narrative is concentrated in the following section:

11. <u>now</u> if I hadn't been with my mother-in-law
12. I would have been absolutely (.) scared out of my mind
13. but because she was there you know

This is external evaluation as the narrator stands outside the story and tells the listener what the point of the story is. A number of Labovian evaluative devices are used: <u>now</u> – **intensifer** (expressive phonology)
if I hadn't been with my mother-in-law I would have been absolutely (.) scared out of my mind – **comparator** (something that could have happened, but didn't)
absolutely – **intensifier** (quantifier)
but because – **explicative** (invoking causality)
    The narrative also contains embedded evaluation, 'but he had that <u>look</u>' (line 8). The use of the adversative conjunction 'but' here functions to indicate that the preceding description of the man:

5. who was sitting (.) erm (.)
6. drinking a bottle of wine or sherry or something
7. looking very er (.) well down (.) dirty and shabby

is not as significant to the point of the story as him having 'that <u>look</u>' (line 8) is. However, the phrase 'that look' can only be understood by reference back to the talk between Gail and the psychotherapist which immediately precedes this past tense narration:

1. G: but men I don't know er (.) if they look
2. intimidating (.) men have a I think it's called the hungry look
3. [P smiles] you know some men (.) just just look have a look
4. P: mm
5. G: which yes it's frightening
6. P: right
7. G: it's a very intense look
8. P: right so there's something about certain people
9. G: yes
10. P: you find (.) anxiety provoking
11. G: yes if I'm on my own if I'm not on my own then it doesn't
12. concern me (.)

(Gail, 15: 790–809)

Taking a strictly Labovian approach, this present tense, eventless dialogic sequence would be excluded from the analysis; it would be seen as extraneous talk. However, it is clear that the point of the narrative that follows is deeply embedded in this talk. The overriding point of the shabby man story has nothing to do with the specific past events of that day and everything to do with how Gail feels now (at the time of the interview), how she experiences the ongoing effects of what happened to her in the past, and how she is choosing to convey that experience to her interlocutor.

Conclusion

Throughout this chapter I have drawn attention to the event-centricity of the Labovian approach and suggested that an experiential approach not only 'fits' many narratives better, but will also enable researchers to produce richer, more comprehensive analyses and interpretations of the full range of forms that personal experience narratives can take. In other words, I am arguing that it makes no sense to treat the complexity and subtlety of the narration of experience as though it *should* have an orderly, complete structure by reducing it to the one type of text that conforms to the paradigmatic model.

Given that many of the limitations of the Labovian approach arise from its event-centric definition of narrative and the implications this has for identifying narratives, there are many ways in which narrative analysts can utilize the valuable aspects of Labov's work by using more inclusive definitional criteria. I formulated an experiential definition of the oral personal experience narrative for use with my data corpus of narratives of traumatic experience:

> texts which bring stories of personal experience into being by means of the first person oral narration of past, present, future or imaginary experience.

> (Patterson, 2000: 128)

This definition is broad enough to include all aspects of personal experience narration without being so broad as to suggest that everything anyone says may be counted as narrative. One is then free to apply the full Labovian model and method to those sections of transcripts that conform to the Labovian definitional criteria, but also to use Labovian tools and concepts as appropriate throughout. In my view, the necessary linguistic concepts and tools needed for performing systematic analyses are thin on the ground of narrative research so it is important that we make appropriate use of those that are available to us, as well as developing new ones.

Notes

1   See, for example, Attanucci (1993); Bell (1988); Ferrara (1994); Harris (2001); Koven (2002); Peterson and McCabe (1983); Polanyi (1981); Riessman (1990).
2   See Bakhtin (1981); Hermans (1996); Kerby (1991); Plummer (1995); Ricoeur (1991); Rosenwald and Ochberg (1993); Sampson (1993); Sarbin (1986); Widdershoven (1994).
3   The theoretical problems and limitations of the Labovian approach, when used in isolation, are discussed by a number of theorists who seek ways of incorporating the very valuable insights of Labov's work into a more holistic approach to data. See, for example, Agar and Hobbs (1982); Ferrara (1994); Koven (2002); McLeod (1997); Mishler (1986); Ochs (1994); Polyani (1979); Riessman (1993).

4   Unless referenced otherwise, all extracts in this chapter are taken from a data-corpus of personal experience narratives of trauma compiled by the author. All names and identifying features have been changed. Full details of the methodological and ethical issues concerning this data can be found in Patterson (2000).

5   Polanyi's 'state clauses' are similar to Riessman's concept of 'habitual narratives' (Riessman 1993:18–19) but Riessman uses 'habitual' at the level of the narrative whereas Polanyi identifies recurring states at the level of the clause.

Suggestions for further reading

- Langellier, K.M. (1989) and Mishler, E.G. (1995) are recommended to researchers as articles that can help to clarify which approach, or understanding of narrative, underpins one's own research.
- Readers who are interested in the philosophical issue of the relationship between life and story will find that Bal (1985), Mitchell (1981), Ricoeur (1981, 1984) and Widdershoven (1994) are all very useful texts. See also Patterson's (2002) analysis and discussion of 'liminal zone' stories for evidence that personal experience narratives are primarily about experience rather than events.
- From Labov's own work, his 1967 paper with Waletsky, his book *Language in the Inner City* and his more recent (1997) paper in *The Journal of Narrative and Life History*, now *Narrative Inquiry*, are good places to start. More recent papers can be found on his website. The 1997 Labov-dedicated volume of *The Journal of Narrative and Life History* is a very useful initial resource.

References

Agar, M. and Hobbs, J.R. (1982) Interpreting discourse: Coherence and the analysis of ethnographic interviews. *Discourse Processes* 5: 1–32.

Attanucci, J.S. (1993) Timely characterizations of mother–daughter and family-school relations: Narrative understandings of adolescence. *Journal of Narrative and Life History* 2: 99–116.

Bakhtin, M.M. (1981) *The Dialogic Imagination*. Austin: University of Texas Press.

Bal, M. (1985) *Narratology: Introduction to the Theory of Narrative*. Toronto: University of Toronto Press.

Bell, S.E. (1988) Becoming a political woman: The reconstruction and interpretation of experience through stories. In A. D. Todd and S. Fisher (eds) *Gender and Discourse: The power of Talk*. Norwood, NJ: Ablex.

Culler, J. (1981) *The Pursuit of Signs*. London: Routledge & Kegan Paul.

Ferrara. K.W. (1994) *Therapeutic Ways with Words*. Oxford: Oxford University Press.

Gee, J.P. (1991) A linguistic approach to narrative. *Journal of Narrative and Life History* 1(1): 15–39.

Genette, G. (1980) *Narrative Discourse*. Oxford: Basil Blackwell.

Gülich, E. and Quasthoff, U.M. (1987) Narrative analysis. In T. A. van Dijk (ed.), *Handbook of Discourse Analysis*. London: Academic Press.

Harris, S. (2001) Fragmented narratives and multiple tellers: witness and defendant accounts in trials. *Discourse Studies* 3 (1): 53–74.

Hermans, H.J.M. (1996) Voicing the self. *Psychological Bulletin* 119(1): 31–50.

Kerby, A. P. (1991) *Narative and the Self.* Bloomington: Indiana University Press.

Koven, M. (2002) An analysis of speaker role inhabitance in narratives of personal Experience. *Journal of Pragmatics* 34: 167–217.

Labov, W. (1972) *Language in the Inner City: Studies in the Black English Vernacular.* Oxford: Basil Blackwell.

Labov, W. (1982) Speech actions and reactions in personal narratives. In D. Tannen (ed.), *Analyzing Discourse: Text and Talk.* Washington DC: Georgetown University Press.

Labov, W. (1997) Some further steps in narrative analysis. *Journal of Narrative and Life History* 7: 395–415.

Labov, W. and Waletsky, J. (1967) Narrative Analysis: Oral Versions of Personal Experience. In J. Helms (ed.) *Essays in the Verbal and Visual Arts.* Seattle: University of Washington.

Langellier, K.M. (1989) Personal narratives: Perspectives on theory and research. *Text and Performance Quarterly* 9(4): 243–76.

Langellier, K. and Peterson, E.E. (1992) Spinstorying: An Analysis of Women Storytelling. In E.C. Fine and J.H. Speer (eds) *Performance, Culture and Identity.* Westport, CT: Praeger.

Linde, C. (1993) *Life Stories. The Creation of Coherence.* New York: Oxford University Press.

McLeod, J. (1997) *Narrative and Psychotherapy.* London: Sage.

Mishler, E.G. (1986) The analysis of interview-narratives. In T.R. Sarbin (ed.) *Narrative Psychology. The Storied Nature of Human Conduct.* New York: Praeger.

Mishler, E.G. (1995) Models of Narrative Analysis: A Typology. *Journal of Narrative and Life History* 5(2): 87–123.

Mitchell, W.J.T. (ed.) (1981) *On Narrative.* Chicago: University of Chicago Press.

Ochs, E. (1994) Stories that Step into the Future. In D. Biber and E. Finegan (eds) *Sociolinguistic Perspectives on Register.* New York: Oxford University Press.

Onega, S. and Landa, J.A.G. (1996) *Narratology : An Introduction.* New York: Longman.

Patterson, W. (2000) Reading trauma: exploring the relationship between narrative and coping. Unpublished PhD thesis. The Nottingham Trent University, UK (electronic copy available from the author: wendy@journalofhandsurgery.com).

Patterson, W. (2002) Narrative imaginings: The liminal zone in narratives of trauma. In W. Patterson (ed.) *Strategic Narrative. New perspectives on the power of personal and cultural stories.* Maryland: Lexington Books.

Personal Narratives Group (1989) *Interpreting Women's Lives: Feminist Theory and Personal Narratives.* Bloomington and Indianapolis: Indiana University Press.

Peterson, C. and McCabe, A. (1983) *Developmental Psycholinguistics: Three Ways of Looking at a Child's Narrative.* New York: Plenum.

Plummer, K. (1995) *Telling Sexual Stories: Power, Change and Social Worlds.* London: Routledge.

Polanyi, L. (1979) So what's the point? *Semiotica* 25: 3–4.

Polanyi, L. (1981) What stories can tell us about their teller's world. *Poetics Today* 2: 97–112.

Polanyi, L. (1985) Conversational Storytelling. In T.A. van Dijk (ed.), *Discourse and Dialogue, volume 3 of Handbook of Discourse Analysis 4.* London: Academic Press.

Ricoeur, P. (1981) *Hermeneutics and the Human Sciences* (edited by J. B. Thompson). Camb: Cambridge University Press.

Ricoeur, P. (1984) *Time and Narrative* volume 1 (translated by K. McLaughlin and D. Pellauer). Chicago: University of Chicago Press.

Ricoeur, P. (1991) Life in Quest of Narrative. In D.Wood (ed.) *On Paul Ricoeur: Narrative and Interpretation*. London: Routledge.

Riessman, C.K. (1990) *Divorce talk: Women and Men Make Sense of Personal Relationships*. New Brunswick, NJ: Rutgers University Press.

Riessman, C.K. (1993) Narrative analysis. *Qualitative Research Methods*. 30. Newbury Park, CA: Sage.

Rosenwald, G.C. and Ochberg, R.L. (eds) (1993) *Storied Lives. The Cultural Politics of Self-Understanding*. New Haven: Yale University Press.

Sampson, E.E. (1993) *Celebrating the Other. A Dialogic Account of Human Nature*. Hemel Hempstead: Harvester Wheatsheaf.

Sarbin, T.R. (1986) *Narrative Psychology. The Storied Nature of Human Conduct*. New York: Praeger.

Toolan, M.J. (1988) *Narrative A Critical Linguistic Introduction*. London: Routledge.

Widdershoven, G.A.M. (1994) Identity and Development: A Narrative Perspective. In H.A. Bosman, T.L.G. Graffsma, H.D. Grotevant and D.J. de Levita (eds) *Identity and Development: An Interdisciplinary Approach*. London: Sage.

Chapter 2

Experience-centred and culturally-oriented approaches to narrative

Corinne Squire

Introduction

This chapter examines how we can study narratives as stories of experience, rather than events; considers the problems associated with experience-centred narrative research; looks at ways to tackle such problems, particularly, adopting a more socially and culturally-directed research framework;[1] and returns to some research described in the previous chapter, while also referring to additional studies, and drawing on my research about people's stories of living with HIV in South Africa.

As noted in the previous chapter, when we consider personal narratives as event-centred, we tend to neglect three important narrative elements:

(a) Talk that is not about events but that is nevertheless significant for the narrator's story of 'who they are'.
(b) Representation itself. The uncertain, changeable nature of written, spoken and visual symbol systems means that stories are distanced from the happenings they described, have many meanings, and are never the same when told twice.
(c) Interactions between storyteller and listener, researcher and research participant, in the co-construction of stories.

Towards its end, Wendy Patterson looked at research that addresses these omissions by focusing not on the syntax (Mishler, 1986) of storied 'events', but at a second focus of narrative work: the semantics of narrated 'experience'. This chapter looks in more detail at such research.

I am going to describe this second type of narrative research, following Patterson, as experience-centred narrative research. The work rests on a phenomenological assumption that experience can, through stories, become part of consciousness. It also takes a hermeneutic approach to analysing stories, aiming at full understanding rather than, as in William Labov's case, structural analysis – although Labov himself does indeed describe this work as hermeneutic. This work does not provide useful methodological guidelines, like Labov's. Instead, it offers an appealing conceptual technology. It is the dominant conceptual framework within which current social science narrative research operates. It is perhaps most often related to the work of Paul Ricoeur (1984, 1991), which provides a helpful reference point for this chapter.

What is a narrative of experience?

The experience-centred approach assumes that narratives:

- are sequential and meaningful
- are definitively human
- 're-present' experience, reconstituting it, as well as expressing it
- display transformation or change.

Personal narratives as sequential and meaningful

Experience-centred narrative research distinguishes personal narratives from other kinds of representations as being sequential in time and meaningful. Unlike event-centred research, it assumes 'personal narrative' includes all sequential and meaningful stories of personal experience that people produce. Such stories may be an event narrative; but may also be more flexible about time and personal experience, and defined by theme rather than structure. An experience-centred narrative might address a life turning point (Denzin, 1989), such as a realization about sexuality, or having children. It might address a more general experience, such as living through a trauma and its consequences, as Patterson's research described in Chapter 1. It may go beyond the past tense first person recountings that interested Labov, to include present and future stories about others as well as oneself. It may address generalized states or, as Patterson emphasizes, imaginary events, as well as particular events that actually happened. It may appear in different places across an interview or interviews, and in contradictory ways.

A personal narrative could also, within the experience-centred tradition, be a life history or biography, produced in several interviews, perhaps over months or years, as in Molly Andrews's (1991) life history research with lifetime political activists. A personal narrative could be the thematic biography produced when someone tells the story of a long-term aspect of their life such as chronic illness (Bury, 1982) or career (Freeman, 2004). In these instances, sequence and meaningfulness are guaranteed by the research participant's following a life or theme; but some 'non-story' material – for instance, description and theorizing – will probably be included.

A personal narrative may also, from the experience-centred perspective, be the entire 'narrative' told to and with a researcher – a position Cathy Riessman (2000, 2002) arrives at, when looking for ways to understand her interviews with south Indian women about infertility. Here, 'sequence' spans dialogue, not just what the interviewee says; and meaningfulness is located in interviewer–interviewee interaction as well as the interviewees' words. Ricoeur (1991) describes this intersection of the life-worlds of speaker and hearer, or writer and reader, as an inevitable, constitutive characteristic of narrative.

For some experience-centred narrative researchers, 'personal narrative' can involve interviewing several people about the same phenomena, as with Elliot Mishler's interpretation of a man's story in the light of an interview with his wife, described in the previous chapter. Like Labov, some experience-centred researchers privilege speech as closest to personal experience, but experience-centred research also increasingly addresses written materials – published and unpublished, documentary and fiction – as with the diaries, letters, autobiographies and biographies that form Maria Tamboukou's data in her (2003) study of women teachers in the late nineteenth and early twentieth centuries. There is, too, growing interest in gathering and analysing visual materials and conducting interviews around them, as with Alan Radley's and Diane Taylor's (2003a, b) research on photo diaries produced by people during hospital stays, followed by interviews with them on their return home.

To understand 'meaning', experience-centred narrative researchers often expand the contexts, as well as the materials, that they study. They may include participants' and their own reflective written or oral comments on interviews, sometimes just afterwards, sometimes as a 'second take' years later, as in Andrews's (2003, 2004) research, which sustains longstanding interviewee relationships. Researchers may look at hard-to-transcribe fragments, contradictions and gaps within narratives, as well as the words themselves; or at the paralanguage of for instance tone, pauses and laughter 'around' words. They may draw in related materials, such as the larger cultural and national narratives about femininity, reproduction, and political activism that Riessman referred to in her study of south Indian women's infertility stories.

Thus, the previous chapter's definition of experience-centred narratives, as 'texts which bring stories of personal experience into being by means of the first person oral narration of past, present, future or imaginary experience' (p.37) and which may be fragmented and contradictory, is expanded by some in the experience-centred tradition to include *non-oral* media, and some non-first person and non-experiential material. All such material is contained within the tradition's broader understandings of narrative sequence and meaningfulness.

Narratives as means of human sense-making

Experience-centred narrative researchers think we can understand personal experience stories because of narratives' second defining feature: narratives are the means of human sense-making. Humans are imbricated in narrative. Labov too thinks there is a special relationship between people and stories. For him, event narratives express, in fairly invariant form, humans' most vivid experiences, those of sex, death and mortal injury. But the experience-centred approach assumes that sequential temporal orderings of human experience into narrative are not just characteristic of humans, but *make* us human. 'Time becomes human to the extent that it is articulated through a narrative mode', Ricoeur (1984: 52) puts it. Adapting Socrates, he declares that the 'examination' of a life, without which life is not worth living, consists in the recounting of it (1991).

For the psychologist Jerome Bruner, too, humans are, as a species, *homo narrans,* with an inborn tendency to tell and understand stories (1990). This perspective draws on the Aristotelian account of human morality as developed and transmitted through the meaning-making activity of storytelling. All stories are thus, to some extent, morality tales (MacIntyre, 1984). Stories are also, because human, deeply social; not just because they always involve hearers as well as speakers, as Labov might argue, but because storytelling constitutes and maintains sociality (Denzin, 1989). Even if you tell your story to yourself, or to someone who does not understand it, you are still speaking as a social being, to an imagined social 'other' who understands your tale.

At the same time, some experience-centred narrative researchers, particularly those influenced by psychoanalysis, think that important aspects of human experience escape narrative and cannot be storied into sense. Some such researchers, such as Stephen Frosh (2002), present narrative as nevertheless an important route towards such unrepresentable meanings. Wendy Hollway and Tony Jefferson (2000) similarly refer to the 'emotional' rather than the temporal sequencing of stories, as offering a route into the logic of the unconscious.

Narrative as representation and reconstruction

A third assumption of the experience-centred perspective on narrative is that narrative involves some reconstruction of stories across times and places. Narratives cannot be repeated exactly, since words never 'mean' the same thing twice (see Andrews, this volume),[2] and stories are performed differently in different social contexts. For Ricoeur and Bruner, narratives convey experience through reconstituting it, resulting in multiple and changeable storylines – like those pointed out in Mishler's and Langellier's work, examined in Chapter 1. These uncertainties of language can even be understood as a route to the unconscious, if the unconscious is itself defined, following Lacan, as like a 'language', and as existing, like stories, in and through the uncertainties of representation (Frosh, 2002).

Ricoeur describes narratives as jointly 'told' between writer and reader, speaker and hearer. In telling and understanding stories, we are thus working on the relation between 'life as a story in its nascent state' (Ricoeur, 1991: 29) and its symbolic translation into recounted narrative. Here we move towards what Mishler describes as the third focus of narrative research, its *context* – beginning with the research situation's interpersonal context, but taking in broader social and cultural contexts also. In my South African research on experiences and requirements of support for living with HIV, for example, many levels of context were in play. The interviewees were all black, mostly women, almost all working class, and largely under the age of 30. Speaking to a white middle class female university researcher from the overdeveloped world, in most cases older than them, certainly affected the stories they told. But interviewees were also speaking to the other potential hearers of their words, who would listen to archived tapes, or read papers or reports, or hear talks about the research. They were speaking, too, in the broader context of contemporary national contests over HIV issues, and the continuing global history and politics of the pandemic, over which they had little power but strong interests. At a time when they perceived scant interest in hearing them outside local HIV communities, they were highly concerned about what would happen to the research. They wanted the tapes archived. Sometimes, they even spoke directly into the tape recorder, addressing future audiences.

The interest in reconstruction and co-construction in experience-centred narrative research leads some researchers to view any personal story as just one of many narratable 'truths'. Ricoeur, however, distinguishes narrative from reason. Stories are for him, as for Labov, an imperfect, 'practical wisdom'. They convey and construct moralities, but they are time-dependent, caught in 'tradition', which for Ricoeur involves a varying balance between sedimentation and innovation. They are important sources of the 'truths' of a tradition, but they do not have the generality of a grand theoretical 'truth'.

However, some experience-centred researchers view narratives as representing, fairly transparently, both experience and the realities from which it derives. Such researchers may also assume that stories can represent the psychic realities of the narrator – including sometimes their unconscious elements – without much social mediation. Researchers using the biographic–narrative interpretive method such as for instance Prue Chamberlayne, Michael Rustin and Tom Wengraf (2002), expect to find in their interview transcripts both the story of an objective 'lived life' that can be corroborated by, for example birth and death registers and newspapers, and a 'told story', containing meanings specific to the narrator, including some unconscious meanings, relatively independent of the social contexts of storytelling. In stories about living with HIV, the 'lived life' might include date of diagnosis, medical history and support services used. The 'told story' might cover the speaker's journey through getting ill, getting tested; coming to terms with HIV both consciously and unconsciously, telling others about their status, and finding effective treatments and ways of living. The objectivity of the 'lived life', and the relatively asocial analysis and potentially unconscious nature of the 'told story' are often questioned. However, for some researchers, the distinction offers a starting point for identifying and defining narratives.

Narrative as transformation

Fourth, experience-centred research assumes that narratives represent personal changes that go beyond the formal 'resolutions' of Labovian event narratives. It addresses themes, rather than clauses. For Bruner (1990), for instance, stories involve the violation of normality and an attempt, through human agency, at its restoration. Michele Crossley (2000) applies this criterion to gay men's stories of living with HIV over a long period of time, and differentiates three separate kinds of story. One addresses HIV directly and comes to terms with it, even deploying a discourse of 'growth'; one normalizes HIV's impact throughout; the third is propelled into mourning by the losses involved with HIV and never makes its way out of it.

This interest in narrative change often impels experience-centred researchers to look for improvement in stories, as well as trying to understand them. Ricoeur suggests that by hearing a 'story not yet told', the psychoanalyst offers the analysis and the possibility of producing a better story, 'more bearable and more intelligible' (1991: 30). From an experience-centred perspective, all hearers and speakers of stories might be involved in such projects, including researchers and research participants. Experience-centred researchers are, therefore, often interested in what constitutes a 'good' human story. Crossley, for instance, assesses the melancholic stories she found in her narratives of long-term HIV survivors as the least adaptive. This emphasis on transformation leads to some experience-centred narrative research being associated, sometimes controversially, with social, psychological and sometimes quasi-clinical value judgements about stories.

Obtaining narratives of experience

When we start looking at how we might obtain narratives, more differences within the experience-centred approach emerge, depending on what definition of 'narrative' the researchers adopt.

Narrative materials

The range of materials that can be incorporated into experience-centred narrative research is wide, but there is one area of broad agreement: While some narrative researchers, predominantly working in clinical or observational settings, reconstruct material by writing notes concurrently or afterwards, most view the sequencing and particularity involved with stories as requiring a concurrent representation. This means that almost all experience-centred narrative researchers try to obtain a full written, aural or visual record of research participants' stories.

Researchers who take a broad view of 'narrative' and are interested in narratives' context may use a number of such records – oral, written and visual texts, field notes, participants' and their own commentaries, alongside related cultural representations and records of important realities in their own and their interviewees' lives. Riessman, for instance, (2000) situates her work on south Indian women's narratives of reproductive problems in relation to dominant cultural narratives of women's fertility, and south Indian political narratives. The value of this becomes clear when she analyses an interview with Gita, a woman who positions herself not as an infertile woman, but as a political actor, surrounded by stigmatizing discourses of femininity and reproduction (Riessman, 2002). Revisiting her materials several years on, Riessman (2005) includes more material about the context of the research, specifically about her own relation to discourses of feminism and postcolonialism, that leads her to understand Gita's story as potentially less heroic than in her earlier reading of a narrower range of narrative contexts.

Researchers who view narratives as relatively unmediated expressions of personal experience, such as Chamberlayne and her colleagues (Chamberlayne et al., 2002), may see context as important, but they treat it separately from the personal story. Researchers who are more interested in context may also concentrate on personal stories, simply because these seem the most practical and effective means of researching particular issues. Spoken personal testimony is indeed a strong cultural currency, with powerful effects, constituting, in the 'west' and beyond, what Kenneth Plummer (2001) calls an 'autobiographical age'. This is why my own research on HIV has focused on personal narratives, rather than other materials. In South Africa in 2001, when I did the interview study about HIV support, people living with HIV often felt unable to talk openly about their status. Even in politics and popular media, HIV was minimized or referred to other countries or other people, rarely owned publically. In this context, many research participants saw the interviews as a way of 'speaking out' for themselves and others. Their words practised and prefigured a new acceptance and openness about HIV in South Africa.

Ethical issues also affect what narrative materials are collected. In South Africa, I audio-recorded interviews in community organizations' offices, treated research participants as expert informants about HIV support and asked no questions about modes of infection, 'risk behaviours' or HIV as a medical condition. These constraints on content and context offered research participants an anonymity that visual recordings, or audio-recordings in domestic settings or clinics, could not. They provided a framework for referrals, should people want to access more support; and they clearly distinguished the research from studies of people's medical knowledge or individual efficacy. Similar issues of anonymity, confidentiality, referrals and implicit pathologization might arise when gathering Labovian event narratives. However, research that collects longer 'experience' narratives is more likely to encounter such issues, especially when it extends its definitions of 'materials' to include diverse media and extensive contextual elements.

Finally, experience-centred researchers who are interested in what is *not* clearly represented in narratives, try to include such elements within their materials. Hollway and Jefferson (2000), for example studying fear of crime in northern England in long, open-ended interviews, were concerned not just with what people said, but with contradictions, silences, hesitations and emotionally marked aspects of the interviews. As we shall see in the next section, such elements are harder to define, record and transcribe than symbolic language or images; they also present large problems for narrative analysis.

The processes of experience-centred narrative research

How is experience-centred narrative research carried out? As with Labovian event narrative research, general guidelines for qualitative research apply (Denzin and Lincoln, 2000; Seale et al., 2004). However, different definitional emphases again lead to divergent approaches. I shall concentrate on oral interview research, the most common form; research on experiential images and writing shows similar variability, but requires more specific considerations than I can offer here.[3]

Event-centred narrative researchers gather corpuses of stories. Experience-centred narrative researchers are more likely to aim for a certain number of interviews or interviewees. Researchers who study life narratives, or who aim for fully biographical accounts of at least parts of interviewees' lives, tend to use small numbers of interviewees, sampled theoretically, often on an opportunistic and network basis, with little randomization within this sampling frame. Interviews may involve several meetings and last many hours, but involve relatively small numbers of participants – 15 for instance in Andrews's (1991) life history study of older political activists. Hollway and Jefferson (2000) generated two interviews per participant and (like Mishler) interviewed family and other networks.[4] Notes on the interviews and their contexts will usually be made roughly concurrently. Broader contextual material, if collected, may be gathered beforehand – as in approaches influenced by oral history – or in parallel, as with Riessman's south Indian work.

Researchers who are interested less in biography, more in narrative themes' commonalities and differences across groups of individuals, tend to use larger interviewee numbers, and quota sampling and a degree of randomization, within a still theoretical sampling frame. Interviews here are typically one or two hours in length. In my South African research, for instance, I wanted to examine how people talked about HIV in differently resourced situations, and how gender might affect such talk. Interviews with 37 people in different neighbourhoods were a way both to look across local variabilities in resources and to obtain a reasonable number of male interviewees (eight), since men were, as in many interview studies, less likely to volunteer.

Pragmatic and ethical considerations are important, again, for sampling. It may be difficult for some participant groups to find time or personal resources for long interviews – for instance, in HIV research, if interviews are conducted far from home, or if participants have health problems. With sensitive research topics, it can be hard to recruit a sample for qualitative interviewing. The resultant small number of participants may, out of the researcher's concern to learn as much as possible from this group, be asked to participate in more intensive research, perhaps using a life history or biographical approach.

Most experience-centred narrative interviewing is semi-structured. Within this format, researcher involvement shows a continuum, depending on where the researcher thinks 'narratives' live. If you place the story within the person, you may simply ask for 'their story', intervening as little as possible. Hollway and Jefferson's (2000) 'free association narrative interviewing' for instance, concerned with narrators' emotional sequencing of their stories, is highly participant-centred in the interviewing phase. Somewhat like an analytic session, it allows silences and other awkwardnesses that may be difficult in a research – or indeed a conversation – context, and that may also present problems in terms of researcher's and participant's power within the research process. Researchers may partly constrain such open processes by asking for instance for a family or career 'story', and allowing 'active listening' that is, non-verbal responses by the researcher at conventionally appropriate points (Chamberlayne et al., 2002).

If you assume that reality is to some degree separate from personal story, you may triangulate, asking interviewees about real events, or looking for evidence of them elsewhere, for instance in newspaper reports (Chamberlayne et al., 2002). If you want to gather and analyse full biographical accounts, you may ask questions about 'conventional' aspects of lives – family, work, friends – if they are not spontaneously covered, and about events marked by the speaker as important but not expanded on (Wengraf, 2004). If you are convinced of the importance of narratives' co-construction, you will engage throughout in active narrative interviewing, an interaction that stretches to something like conversation, or co-research. If context is assumed to be a large aspect of research, you may, like Riessman in her south Indian work, be particularly alert to social and political factors as they affect the ongoing interview. In my South African research, interviewees sometimes explicitly referred to the country's post-apartheid, developing world context of political change and activism, alongside continuing structural disadvantage and poverty, high HIV prevalence and low treatment access. However, these factors were highly salient even when implicit.

If you want to collect and study stories about particular experiences, you may elicit them, with formulations like, 'can you give me an example?' or 'tell me more about when ...'. If, however, you see 'narrative' as the whole interview, or as a wider representational formation of which the interview is a part, you may not be concerned with gathering obvious 'stories'. You might even see such procedures as skewing the research. In asking South African interviewees about HIV support, I deliberately avoided such formulations, so as not to force individualization and particularization in people's talk.

Research need not stop with the first interview. You may return for chronological follow-up, a longer story, or to check facts, examine interpretations, or explore highly emotional issues. Hollway and Jefferson use second interviews to return to points in the first interview that their theoretical frame pointed to as significant: contradictions, silences, hesitations, strong or unusual patterns of emotion. Re-interviews and other post-interview interactions can also be viewed as ways to give interviewees more power over the materials; to enable them to 'look back' historically, or to continue the conversation: For Andrews and other life history researchers, such interactions can extend over decades.

Much qualitative research, modifying ethical considerations developed initially for quantitative, often medical research with 'human subjects' gives guarantees about the time-limited availability of materials. This may not be appropriate for narrative materials with which interviewees are heavily invested. Many of our South African research participants would not have agreed to participate without being convinced of the long-term survival of their interviews. However, the quantitatively derived ethics codes of many universities, in combination with the codes of professional bodies such as, in Britain, the British Psychological Society, British Sociological Association and the Economic and Social Research Council, do provide extensive participant rights over research processes and access to materials such as tapes and transcripts. These rights are often more significant for experience-centred narrative research than for the more minimal research processes of event narrative research.

How do we analyse narratives of experience?

In Labovian narrative analysis, defining, categorizing and assessing the 'evaluations' that give meaning to event narratives are difficult. Analysing the human meanings of experience–centred narratives is an even more controversial project.

Going round in hermeneutic circles

For Ricoeur, 'the hermeneutical problem begins where linguistics' – Labovian analysis, for instance – 'leaves off' (1991: 27). Some narrative analysts move from Labovian linguistics towards wider interpretive frames (Mishler, 1986; Riessman, 1993); others start off looking for large-scale 'meanings'. The search for a valid interpretive frame is perhaps the research stage that causes most argument and concern.

The simplest approach is to begin describing the interviews thematically, and from this, to develop and test theories that give a predictive explanation of the stories, moving back and forth between the interviews themselves and generalizations about them in a classic 'hermeneutic circle', using a combination of top–down and bottom–up interpretive procedures. This approach may not seem at first to differ greatly from many other qualitative procedures, for instance a thematic content analysis. However, experience–centred narrative analysis is distinguished by its attention to the sequencing and progression of themes within interviews, their transformation and resolution. Thus, it foregrounds the specifically narrative aspects of texts' meanings.

How the analysis is done depends once more on researchers' idea of what 'narrative' is. Riessman (2002) for instance describes expanding her initial definition of Gita's own 'experiences-of-pregnancy "narrative"', to include Gita's account of family reactions. This allowed her to analyse Gita's progressive and successful positioning of herself in her narrative as someone who is defined *by others* as having fertility problems. Hollway and Jefferson (2004) use a Kleinian theory of the narrator as an anxious and defended subject, and the biographical narrative as a means of managing psychic difficulties, to understand the contradictory attitudes of an unemployed working-class man, Tommy, towards his family, his fondly remembered 'poor but happy' childhood, his contemporary distance from most of his relations; and his conflicted attitudes towards his father. My own work (1998, 2003, 2007), assuming connections between individual and cultural narratives, analyses people's deployments of political, religious, psychological and western and traditional medical narratives, within their personal narratives of HIV.

Many researchers do not expect a single interpretation to emerge. They argue that there are multiple valid interpretations, multiple narrative 'truths' (Freeman, 2003); for them, the hermeneutic circle never closes. How, though, might we build a persuasive case for a particular interpretation? As described above, researchers themselves continually check their evolving interpretations against the materials and actively seek out contrary cases. They may also submit their analyses to external assessment by interested others (Chamberlayne et al., 2002). For some, the value of such external testing is restricted by the difficulty of others achieving sufficient familiarity with the materials to be able validly to interpret them. Feedback from respondents may also be a check on analyses (Andrews, 2003). My research used a combination of such procedures. My use of the religious conversion genre to analyse some interviewee stories came not simply from observed structural parallels between the genre and the interview narratives, but also from research assistants' independent comments on the faith-oriented nature of interviewees' HIV talk; interviewees' frequent mentions of religious faith; and the prominence of religious discourse in South Africa.

Analysis raises, again, some ethical questions. Ethical approval for experience-focused narrative research should, but rarely does, involve considering the ethics of interpretation, within the frame of researchers' and research participants' different powers over the data. Presentation of data can be problematic. Reproducing larger amounts of data than with an event-centred approach, sometimes glossing whole lives, it becomes harder to guarantee anonymity, especially when researching an understudied topic with a small community of potential respondents. To obviate this problem, researchers can – as those working with therapeutic materials often do – omit or change more specific data, guaranteeing confidentiality at the expense of some of the data's richness.

The ethics of discussing analyses with participants is widely debated, though all agree on the need for interpretive responsibility. Hollway and Jefferson provide transcripts but do not invite participant input into interpretation. From their psychoanalytic perspective, the participant may not know what she/he is 'saying' in the story (2004). Chamberlayne and colleagues feedback interpretations, particularly of semantically open-ended visual materials, and note responses, but do not necessarily change their accounts. Interviewee rights over material can, however, be conceived in a much stronger way that overlaps with interpretation, allowing participants to comment, rewrite and add their own analyses. Andrews for instance engages in long-term conversations with her participants over interpretations, exchanges which generate new materials and themselves become part of the analysis.

The place of the researcher

For Ricoeur, written and told stories are reconfigured in their readings or hearings: 'the process of composition, of configuration, is not completed in the text but in the reader' (1991: 26). Understanding requires, as for Labov, re-actualizing the act that produced the story, but in Ricoeur's account considerable indeterminacy attends the process. It is, though, possible, because for Ricoeur, as for Labov, human action and experience, like human symbols, all have a narrative structure (Ricoeur, 1991: 28–9). Yet narratives are not autonomous for Ricoeur, as they are in Labov's work. The worlds of readers and texts, speakers and listeners must be brought together, co-inhabited, in order for understanding to occur. Moreover, the tradition is, as we have seen, concerned with the possibilities of multiple interpretations, among which researchers' reflexive analyses of their own contributions sit easily. Riessman's accounts of her own implication in analytic processes (2002, 2005) again, provide good examples. Hollway and Jefferson formulate the process differently, as an examination of researcher countertransference, drawing on their psychoanalytic frame (2004). Andrews explores the issue of researcher stance and its historical specificity later in this volume.

The social world

Narrative is intrinsically social to some extent for all experience-centred researchers, since it uses the social medium of language and is produced by social subjects. At the same time, narrative remains, in this tradition, a production of individualized subjectivities. Ricoeur, having and eating his poststructuralist cake, puts it like this: 'we can become our own narrator' (1991: 32) while at the same time 'in place of an *ego* enamoured of itself arises a *self* instructed by cultural symbols, the first among which are the narratives handed down in our literary tradition' (1991: 33). This dualism is acted out in analysis, usually by paralleled top-down and bottom-up approaches. Top-down analyses tend – except in the case of psychoanalytic accounts – to be more socially oriented. My analyses for instance draw on existing research about religious and HIV discourses in South Africa, and relate it to the interview data. In Bamberg and Andrews's (2004) collection of papers on 'counternarratives', stories in interview materials are analysed as told 'against' dominant cultural narratives of, for instance, 'mothering' or ageing. Andrews (2004) argues that the explanatory power of this analysis is not vitiated by the frequently inexplicit 'countering' process, the fine grain of the materials, or the possibility of other levels of reading. Wengraf puts the cases more strongly when he advocates reading 'potentially symptomatic and revelatory expressions of historically evolving psychologies', within the personal biographies that emerge in his research – 'in a historically evolving context of micro and macro social relationships' (2004: 117) involving, for instance, employment and social welfare histories within particular communities. At the same time, he advises caution with such rich interpretive moves.

From social analysis to advocacy is a small step. Some experience-centred researchers include within their analysis a privileging of some stories over others: Crossley for instance sees the narratives of long-term HIV survivors that manage to consider the future as the most useful. Many researchers suggest that narratives that are not 'closed off', and that contain multiple possibilities within them, are better than more apparently dogmatic stories (Freeman, 2004; Wengraf, 2004). Even those who do not deliberately judge narratives often do so by default. It was indeed difficult in listening to our South African interviewees to get away from the sense that in general, narratives that managed to represent a future were 'good' stories – especially as such stories seemed commoner when interviewees had access to resources such as treatment and support groups. This kind of assumption is, however, indicative of the problems emerging around experience-centred narrative research.

Criticizing experience-centred narrative research

Interpretation as prescription

Experience-centred narrative research makes strong, sometimes prescriptive assumptions about the stories it claims to inhabit. The approach often assumes that hermeneutic immersion warrants the drawing up of a narrative typology of a particular text; judging which are 'good' narratives; and, on the presumption that narratives reflect lives, associating these 'good' stories with successful life adjustment. Of course, any hermeneutic project asserts some interpretive authority. Moreover, some researchers base their assumptions on well-specified, and therefore challengeable, psychoanalytic or narrative theories. However, others use nebulous criteria such as narrative 'openness' and 'reflexivity'; assert interpretive authority based on materials to which their readers have little access; or rely on assumptions about the nature of 'narrative' like those we considered earlier, whose cracks now start to show.

What is narrative 'coherence'?

A related issue is that some experience-centred research criticizes partial, fragmented or contradictory narratives for their incoherent representations of experience. For example, we tend to expect life narratives to mention family members, education, work, leisure and major life-defining events, and to provide more or less resolved accounts of them. I would argue however that we cannot tell what events 'ought' to be mentioned in life stories or how they 'should' be talked about. For example, one of our South African interviewees, telling how she and her boyfriend accepted and lived with her positive status and his refusal to test, said of their relationship, 'all of the children are his and it's been a long time that we've been staying together'. This account does not fit well with conventional western health education narratives of couples' HIV acceptance and risk reduction through talking and testing, or with almost any canonic social science or clinical account of 'good' heterosexual relationship as involving strong emotionality and communication. That does not make it a 'bad' story. There are many other frames within which it could be read – and within which our interviewee might indeed be expecting myself and the research assistant to understand it, involving for instance the highly mobile, resource-deprived, informal settlement in which she lives, and ways of representing emotions that do not involve talking about them a lot.

Even with difficult to understand stories like that told by a man with schizophrenia, considered by Phil Salmon and Riessman in Chapter 4, the establishment of a language community can be worked at so the stories can get 'heard'. But we have to accept that we are always powerfully limited in story understanding. My and my South African informants' story worlds are hard to bring into congruence and will retain relative autonomy, and this is true to a degree of all storytellers and hearers. The experience-centred approach's emphasis on story worlds coming into congruence, despite its awareness of mismatches between storytellers and researchers, tends to downplay such incongruence.

Is there a 'subject' of experience?

The experience-oriented approach initially suggests that experience is rooted in a 'subject' of those experiences, which has some unity and agency. This position is now sometimes asserted 'against' postmodernism's alleged preoccupations with an entirely fragmented and socially determined subject, which is then presented as elitist, relativist and non-political. At other times, the experience-oriented approach claims a kind of partial, continent subjective unity along the lines perhaps of Spivak's (1993) 'strategic essentialism' and interest in collective action, or Ian Hacking's (1998) assertions about the need for a level of subjective continuity to underpin moral and political personhood (see also Freeman, 2003). Its default first approach, however, can lead experience-focused research into the individualized, prescriptive approaches we have described, and to psychobiographies of data, which assume an authorial subjectivity 'behind' the material. This approach cuts researchers off from all the other literary and cultural studies work on narrative which takes more complicated approaches to subjectivity.

Analysing experience, forgetting language

A focus on 'experience' also tends to reduce the significance of language in narrative research. Even if language is seen as reconstructing experience and not as a direct translation of it, language's patterns and effects tend to be uninteresting to experience-centred researchers. Links between interpersonal and cultural forms of language, such as those in which I am interested, are neglected. Moreover, 'performance', a term frequently used in current narrative research, takes on a Goffmanian meaning, signifying the presentation of different narrative identities in different contexts, with a unified subject behind them. The present popularity of the term derives from Judith Butler's (1993) usage. But her complicated account of 'performance' as predicated on the non-repeatability of significations and a non-repeatable, non-identical subject, is often jettisoned in narrative research. Performance in Butler's sense does not suggest any simple assumptions about agency or language's expression of it.

Relativism

Lastly, even those who work within the experience-centred tradition while also being aware of the complexities of language and subjectivities can end up, by prioritizing experience, with a relativist set of equally valid interpretations. It may seem as if there is no place to stop the interpreting, and no way to judge between interpretations, all of which may be 'truthful' in their own contexts.

Cultural genres and personal narratives

One way around some of these problems is to look at the social and cultural character of personal narratives. A valuable example is Kenneth Plummer's *Telling Sexual Stories* (1995), which traces the emergence of intimate disclosure narratives in the twentieth century west within the larger context of the contemporary cultural and political power of autobiography (see also Plummer, 2001). Plummer gives detailed accounts of, for instance, lesbian and gay coming-out narratives: their structure; the historical and social contexts which enabled their development;

how they have changed; and their effects. He argues that such stories must have an audience at least partly prepared to hear them if they are to achieve currency, but that stories also themselves 'gather people together'. Stories operate within 'interpretive communities' of speakers and hearers that are political as well as cultural actors. They build collective identities that can lead, albeit slowly and discontinuously, to cultural shifts and political change. Personal stories thus often operate as bids for representation and power from the disenfranchized. Plummer (2001) points out that the trend since the nineteenth century has been towards stories told by the less powerful, in a collective mode where one person's story 'stands in' for many others, as with US slave narratives and the testimonies of peoples under occupation.

Within the intimate disclosure genre, there are many variations. My own concern with HIV positive people's ways of talking about the epidemic in South Africa started from the assumption that cultural and personal narratives are interconnected. My specific interest in how people's stories drew on the conversion narrative genre developed first from a recognition of how often interviewees, when talking about being HIV positive, talked also about religion; and from an awareness of the religious sounding phrases and structures in many interviewees' stories. Here is an example, from an interview with a woman who named herself Linda:

Linda: Okay! In the first place I am glad that I know of my HIV positive status because now I know what to do. Then my husband, the one I am married to, I told him. At first, he could not accept it, he gave me too many problems. I then continued talking about it everyday, I used to chat about it so that it would sink into him that I am HIV positive/Mhm/ Truly, eventually he accepted it. My baby was not discharged yet, so that he/she could be tested as well./Ok/ Then he asked about the baby. I said the baby will be tested at 9 months. I then explained. Truly then I was told that the baby, I was very happy, because I was happy to save my baby. AZT helped me, my baby was tested negative. That made me a very happy person, I didn't think of myself as having HIV because I am still alright. There is no difference I must say. My health is still good. The other thing that made me happy is the group support that we are doing as nursing mothers./Ok/ The thing that really helped was the support groups. It really really helped us because you feel free when you are there I must say. You become very happy and forget that eish, when you get home it is then that you remember that you have HIV, but when you are there you are free. We advise each other very well, even the instructor (facilitator), I must say she tells us what to do. So today I am not ready, I am not yet free, I don't feel like I am open, I am not open yet to stand up and say I have HIV. I am still getting there, you understand?/Mhm/ But I feel alright, most importantly I thank God. God said these things before, he said there will be these incurable diseases, so I believe in God truly. What he talked about, is happening today. So that is something else that

Continued

> inspired me, because God mentioned this before, he said they will happen, they are happening today, unto people, they would not fall in steep places, so I believe in that.

This is, at one level, the story of Linda's personal coming to terms with her HIV status. It also exemplifies the religious 'conversion' genre drawn on by interviewees, who described a struggle to confront HIV status, culminating in a conversion moment, often marked by interviewees saying something like, 'then, I believed,' or – as here – 'truly, eventually he accepted it'. For women who, like Linda, had received antiretroviral treatment during pregnancy, this transformation moment was often revisited in the salvational event of their baby testing negative. As in many religious narratives, there were ongoing doubts and reaffirmations of faith. Linda tells of her continuous struggle to improve, ethically as well as informationally, her relation to HIV. Many interviewees told stories of searching out HIV versions of faith communities to strengthen their beliefs – as for Linda, support groups acted in this way where family and friendship groups did not. The stories also often moved on to a kind of HIV witnessing, aimed at converting others to an accepting, knowledgeable and hence ethical life with HIV. The speaker's own telling of their status to others was frequently the first step in this testimony, as for Linda with her husband. Linda's story becomes explicitly entwined with Christian discourse at the end when she seems to be evoking Isaiah's promises of protection of the faithful and the punishment of the wicked – though personal transgression is certainly not equated here with HIV status.[5] However, this kind of story was also often told with no explicit religious content, still deploying a structure that moved from conflict to conversion and witnessing.

Why do such cultural resonances matter? I am assuming that the interconnection between such genres and personal narratives may potentiate personal narratives' effects. The conversion genre was not simply recognizable to our interviewees, ourselves and to wider South African speech communities; it also worked to turn stories of HIV into morality tales. The stories borrowed ethical force of the conversion genre and gave it to living with HIV, often the object of some quite different religious stories of possession, transgression or silence. The conversion genre was then a powerful one at this specific time and place.

Genres are always mixed up and imperfect. As Derrida (1981) says, the law of genre is to break its own laws. My assumption was that many cultural narratives, rather than just one, would inflect personal narratives, so I also looked at stories' inflection by western and traditional health narratives of HIV; psychological narratives of coming to terms with the condition, and political narratives of self-affirmation and action. It is, too, important to recognize that stories are strongly determined by material circumstances. Interviewees tended to tell longer and more complex stories in conditions where they had access to support – support groups, sympathetic family members, medical treatment, employment and training. Interviewees with little support were, unsurprisingly, less likely to talk about HIV at length.

A genre's imperfections also mean that aspects of people's lives that are hard to make sense of can still appear within a 'genre'; it continues, imperfectly, around them. This is important in the case of HIV, whose relations with stigma, death, sexuality and uncertainty are hard to put into words. Crises of HIV 'faith', for instance, can appear in Linda's narrative of immanent, not-yet-achieved belief; she is ready but also not ready to speak of HIV; she is on the long road to community and faith that conversion narratives set out.

Putting the experience-centred approach in a broader cultural context can make it less prescriptive, less controlled by temporal progression; less focused on coherence; more aware of language; more likely to understand selves in non-essentialist ways and more able to break out of hermeneutic reflexivity with its social referents. But how 'solved' are these problems, actually? Expanding the remit of experience-centred narrative research may just force it to operate with two incommensurable theories of the speaking subject: the agentic, storytelling subject of the experience-focused tradition, at odds with the fragmented, culturally produced, 'postmodern' subject of more culturally-oriented analyses.

Neither does a 'cultural' approach necessarily avoid relativism, guarantee political engagement nor provide a clear concept of the relationship between narrative representations and their effects. It is difficult to say anything definitive about narrative genres, given the multiplicity and incompleteness just described. Moreover, focusing on 'cultural stories' can lead to narrow particularism about specific stories; or to reifying culture, for instance, by collapsing stories into categories such as 'women's stories' from which politics is evacuated. The political shapes of narratives are larger than a 'cultural' analysis can indicate; a move towards broader understandings of them is becoming more common in narrative researchers' work, as Chapter 3 and the final section of this book will demonstrate. From an opposed perspective, some critics accuse culturally-oriented approaches of losing sight of the individual stories. In analysing Linda's story as a conversion narrative, am I erasing the particularity of her language and experience?

Some of these problems can be circumvented. Many stories do not mean infinite stories. Liz Stanley's (1992) set of cultural 'stories' about the Yorkshire Ripper are as she points out also an interested collection, told from a set of resistant standpoints that are far from relativist. The contemporary significance of 'experience' as a place-setter for political claims is too strong to allow us to ignore it on the grounds of its conceptual messiness or political dangers. Plummer makes detailed and subtle arguments about the catalyzing effects of self-disclosure stories in shifting political circumstances. These effects are particular to time and place, but we can expect some generalization. For instance, since our South African interviewees drew on genres of conversion and witnessing to talk about HIV in a situation where HIV identities had been 'othered' as unclean and immoral (Joffe, 1997), it may be that such ethical self-disclosure genres may be useful resources in other situations of narrative pathologization. I would also argue that individual stories are not lost, but reframed in this approach. What we hear from Linda is certainly a 'personal' story – just one expressed within a particular national and representational context.

Some problems remain. Can genres really continue across the unsayable and so 'represent' unrepresentable things, as I have suggested? Critics who point to the seductive and even self-deluding sense that you have solved unsolvable unconscious issues by 'telling your story' would not be convinced. Was there any way for the loss of a child or the shame of sexual transgression really to find a place within the narratives of the South African interviewees? Psychoanalytic approaches to narrative might argue that unconscious significations in and around the research materials are being neglected in this analysis.

In addition, in looking at the genre structure of, for instance conversion narratives, we miss out, inevitably, on smaller, co-occurring language structures, the co-construction of narratives between speakers and hearers, and the limits of such co-construction. Such structures are specially difficult to discern across language differences – which of course exist between the 'language communities' of any interviewer and interviewee, but which are much more pronounced and freighted with historical and political meanings in cases like my South African research, where white middle class UK English met South African English and urban Xhosa, itself mixed with English and containing many Xhosalised English terms.[6] Chapter 3 examines how research on the fine grain of context can help us understand the construction of narratives and identities. This is an issue that is also taken up in the conversation between Salmon and Riessman in Chapter 4, and in Andrews's Chapter 5.

I want finally to mention a valuable counter to many criticisms of experience-centred narrative research: Couze Venn's recent work on a move towards the 'politics of transfiguration' from 'problems of identity' in the Israeli context (2005). Venn joins a Ricoeurian approach to narrative identity and a commitment to Bakhtinian dialogics, with concepts drawn from the work of Derrida and Levinas on hospitality, responsibility, gift and forgiveness. He examines ethnographic materials from two high schools that stage 'dialogues' between Jewish and Arab Israeli students. Such dialogues address, for instance, the concept of land, which for Jewish Israelis, however diverse their own histories, is the end point of an emancipatory narrative. For Arab Israelis and ·Palestinians, it is a place of long term settlement or nomadic travel and use. The dialogues also address the histories of specific events, narrated quite differently by the two communities. Following Ricoeur, Venn notes that narrative approaches history and identity through chronological time, but is also fiction. Histories and personal stories, co-articulated by the school students, interweave materiality and subjectivity. Together, they help create, Venn says, not a reconciliation but a third space between the interminabilities of speech, and the fixed meanings of what is said; between the future and lived worlds. These are already mixed – the school dialogues just foreground and promote this mixing.

Grand narratives, for Venn, may have considerable ambiguities within them which allow them to be 'occupied' by others. The ongoing context of state violence does not encourage dialogue, but within these school programmes, some ability emerges imaginarily to inhabit the story of the other – as in Patterson's example, where the listener is invited into the trauma of the other, and to take Levinasian responsibility for the other. Power differences though remain, even in the unequal languages in which the students must dialogue, which privileges Hebrew, through

familiarity with which Arab students are expected to demonstrate their commitment to Israeli citizenship. Venn is not over-optimistic about the possibilities of
such narrative research in action, but for him, it remains worth doing.

Conclusion

The experience-centred approach has many positive features; for example it focuses
on the constructive powers of narrative, which can be useful for social research
and practice; its biographical interests are salient for the many for whom 'life story'
undoubtedly is expressively or analytically meaningful; and it can extend the notion
of 'story' into communicative realms other than speech and writing, such as the
visual and action. Its interest in the intersections of texts and audience worlds
allows attention to the co-construction of narratives; diversities, uncertainties and
intertextualities in and between narratives; subjectivities that are always in process;
stories with truths rather than a single truth (Freeman, 2003); stories that have social
effects; and stories that may serve useful, even 'improving' functions for people.
As Venn (2005) points out, in relation to Ricoeur's narratology, the approach
can serve the important contemporary function of allowing personal narratives of
identifications to come into congruence with broader narratives of trauma and
conflict, through the storying of memory and history.

   As we have seen, the experience-centred approach also runs into a number of
problems, particularly of over-interpretation. Ways to guard against them might
include listening carefully to research participants. We will probably want to be
able to defend our interpretations to them, except if our interpretive framework
clearly suggests this is not useful – as in Hollway and Jefferson's (2004) case, where
interpretation depends on analysis of unconscious processes that are not expected
to be available to the interviewee. We will be aware that we cannot be fully
reflexive, that there will always be material that lies beyond the realm of our
interpretations and that we may get things very wrong for our interviewees, or
for other audiences. If approaching materials psychoanalytically, we might also
want to keep in mind the 'story' of psychoanalysis itself (Parker, 2003). We will
be trying to situate our work culturally and politically; we will also want to pay
attention to the microcontexts of research through which these broader issues are
lived and clarified.

   Experience-centred and culturally-oriented narrative research is, as this chapter
demonstrates, extremely diverse, with limited common ground. Relating stories
to personal identities, unconscious meanings and cultural representations, for
instance, are theoretically and often methodologically distinct endeavours. The
perspectives tend, however, to be loosely associated, by a kind of pragmatic politics.
Many of them share a similar preoccupation with a politics of representation and
expression (Freeman, 2003), rooted in a long history of class, gender, anticolonial
and sexuality politics driven by personal narratives (Stanley, 1992; Plummer,
1995). Whether they associate narrative research with personal biographies, with
cultural patterns of representation, or with the interpersonally produced 'story'
of the interview process, such narrative approaches often operate as means of
delineating and even theorizing under- or unrepresented lives; and as preliminary,

complementary or even new forms of politics for unpolitical - or differently political-times. It may be that this commonality supercedes theoretical and methodological divergences. It may also, however, be that such commonality is itself limited, in the long run, by the unaddressed contradictions within these narrative approaches.

Notes

1 Portions of this chapter are adapted from Squire (2005; 2007).
2 This slipperiness of meaning can be understood either structurally, in terms of changing nets of signifiers and signifieds, or from a more purely phenomenological or historical perspective.
3 Visual-, object- and writing-based methods need their own considerations – see Bell (2006), Radley and Taylor (2003a, b) and Tamboukou (2003), for examples.
4 Their total of 37 participants included around a third in family groupings.
5 Psalm 37's assurances of protection for the faithful, and Psalm 91's invocation of pestilences may also be referred to here.
6 Given limited researcher time and language skills, full analysis of these complexities was too speculative for me to attempt.

Suggestions for further reading

- On experience-centred narrative research, foundational readings come from Ricoeur (1984; 1991). Recent examples using the perspective are Freeman (for instance, 1993; 2004) and Riessman (for instance, 2002). Bakhtin (1986) provides a good account of dialogic aspects of the approach, taken up in Venn's (2005) work.
- On this approach: compared to others, see Emerson and Frosh (2004), Freeman (2003), Parker (2003), Riessman (2002) and Rustin (2000).
- For more detailed accounts of life history and biographical research, full accounts – from varying theoretical perspectives – can be found in Andrews (1991), Chamberlayne et al. (2002), Hollway and Jefferson (2000) and Mishler (1986).
- Useful addresses to context at levels from the interpersonal to metanarrative appear in Abell et al. (2004), Georgakopoulou (2007), Malson (2004), Mishler (1986) and Riessman (2002).
- Narrative genre is usefully considered in Edley (2002), Jacobs (2004), Plummer (1995; 2001) and Squire (1999). For the linguistic foundation of this work, see Todorov (1990).
- For broader accounts of the power relations involved with stories of 'experience', see Burman (2003) and Tamboukou (2003). For counter-narratives, see Bamberg and Andrews (2004) and Fine and Harris (2001).
- To consider the specialist area of narratives of illness experiences, good texts to start with are Bury (1982), Frank (1997), Kleinman (1988) and Riessman (1990).
- For perspectives on visual and other non-linguistic experience 'narratives; see Bell (2003a, b), Harrison (2004) and Seale (2004).
- These are often good texts to read when trying to find a way to do this kind of research; Karen Throsby's study of IVF failure (now published, 2004) is a recent example.

References

Abell, J., Stokoe, E. and Billig, M. (2004) Narrative and the discursive (re)construction of events. In M. Andrews, S. D. Sclater, C. Squire and A. Treacher (eds) *Uses of Narrative*. New Brunswick, NJ: Transaction.

Andrews, M. (1991) *Lifetimes of Commitment: Ageing, Politics, Psychology*. Cambridge University Press.

Andrews, M. (2003) Conversations through the years: Reflections on age and meaning. Conference Proceedings of the 4th International Symposium on Cultural Gerontology; Tampere, Finland, May.

Andrews, M. (2004) Memories of mother? In M. Bamberg and M. Andrews (eds) *Considering Counter-Narratives*. Amsterdam: John Benjamins.

Bakhtin, M. (1986) *Speech Genres and Other Late Essays*. Austin TX: University of Texas Press.

Bamberg. M. and Andrews, M. (2004) *Considering Counter-Narratives*. Amsterdam: John Benjamins.

Bell, S. (2006) Becoming a mother after DES: Intensive mothering in spite of it all. In Anna DeFina, Deborah Schiffrin and Michael Bamberg (eds) *Discourse and Identity*. Cambridge: Cambridge University Press.

Bruner, J. (1990) *Acts of Meaning*. Cambridge, MA: Harvard University Press.

Burman, E. (2003) Narratives of 'experience' and pedagogical practices. *Narrative Inquiry* 13(2): 269–86.

Bury, M. (1982) Chronic illness as biographical disruption. *Sociology of Health and Illness* 4(2): 167–82.

Butler, J. (1993) *Bodies that Matter*. London: Routledge.

Chamberlayne, P., Rustin, M. and Wengraf, T. (eds) (2002) *Biography and Social Exclusion in Europe: Experiences and Life Journeys*. Bristol: Policy Press.

Crossley, M. (2000) *Introducing Narrative Psychology: Self, Trauma and the Construction of Meaning*. Buckinghamshire: Open University Press.

Denzin, N. (1989) *Interpretive Biography*. New York: Sage.

Denzin, N. and Lincoln, Y. (2000) *Handbook of Qualitative Research*. Thousand Oaks, CA: Sage.

Derrida, J. (1981) The law of genre. In W. J. T. Mitchell (ed.) *On Narrative*. Chicago: University of Chicago Press.

Edley, N. (2002) The loner, the walk and the beast within: Narrative fragments in the construction of masculinity. In W. Patterson (ed.) *Strategic Narrative: New Perspectives on the Power of Stories*. Oxford: Lexington.

Emerson, P. and Frosh, S. (2004) *Critical Narrative Analysis in Psychology*. London: Palgrave.

Fine, M. and Harris, A. (2001) (eds) Under the covers: Theorizing the politics of counter stories. *International Journal of Critical Psychology* 4: 183–99.

Frank, A. (1997) *The Wounded Storyteller*. Chicago, IL: University of Chicago Press.

Freeman, M. (1993) *Rewriting the Self: History, Memory, Narrative*. New York: Routledge.

Freeman, M. (2003) Identity and difference in narrative inquiry, Psychoanalytic narratives: Writing the self into contemporary cultural phenomena. *Narrative Inquiry* 13(2): 331–46.

Freeman, M. (2004) When the story's over. In M. Andrews, S. D. Sclater, C. Squire and A. Treacher (eds) *Uses of Narrative*. New Brunswick, NJ: Transaction.

Frosh, S. (2002) *After Words*. London: Palgrave.

Georgakopoulou, A. (2007) *Small Stories, Interaction and Identities*. Amsterdam: John Benjamins.

Hacking, I. (1998) *Rewriting the Soul*. Princeton, NJ: Princeton University Press.

Harrison, B. (2004) Photographic visions and narrative inquiry. In M. Bamberg and M. Andrews (eds) *Considering Counter-Narratives: Narrating, Resisting and Making Sense*. Amsterdam: John Benjamins.

Hollway, W. and Jefferson, T. (2000) *Doing Qualitative Research Differently: Free Association, Narrative and the Interview Method*. London: Sage.

Hollway, W. and Jefferson, T. (2004) Narrative, discourse and the unconscious. In M. Andrews, S. D. Sclater, C. Squire and A. Treacher (eds) *Uses of Narrative*. New Brunswick, NJ: Transaction.

Jacobs, R. (2004) Narrative, civil society and public culture. In M. Andrews, S. D. Sclater, C. Squire and A. Treacher (eds) *Uses of Narrative*. New Brunswick, NJ: Transaction.

Joffe, H. (1997) The relationship between representational and materialist perspectives: AIDS and the 'other'. In L. Yardley (ed.) *Material Discourses of Health and Illness*. London: Routledge.

Kleinman, A. (1988) *The Illness Narratives*. New York: Basic Books.

MacIntyre, A. (1984) *After Virtue*. Bloomington, IN: University of Notre Dame Press.

Malson, H. (2004) Fictional(ising) identity? Ontological assumptions and methodological productions of ('anorexic') subjectivities. In M. Andrews, S. D. Sclater, C. Squire and A. Treacher (eds) *Uses of Narrative*. New Brunswick, NJ: Transaction.

Mishler, E. (1986) *Research Interviewing: Context and Narrative*. Cambridge, MA: Harvard University Press.

Parker, I. (2003) Psychoanalytic narratives: Writing the self into contemporary cultural phenomena. *Narrative Inquiry* 13(2): 301–15.

Plummer, K. (1995) *Telling Sexual Stories*. London: Routledge.

Plummer, K. (2001) *Documents of Life 2*. London: Sage.

Radley, A. and Taylor, D. (2003a) Images of recovery: a photo-elicitation study on the hospital ward. *Qualitative Health Research* 13(1): 77–99.

Radley, A. and Taylor, D. (2003b) Remembering one's stay in hospital: a study in recovery, photography and forgetting. *Health: An Interdisciplinary Journal for the Social Study of Health, Illness and Medicine* 7(2): 129–59.

Ricoeur, P. (1984) *Time and Narrative*. Chicago: Chicago University Press.

Ricoeur, P. (1991) Life in quest of narrative. In D. Wood (ed.) *On Paul Ricoeur: Narrative and Interpretation*. London: Routledge.

Riessman, C. (1990) Strategic uses of narrative in the presentation of self and illness. *Social Science & Medicine* 30(11):1195–200.

Riessman, C. (1993) *Narrative Analysis*. New York: Sage.

Riessman, C. (2000) Even if we don't have children we can live: Stigma and infertility in South India. In C. Mattingly and L. Garro (eds) *Narratives and the Cultural Construction of Illness and Healing*. Berkeley: University of California Press.

Riessman, C. (2002) Analysis of personal narratives. In J. Gubrium and J. Holstein (eds) *Handbook of Interview Research*. Thousand Oaks: Sage.

Riessman, C. (2005) Exporting ethics: a narrative about narrative research in South India. *Health* 9(4):473–90.

Rustin, M. (2000) Reflections on the biographical turn in the social sciences. In P. Chamberlayne, J. Bornat and T. Wengraf (eds) *The Turn to Biographical Methods in Social Science*. London: Routledge.

Seale, C. (2004) Resurrective practice and narrative. In M. Andrews, S. D. Sclater, C. Squire and A. Treacher (eds) *Uses of Narrative*. New Brunswick, NJ: Transaction.

Seale, C., Gobo, G., Gubrium, J. and Silverman, D. (2004) *Qualitative Research Practice*. London: Sage.

Squire, C. (1999) Neighbors who might become friends: Identities, genres and citizenship in HIV narratives. *The Sociological Quarterly* 40(11): 109–37.

Squire, C. (2003) Can a HIV positive woman find true love? Romance in the stories of women living with HIV. *Feminism and Psychology* 13(1): 73–100.

Squire, C. (2005) Reading narratives. *Group Analysis* 38(1): 91–107.

Squire, C. (2007) *HIV in South Africa: Talking about the Big Thing*. London: Routledge.

Spivak, G. (1993) Interview Sara Danius and Stefan Jonsson. *Boundary 2* 20(2): 24–50.

Stanley, L. (1992) *The Auto/Biographical I: Theory and Practice of Feminist Auto/Biography*. Manchester University Press.

Tamboukou, M. (2003) *Women, Education, the Self: A Foucauldian Perspective*. Basingstoke: Palgrave Macmillan.

Throsby, K. (2004) *When IVF Fails: Feminism, Infertility and the Negotiation of Normality*. Houndmills: Palgrave.

Todorov, T. (1990) *Genres in Discourse*. Cambridge: Cambridge University Press.

Venn, C. (2005) The repetition of violence: Dialogue, the exchange of memory, and the question of convivial socialities. *Social Identities* 11(3): 283–98.

Wengraf, T. (2004) in M. Andrews, S. D. Sclater, C. Squire and A. Treacher (eds) *Uses of Narrative*. New Brunswick, NJ: Transaction.

Chapter 3

Analysing narrative contexts

Ann Phoenix

As interest in narrative has proliferated in recent years, so too have different modes of narrative analysis. Some analysts now focus on the temporal ordering of a plot; some on themes; some on episodes and drama; some on narrative as an interactional accomplishment and some on a combination of these (Riessman, 2001). In Chapter 2, Corinne Squire focused on how we can study narratives as stories of experience, rather than treating them as if they are straightforwardly descriptions of events. This approach fits with what Georgakopolou (2006a: 123) refers to as a 'second wave of narrative analysis' that has 'moved from the study of narrative as text (first wave) to the study of narrative-in-context'. In making this division Georgakopolou (2006a, b) engages with a major debate: whether it is more productive to focus on 'big' or on 'small' stories. Big stories take as their unit of analysis the content of the (auto)biographical story, used to analyse identity and often take cognitive perspectives. By way of contrast, small stories focus on the stories 'we tell in passing, in our everyday encounters with each other' or 'narratives-in-interaction' (Bamberg, 2004: 367; 2006: 146) – that is on how narrative is performed and accomplishes particular tasks, including identity. The 'small story' approach has been fuelled by the 'discursive turn' in the social sciences as some conversation analysts and discourse analysts have begun to conduct fine-grain analyses of the ways in which people 'do' narratives in the context of interactions (for example, Stokoe and Edwards, 2006; Taylor, 2006).

There is currently debate about the utility of the 'small story' approach with many narrative analysts maintaining a commitment to 'big story' approaches or 'life on holiday' as Freeman (2006) puts it, even if they recognize the utility of some 'small story' analysis (e.g. Freeman, 2006; Wengraf, 2006). However, the 'small story' approach allows attention to 'under-represented narrative activities, such as tellings of ongoing events, future or hypothetical events, shared (known) events, but also allusions to tellings, deferrals of tellings, and refusals to tell' Georgakopolou, 2006a: 123). In other words, analysis of the small story enables attention on how people build their narratives and the performative work done by the narratives. This allows insights into the dilemmas and troubled subject positions speakers negotiate as they tell their stories (Billig, 1991; Wetherell, 1998) and so into their understandings of current consensus about what it is acceptable to say and do in their local and national cultures – i.e. what Bruner (1990, 2002) calls 'canonical narratives'. While many conversation and discourse analysts would eschew readings of unconscious motivations, attention to 'the small story' can also facilitate such readings, since ways of telling can signal implicit and unconscious links or free associations between ideas (Hollway and Jefferson, 2000).

There are three advantages that accrue when narrative analysts attend to the doing of narrative. First, it permits the study of identity, focusing on the local practices through which it is produced in particular times and places (Bamberg, 2004, 2006; Georgakopolou, 2006a, b). Second, it attends to the stories and life stories told and how they are occasioned, but also attends to material that is not neatly storied into beginning, middle or end or that appears incoherent – which can be most of an account. It therefore allows both a focus on episodes or event stories ('big story') and aspects of narrative identities that are diachronic in that they present different time frames ('small stories') by attending to what is presented in the interview situation and what is being claimed on the basis of experience (Battersby, 2006; Järvinen, 2004). The small story approach can thus produce a fruitful synthesis of the biographical and contextual approaches discussed in previous chapters in this book. Third, it foregrounds the context within which particular narratives are produced. What constitutes context is, however, subject to debate. In particular, there is disagreement about how to analyse narrative contexts and whether or not it is warranted for analysts to orient to the wider context if narrators do not (e.g. Manstead and Wetherell, 2005). Yet, despite disagreement about how to do so and/or what constitutes context, there is general agreement that it is important to attend to it in narrative analysis.

There are various ways in which researchers attend to small stories and to the wider cultural context. For example, focusing on the minutiae of the interactional context can facilitate analysis of wider canonical and cultural contexts since 'personal standpoints are built from often deeply contradictory and fragmented patchworks of cultural resources' (Wetherell, 2005: 170). Gubrium (2006) advocates that analysts should pay detailed attention to what narrators say, how they say it and the narrative context in which they produce a particular account while also orienting to the cultural.

> [I]f we take the time to understand how members of society use culture to interpret and represent their own and others' lives, we stand to diversify what it means to become who and what we are. In the process, we glean a more culturally nuanced and narratively active understanding.
>
> (Gubrium, 2006: 250)

Squire (Chapter 2) also suggests that it is beneficial to consider 'the social and cultural character of personal narratives'. The understanding of how narrators use culture in their narratives requires that analysts go beyond what narrators say in order to recognize how narrators draw on the wider culture.

This chapter combines the biographical and the contextual approaches to narrative analysis in order to demonstrate that 'local contexts' (meaning the immediate context in which the interview takes place, including the interviewer–interviewee relationship) and wider, societal contexts are inextricably linked. In order to do so, it focuses on aspects of narrative that illuminate that synthesis. The chapter examines both what speakers orient to in their small story narratives, what appears to be motivating particular ways of telling their stories and the identities that are brought into being or reproduced in talk. Thus, while it fits with small story analysis, the narrative analysis presented here goes beyond conversation-analytic notions of context as developing in sequenced turns. Instead, it extends the notion of context to considerations of how social–cultural issues and dilemmas are evident in talk, even if they are not explicitly oriented to. The form of narrative analysis presented here is a version of psychosocial analysis in that it attempts to give equal importance to individual and to social processes. The chapter builds on the 'experience-centred narrative research' examined in Chapter 2, considering aspects of the ways in which narratives are part of the process of sense-making while also focusing on social and cultural processes.

Bruner (1990, 2002) draws a distinction between canonical narratives (narratives of how life ought to be lived in the culture, i.e. normative cultural expectations) and personal narratives. In keeping with Squire (1998), he suggests (2004: 694) that

> the tool kit of any culture is replete not only with a stock of canonical life narratives (heroes, Marthas, tricksters, etc.), but with combinable formal constituents from which its members can construct their own life narratives: canonical stances and circumstances, as it were.

Polletta (1998) also suggests that narratives are canonical. She maintains that there are 'a limited stock of possible story lines' and so cultural understandings limit the stories that can be told. 'Narrative theorists differ on just how many plots there are, and just how universal they are. But there is agreement that stories not conforming to a cultural stock of plots typically are either not stories or are unintelligible' (Polletta, 1998: 424).

Since canonical narratives provide insights into the ways in which narrators use culture in doing narratives, the chapter highlights the ways in which canonical narratives illuminate how narrators draw upon contextual understandings.

Next sections focus on parts of an interview from a white mother of adult children of mixed parentage (given the pseudonym Clare) interviewed by me, a black woman, in a study of social identities (see Tizard and Phoenix, 2002, for details of the study). They consider how it is possible simultaneously to examine canonical and personal narratives and so the ways in which narratives are simultaneously situated in both the local context of talk and the wider social context, including speakers' (implicit or explicit) understandings of, and orientations to, these contexts. In other words, the chapter treats narratives as situated practices, co-constructed in talk (de Fina, 2003; Fischer and Goblirsch, 2006). The holistic approach to understanding people afforded by narrative analysis, therefore, requires a focus on narrators' situated presentations of themselves and recognition that research interviews are 'relational spaces' where the researcher and the narrator co-construct interviews (Tietel, 2000).

The chapter is divided into two main parts. The first part considers one way in which the wider context is brought into an interview narrative by examining how 'key narratives' serve to present particular identities to the researcher (and to the narrator herself). The second part of the chapter then considers the ways in which narrators establish their entitlement to talk on subjects they recognize to be controversial – in this case for a white mother with children of mixed parentage to warrant her right to talk about racism.

Constructing identities in key narratives

One of the central elements of narrative research is the analysis of key themes that help to organize the way a life story is told (Plummer, 2001). According to Dan McAdams (1997), these themes cluster around recurrent content in stories. The identification of repeated subject matter thus provides a useful means of identifying key themes. Key themes may, but need not, be stories of events. In response to a variety of questions, participants may construct themselves as having particular philosophies and habitual ways of dealing with the world that constitute a projection of identity or that signal their preoccupations. Boenisch-Brednich (2002) suggests that people develop key narratives as a result of important events or processes in their histories. These key narratives are repeatedly told and can be reinvented as the life narrative is reworked. According to Boenisch-Brednich, repeated retelling hones key narratives so that they become well structured, polished and ready for presentation at any time. They are thus often used as 'personal and symbolic mark(s)' (Boenisch-Brednich, 2002: 75). Once developed, then, key narratives are often produced as well-worn accounts that are used to explain and justify people's actions and decisions.

In keeping with the 'small story' emphasis, analysis of key narratives de-emphasizes the structural search for narrative-as-event and overcomes the difficulties that accompany the fact that not all research participants produce narratives of events (as discussed in Chapter 1) and that narratives of events do more than just describe events. Instead, the focus is on accounts that construct emotions, worldviews, characters or events in ways that illuminate why particular accounts are produced in particular ways – i.e. on sense-making processes. This section presents an example of a key narrative that demonstrates that canonical and personal narratives can both be produced in the same piece of talk. It demonstrates how culture is visible in the narrative context of 'big' and 'small' stories.

Recurrent key narratives are personal, canonical and evaluative

It is relatively easy to spot recurrent content when narrators repeatedly retell the same story – even if they use different words – but recurrent themes are often embedded within different sorts of stories. For example, the event narrative below was produced by Clare in response to a question on when she first became aware of people's colour, but reiterates and produces afresh one of her key narratives.

Q. If you think back to your childhood, when did you first become conscious of
   people's colour?
Clare. ...My last year in school, we had a girl grafted in from another area who
   was genuinely black. My god did they lead her a dog's life. [...] and to my
   shame, the first and only time in my life I didn't have the courage to stand up
   for her. [...] and when this girl had left [after six months of bullying], I told
   her [grandmother] and all she said to me was 'And what did you do?' and
   I said 'nothing' and she literally backhanded me across the kitchen. She
   never said another word about it.
Q. How did you feel about that?
Clare. It broke my heart. It absolutely slaughtered me.
Q. That your grandmother was angry, or=
Clare. =Yes, she wasn't angry. She was disgusted with me and she was quite
   right, but my only alibi was that I was the smallest person in that year. I was
   minute. Everybody was bigger than me. I was continuously knocked about
   and I was too frightened. But I learnt a lesson. It is worth standing up for
   your convictions if it is something you really feel about. It is worth it, maybe
   you will get a thump, but that's not the end of the world.

In answer to the question, Clare presents a rich event narrative ('big story')
that contains explanations of the emotions she felt and explicit justifications
of her reported actions. It would be possible to spend the rest of the chapter
doing a detailed discourse analysis of what she says. However, the focus
here is on the key narrative that emerges as she does the work of narrative
construction.

Clare's narrative is explicitly relational in that it is populated with a black
girl who comes to her school and by Clare's grandmother who appears both
heteroglossically – that is to say, presented by the narrator as someone else's
words – Bakhtin, (1981) in that Clare reports her grandmother as saying 'And what
did you do?', and as a silent presence. In relatively few words, Clare constructs
her grandmother as a significant, uncompromising and harsh agent of moral
socialization.

The short narrative presents both exculpatory discourses for why she did not
stand up for her black peer who was subjected to racist bullying ('I was the
smallest person in that year ... I was too frightened') and explains that it was
the only time she has not stood up to racist bullies – an event she is retrospectively
ashamed of. Clare's account also idealizes her grandmother's reported wordless
aggression in response to her reported non-intervention to stop racist bullying.
The suggestion is that this was the last time she let fear stop her from doing what
she believed to be right. At the same time Clare's narrative makes clear that she
is opposed to racism. This is part of her repeated construction of herself in the
interview as a moral agent who has had a difficult life, but does the right thing,
even in difficult circumstances. Central to doing the morally praiseworthy thing is
'standing up' against racism or otherwise dealing with it. Clare also repeatedly
makes clear that she has brought up her children (who are of mixed black–
white parentage) with the same philosophy. Her interpretation of the above event
sets up a key narrative that, as Boenisch-Brednich (2002) suggests, is common

for key narratives, recurs in the interview: '… it is worth standing up for your convictions …'.

This key narrative is clearly embedded in a personal narrative, but it also implicitly constructs a canonical narrative in that it makes clear that, in Clare's worldview, racism is illegitimate and has to be opposed. It constructs her grandmother as a hero figure (one of the canonical narratives Bruner (2004) suggests is readily available in (western) cultures) in her implacable opposition to racism and, as Clare suggests that she has always opposed racism since, it also constructs her as a hero. In positioning herself in this way, Clare is using identity as a resource (Antaki and Widdicombe, 1998) to set up a moral worldview and warrant her position in it. In doing this, she fits with Polletta's (2006) suggestion that 'stories are normative', meaning that they make a moral point. It is not the event per se that sets up this key narrative for Clare. Instead, the recurrent theme arises from how, in retrospect, she presents an analytic narrative about it.

Interlinked local and societal contexts

Both the event and the evaluation are locally situated (in that Clare knows that the study in which she is participating is about social identities and that one point of interest is the racialized identities of her children). Yet, while the narrative context is clear in the ways in which Clare establishes 'small story', diachronic concerns (in expressing emotion, giving explanations and evaluations), the narrative also draws on wider societal contexts. In Bruner's (1990) terms, Clare's story presents the canonical narrative that racism is unacceptable and should be challenged. This taken for granted assumption demonstrates a more implicit way in which Clare's accounts are relational and societal: she assumes that we (interviewee and interviewer) share cultural understandings that racism is unacceptable and that it is morally imperative to oppose it.

This assumption is common in the current UK context (Billig, 1991) and Clare may have been more inclined to take it for granted because she was speaking to a black interviewer. There is a further way in which the cultural context is evident in the above short extract from Clare's interview. Dan McAdams (2006) argues that, although everybody's life story is unique, it is common for people in midlife to present culturally sanctioned scripts. In the USA (where he has done his research), these often involve tales of redemption where satisfactory outcomes are crafted from an unpromising start. Redemptive stories are evident when Clare says: 'But I learnt a lesson. It is worth standing up for your convictions if it is something you really feel about. It is worth it, maybe you will get a thump, but that's not the end of the world'. Both the local and societal contexts are condensed, therefore, in her short narrative.

Clare's interview provides a second and related key narrative that forms the backdrop to her moral outlook. This is presented when she is asked to clarify what she means when she says that she is 'totally and extremely proud' of 'being Yorkshire' (having been born and brought up there although she has lived in London for most of her adult life).

Q. What does that mean to you then, to be Yorkshire. What do you mean?
Clare. Strength, the strength to be an individual. I don't mean physical strength.
I mean general strength. Getting on with life and making the best of what
you have got and not moaning about what you might have because that is a
waste of time. And being as good as you can be at what you do and not
wasting one minute of your life worrying about what you never will be able to
do. That all sums up Yorkshire to me.

The ideas presented in this 'small story', about continually striving to get on with things in the best way possible and being strong enough to deal with everything are attributed to being Yorkshire. They both present a canonical narrative and make an identity claim about the sort of person Clare is that parallel the ways in which she narrates herself as dealing with racism. As Margie Wetherell (1996) suggests, such habitual patterns are what psychologists generally consider to be personality. What Clare is doing is constructing personality traits for herself that warrant her as a praiseworthy and strong moral agent who uncomplainingly makes 'the best of what you have got' and who opposes racism. Her construction of herself as 'Yorkshire' parallels Dan McAdams' (1997) research findings that, in midlife, US citizens who are productive and caring (i.e. generative) tend to tell life stories that construct themselves as always having operated according to deep personal beliefs and that underline the value of moral clarity. According to McAdams, these 'personal myths' provide lives with a sense of unity and purpose. The 'small story' narrative above is, however, not only personal in that Clare explicitly relates herself with a social group – Yorkshire people. 'Yorkshire' is used to symbolize the qualities she wants me, the interviewer, to accept that she possesses. Presented as it is, early in the interview, this is an instance of using identity as a resource (Antaki and Widdicombe, 1998) to warrant the other narratives she constructs in the rest of the interview.

There is much debate currently about the relationship of a narrative to identity and to experience. Shelley Day Sclater (2003) points out that it is important not to assume a one-to-one correspondence between selves, identities and the stories people tell. However, Clare makes identity claims as part of her key narratives. In order to analyse her narratives then, it is important to understand the meanings she makes from her personal biography as she 'does narrative' and how this is central to her identity construction. Narrative analysis of Clare's interview demonstrates how she uses her biography to make meaning and construct identities and indicates how key narratives can direct researchers to research participants' concerns and local and wider narrative contexts.

Establishing an entitlement to talk about racism

The participants in any conversation, including interviews, have to establish their right to speak on the topics being discussed. According to Potter (1996), they do this by claiming 'category entitlement' and so authority to speak – for example by establishing their membership of a particular group that has expert knowledge or privileged experience about the topic being discussed. Potter suggests that successful claims to category entitlement allow people to speak without having to explain the source of their knowledge. In interviews, interviewers as well as interviewees make claims to category entitlement. Abell et al. (2006: 224) suggest that interviewers 'mobilize category memberships in order to construct rapport, or to construct difference with respondents'. Interviewers' self-disclosures aim to produce loquacity from interviewees, but interviewees too make assumptions about interviewers that influence the claims they (the interviewees) can make to category entitlement. Song and Parker (1995), for example suggest that interviewees can make assumptions about the interviewer's cultural identity and, as a result, modify what they say and how they say it in line with these assumptions. This means that, although interviews are often considered to be self-contained events, research participants bring their histories of previous positioning and their expectations of the interviewer and the interview to the research context. Not surprisingly then the deployment of category entitle-ments can be defensive, designed to defend the speaker from being viewed unfavourably.

Analysis of the process of warranting oneself as entitled to talk on a particular topic, therefore, provides evidence of the assumptions that interviewees are making about the interviewer and interaction as well as about the wider social context. This is a further way in which narratives include wider sociocultural narratives.

Clare, a white woman with children 'of mixed parentage', was interviewed by me, a black woman for a study on social identities where she knew that racialization would be one topic discussed. She no doubt also knew that the subject of mixed parentage generates both political and popular discussion. In that context, doing the interview potentially placed her in what Wetherell (1998) calls a 'troubled subject position' because she was likely to be aware that many people believe that children of mixed parentage may face particular problems. Since Clare did not know me, she may have assumed that, as an interviewer asking her questions about racialized identities, I wanted to hear her opinions about this. The social context is thus one which sets up a potentially troubled subject position where the narrator is being asked to tell her story without knowing whether the interviewer is a sympathetic ally or potentially threatening adversary. She has, therefore, to warrant herself as not racist (in order to be consistent with her canonical narrative) and to establish that she brought up her children well. The local context in which Clare was interviewed was, in Bakhtin's (1981) terms, constructed from many voices (some remembered and some imagined – e.g. the interviewer's).

It is not surprising, therefore, that Clare established her credentials to speak authoritatively about racialization before I asked any questions about it. She did this by positioning herself as someone who has been subjected to racism many times and has dealt with it decisively and firmly (and, therefore, in concert with her key narrative discussed above). She mentioned early in the interview that her children's father was black – something she knew that I already knew since I had interviewed one of her children. The 'big story' event narrative below was given in response to a question about social class, which preceded questions on racialization.

Q. So when you actually left home, what sort of class did you think you were
     then?
Clare. I went straight into another fairly poor working class home. I mean we
     flitted from room to room.
Q. This was after you started your relationship with=
Clare. =Yes
[…]
Q. But when you were with the children's father, did you feel that class was
     important or not?
Clare. I wasn't given a choice. He was black. I was white and it was made quite
     clear that that made me slightly lower than dog dirt.
Q. Who made that clear?
Clare. Every landlord and landlady, or employer that we went to see.
Q. What about what it made him feel? Did they treat him in the same way?
Clare. They didn't dare. He was massive, which proves what my grandmother
     actually always said, that most people who have strong prejudices actually
     are just too stupid to think things out and most stupid people are also
     cowards.
Q. …when you had this relationship? How was that treated then – the fact that
     you were a white woman and that he was a black man?
Clare. The first flat we ever went to when I was pregnant with William sums up
     the whole thing. I was shown to this grubby little room. I was not him, he
     wasn't with me, absolutely filthy little room in (London) and I said to the
     woman. 'Do you object to children?' And she kind of looked a little bit – you
     know and said 'Well, you know'. And I said 'My husband is black'. And she
     said 'Well if he is a black, you can get rid of it can't you?' And there was no
     legal abortion and that was her attitude.
Q. What was the response?
Clare. I wouldn't put it on tape. It is rude. But it was fairly basic and left her in
     no doubt as to what I felt.

In the above excerpt, Clare presents herself as having experienced 'prejudice' when
looking for rooms more often than her black Trinidadian (now ex-) husband
did. She uses heteroglossia by echoing her grandmother's words – something she
frequently does in the interview – to make a moral point. The actual 'bounded
event' she describes stands as a condensation of all the occasions on which she
was treated badly when attempting to rent a room and she constructs herself
as responsible for dealing with it. There is a switch from 'we' in the general
account to 'I' and the reported 'I' deals with the racist episode with resolution
and, in so doing, implicitly defends her unborn child and absent husband. Her
account is vivid, compelling and dramatic, to the extent of presenting reported
speech from an episode a quarter of a century earlier. It is consistent with the
identity claims of being 'Yorkshire', resolute and 'standing up' against racism
(presented above, although they occurred later in the interview). She, therefore,
consistently warrants her entitlement to speak and, more importantly, to be taken
seriously on racialization and racism by being the hero of her account. Her
category entitlement is based on warranting her expertise by establishing two
issues: first, that she has experience (indeed more than her black ex-husband)

of being subjected to racism and of dealing with it in ways that defended her black husband and her unborn (mixed parentage) child and, second, that she has been in a 'mixed' black–white relationship and has children of mixed parentage.

Clare consistently deployed such narrative events in order to establish her category entitlement. For example, the 'small story' excerpt below was also presented before I introduced the issue of racialization in the interview.

Q. You said that your mother was very bigoted. Can you explain what you meant by that?

A. My mother had never, to my personal knowledge, met a negro. Yet she hated all blacks, because my father did. The fact that my father came from Mississippi had nothing to do with it.

[...]

And just in case you didn't notice, I am fairly brown. I am a typical Breton peasant. And I was quite often made to walk behind my mother so – especially in the summer because I go very dark. I go much darker than my kids without trying. This is half a day on Southend. That's all it takes. But if I got too brown, my mother would not walk in the street with me?

Q. So how did she explain that?

A. She didn't. Mother didn't explain anything. She just told you, and if you argued, she hit you.

Q. So was she the same to your half sister?

A. No she wasn't (inaudible). It was slightly different. She was also blonde, blue eyed and very pale skin. [...]

Here Clare implies that her mother treated her in a racist way – pretending not to be with her when she became suntanned. This is not an unknown response of white mothers to children of mixed parentage, but Clare's recounting of this incident constructs a discursive space for herself as someone who has been subjected to different forms of racism – more so she suggests than was her black ex-husband and in ways that her children never were, since she did not treat them like this. In constructing this discursive space, Clare also constructs a position for herself that is akin to having been a child 'of mixed parentage'. This is a delicate position to set up for herself in that she knows that I know she is not of mixed parentage. Therefore, the choice of this episode and way of recounting it functions proleptically. Clare does not, for example, claim to know what it feels like to be a mixed parentage child because of how her mother treated her. That would have opened the possibility that I could have challenged that claim. Instead, the version she presents defends, in advance, against that possibility while indicating that she had 'insider' experience of mixed parentage before her children were born. The point here is that narrators actively set up their entitlement to talk by warranting themselves through particular kinds of experience and positioning themselves in specific ways, which include anticipation of what they assume the interviewer wants to hear.

One way in which Clare demonstrates agentic choice in how she constructs her story is in her dismissal of the relevance of her birth father's origins in the US state of Mississippi. The fact that Clare mentioned Mississippi as a free association when she did not have to suggests that she may entertain the possibility that the ideas her father brought to his relationship with her mother, as a result of his upbringing, amplified her mother's racism. This has not previously been mentioned in the interview and, since I forgot to return to discuss it after her lengthy discussion of her mother's behaviour, her dismissal of its relevance remains enigmatic. However, her mention of it demonstrates how the wider social context is an inextricable part of her doing of narrative. She defends against the implicit possibility that I would excuse her mother's behaviour and blame it on her father's origins – particularly since she might assume that I knew that Mississippi has a racist history. My doing so would have vitiated the force of the small story that established her category entitlement in having been subjected to racism in childhood from her own mother. It would also have prevented Clare from setting up a narrative foundation for the key narrative discussed in the previous section that she is implacably opposed to racism and so for the identity claims that go along with this – of herself as not 'bigoted' or 'prejudiced'. Her doing of narrative in the excerpt above is thus proleptic in defending against the possibility that I might excuse her mother's behaviour by blaming her father and so undermine her claims to category entitlement and the basis for one of her key narratives. The work required to unpack and analyse this short piece of narrative demonstrates that, as Polletta (2006) suggests, stories are allusive – they require interpretation.

Conclusion: analysing local and societal contexts in narratives

This chapter has analysed processes of meaning-making in narrative talk by examining how key narratives and the warranting of entitlement to speak (category entitlement) establish identity claims. The chapter demonstrated some of the ways in which canonical narratives are represented in personal narratives and local and wider societal contexts are interlinked in 'small' or 'big' story narratives. A focus on context, however, also necessitates a focus on the ways in which narrators construct their autobiographies. Indeed, recognition of the importance of the local and wider social contexts means that it is possible to see the preoccupations of the narrator and the identity claims they make on the basis of their autobiographical histories and the experiences they claim as the interview is co-constructed with the interviewer. A focus on narrative issues such as these thus demonstrates the utility of synthesizing biographical and contextual narrative approaches.

Suggestions for further reading

- Bamberg, M. (2006) Stories: Big or small. Why do we care? *Narrative Inquiry* 16(1): 139–147.

In this short article the developmental psychologist Michael Bamberg argues that 'small' and 'big' stories represent very different approaches to narrative enquiry. He argues for the small story approach, which he suggests is able to enrich traditional narrative enquiry, and not just in a complementary way, but by dislodging 'big' story approaches from their privileged position as the best way to analyse identity. Instead, he supports the notion that a 'new narrative turn will have to place emphasis on how selves and identities are "*done*" in interactions – i.e. how identities are emerging and are managed by use of narratives-in-interaction' (p.147). The article gives an idea of one set of disagreements about how to theorize narratives and do narrative analysis while arguing for a 'small' story position.

- Bruner, J. (2002) *Making Stories: Law, Literature, Life*. New York: Farrar, Strauss and Giroux.

  Jerome Bruner is one of the most eminent psychologists of the twentieth and twenty-first centuries. Over the seven decades of his career, he worked in psychology departments in Oxford and Harvard Universities (UK and USA) as well as moving into the Faculty of Law at Harvard when in his eighties. This book is based on a series of lectures he gave in Italy and so is both a short text and easy to read because it was designed to be spoken. The book sets out Bruner's ideas about the centrality of storytelling to the construction of the self. Bruner argues that stories pervade our daily lives and that it is through stories that we make sense of the world. He uses the examples of literature and legal cases to examine the complexity of making stories.

- McAdams, D.P. (2006) *The Redemptive Self: Stories Americans Live By*. Oxford University Press.

  Dan McAdams is a professor of psychology. This book brings together 15 years of research done in collaboration with his students; it attempts to develop a new psychology of American (US) identity as expressed in cultural and historical American texts and images and in the life stories of mainly middle class 'caring and productive American adults in their midlife years'. McAdams suggests that the key to American identity lies in the stories Americans live by and that the most powerful life story in the US today is the story of redemption. On a broad societal scale and in their private lives, McAdams argues that Americans transform suffering into a positive emotional state and move from pain and peril to redemption. Hence, US identity is of the redemptive self. The book presents many case studies. It won the 2006 William James Award from the American Psychological Association for best general interest book in psychology and the 2006 Theodore Sarbin Award from the American Psychological Association for its contribution to theoretical and philosophical psychology.

References

Abell, J., Locke, A., Condor, S., Gibson, S. and Stevenson, S. (2006) Trying similarity, doing difference: the role of interviewer self–disclosure in interview talk with young people. *Qualitative Research* 6(2): 221–44.

Antaki, C. and Widdicombe, S. (eds) (1998) *Identities in Talk*. London: Sage.

Bakhtin, M.M. (1981) *The Dialogical Imagination: Four Essays*. Edited by M. Holquist, translated C. Emerson and M. Holquist. Austin, TX: University of Texas Press.

Bamberg, M. (2004) Talk, small stories, and adolescent identities. *Human Development* 47: 366–9.

Bamberg, M. (2006) Stories: Big or small. Why do we care? *Narrative Inquiry* 16(1): 139–47.

Battersby, J. (2006) Narrativity, self, and self-representation. *Narrative* 14(1): 27–44.

Billig, M. (1991) *Ideology and Opinion*. London: Sage.

Boenisch-Brednich, B. (2002) Migration and narration. *Folklore* 20: 64–77. http://www.folklore.ee/folklore/vol20/brednich.pdf [Accessed 6 February 2007]

Bruner, J. (1990) *Acts of Meaning*. Cambridge, MA: Harvard University Press.

Bruner, J. (2002) *Making Stories: Law, Literature, Life*. New York: Farrar, Strauss and Giroux.

Bruner, J. (2004) Life as narrative. *Social Research* 71(3): 691–710.

de Fina, A. (2003) Crossing borders: Time, space, and disorientation in narrative. *Narrative Inquiry* 13(2): 367–91.

Fischer, W. and Goblirsch, M. (2006) Biographical structuring: Narrating and reconstructing the self in research and professional practice. *Narrative Inquiry* 16(1): 28–36.

Freeman, M. (2006) Life 'on holiday?' In defense of big stories. *Narrative Inquiry* 16: 131–8.

Georgakopolou, A. (2006a) Thinking big with small stories in narrative and identity analysis. *Narrative Inquiry* 16(1): 122–30.

Georgakopolou, A. (2006b) Small and large identities in narrative (inter)action. In A. de Fina, D. Schiffrin and M. Bamberg (eds) *Discourse and Identity: Studies in interactional sociolinguistics 23*. Cambridge: Cambridge University Press.

Gubrium, A. (2006) 'I was my momma baby. I was my daddy gal': Strategic stories of success. *Narrative Inquiry* 16(2): 231–53.

Hollway, W. and Jefferson, T. (2000) *Doing Qualitative Research Differently*. London: Sage.

Järvinen, M. (2004) Life histories and the perspective of the present. *Narrative Inquiry* 14(1): 45–68.

McAdams, D. P. (1997) *The Stories We Live By: Personal Myths and the Making of the Self*. New York: Guilford Press.

McAdams, D. P. (2006) *The Redemptive Self: Stories Americans Live By*. Oxford University Press.

Manstead, A. and Wetherell, M. (eds) (2005) 'Dialoguing across divisions. Special issue. *The Psychologist* 18: 544–54.

Plummer, K. (2001) *Documents of Life 2: An Invitation to a Critical Humanism* (2nd edn). London: Sage.

Polletta, F. (1998) Contending stories: Narrative in social movements. *Qualitative Sociology* 21(4): 419–46.

Polletta, F. (2006) Designing the new World Trade Center: Personal storytelling in public deliberation, 19 November 2006. http://storyteller-and-listener.blog-city.com/francesca_polletta.htm [Accessed 3 March 2007]

Potter, J. (1996) *Representing Reality: Discourse, Rhetoric and Social Construction*. London: Sage.

Riessman, C.K. (2001) Analysis of personal narratives. In J. R. Gubrium and J. A. Holstein (eds) *Handbook of Interviewing*. Thousand Oaks, CA: Sage.

Sclater, Day S. (2003) What is the subject? *Narrative Inquiry* 13(2): 317–30.

Song, M. and Parker, D. (1995) Commonality, difference and the dynamics of disclosure in in-depth interviewing, *Sociology* 29(2): 241–56.

Squire, C. (1998) Narrative analysis and feminism. In C. Griffin, K. Henwood and A. Phoenix (eds) *Standpoints and Differences*. London: Sage.

Tietel, E. (2000, November). The Interview as a Relational Space [20 paragraphs]. *Forum Qualitative Sozialforschung/Forum: Qualitative Social Research* 1(3). [On-line Journal]. Available at: http://qualitative-research.net/fqs/fqs-eng.htm [Accessed 11 February 2007]

Tizard, B. and Phoenix, A. (2002) *Black, White or Mixed Race? 'Race' and Racism in the Lives of Young People of Mixed Parentage* (2nd edn). London: Routledge.

Wengraf, T. (2006) Interviewing for life histories, lived situations and experience: The biographic-narrative interpretive method (BNIM). A short guide to BNIM interviewing and practice. Version 6.1b – 20/01/06 (available through Tom Wengraf [ascy82@dsl.pipex.com]).

Wetherell, M. (1996) The distributed self: a social constructionist perspective. In R. Stevens (ed.) *Understanding the Self*. London: Sage.

Wetherell, M. (1998) Positioning and interpretative repertoires: Conversation analysis and post-structuralism in dialogue. *Discourse & Society* 9: 387–412.

Wetherell, M. (2005) Unconscious conflict or everyday accountability? *British Journal of Social Psychology* 44(2):169–73.

Chapter 4

Looking back on narrative research: An exchange

Phillida Salmon and Catherine Kohler Riessman

Part I: Phillida Salmon

> 'I was a Post Office clerk. So I jumped off Westminster Bridge and I went for a ride in a police launch.'

This was Percy, a man I interviewed once every week over a year, as part of an MRC research project into schizophrenic thought disorder. It's Percy's 'story', but as a story, it doesn't work. Why it fails seems important for understanding what we mean by narrative.

A fundamental criterion of narrative is surely that of contingency. Whatever the content, stories demand the consequential linking of events or ideas. Narrative shaping entails imposing a meaningful pattern on what would otherwise be random and disconnected. The 'and then' of stories includes temporal ordering, but goes beyond this in presenting some kind of humanly understandable connection. In Percy's account, his use of 'so' suggests a logical succession; but to his audience, the link is completely missing.

Percy's story also falls short on other crucial narrative requirements. The narratives we tell necessarily draw on our basic understanding of human life: of what it means to be human. In the terms of Berger and Luckmann (1966), this involves a discourse of agents as against objects, a discourse of subjectivity, of motives, purposes, feelings. And storytellers speak from a moral stance; whether explicit or implicit, narratives contain some kind of evaluative orientation. No matter how often and how variously I tried to prompt him, Percy never made any reference to his own subjectivity or that of others. Nor did he ever formulate his apparent suicide attempt and subsequent rescue in terms other than those which seemed, bizarrely, to suggest nothing more than a jaunt.

As Peter Barham and Robert Hayward (1991) argue, the social exclusion of schizophrenics is the outcome of their inability to present their lives as socially intelligible projects. Being accountable to others – to story our actions and our experience in socially and culturally comprehensible ways – is crucial to our whole standing as persons, as recognized members of human society. And growing into narrative capabililily is perhaps fundamental in the coming of young people into full personhood. In family politics, as Judy Dunn (1990) has shown, stories serve a vital function in excusing, justifying, blaming or securing hoped-for things. The stories of very young children lack economy, coherence and plausibility: it takes time and practice to produce credible, rhetorically persuasive, socially effective narratives.

Here, for example, in a study by Maya Hickmann, is a four-year-old boy telling an adult the story of a short film he has just seen.

Penny was in the box ... The next day it wasn't ... He was mad at the giraffe ... cause he took the penny ... Yeah, but he di- bu- but he thought he was tricking him ... see because ... bec- be- he-he-he didn't know that he had the penny (1985: 247).

For the listener, this narrative makes little sense, because of the use of words like 'the' and 'he', without referential expressions which would explain them. Yet in his hesitations, false starts and self-corrections, this child is clearly struggling towards greater clarity. In developing narrative capacity, young people show an increasing appreciation of their listeners' position. And this comes about through direct interaction with those to whom they tell their stories. By their reactions, their puzzlement, prompts and questions, listeners make clear what is lacking in comprehensibility, and oblige the child to reach for words and phrases that will clarify the tale.

Studies of children's talk have shown that the development of expressive capacity is fostered by adults who receive and respond to what the child is trying to say, without a continuous corrective questioning of the way they say it. A tolerance of some ambiguity, a willingness to wait for meaning to emerge: this is the kind of generous listening which facilitates a flowering of narrative art. In responding to and elaborating what matters in communication – the meaning being expressed – adults offer children a kind of Vygotskian scaffolding for the complex task involved in telling a story.

It is evident that adults make a profoundly helpful contribution to children's narrative powers. Could the same kind of help enable schizophrenics to render their experience in comprehensible narrative terms? For Percy, this was clearly not the case, as I found through my prolonged and ultimately fruitless attempts to elicit from him a humanly meaningful account of his life. But Percy had spent 28 years in a psychiatric back ward, living within a regime which took no account of his individual subjectivity and denied him any kind of engagement with the ordinary social world.

For others, not yet so totally excluded from that world, the direct involvement of active and challenging listeners may be crucial. Rufus May (2002), the self-styled 'mad psychologist', speaks of the effectiveness of challenges to his bizarre and emotive behaviour by a fellow-patient; 'This had a memorable impact in getting me to become more accountable for my actions, and to take more responsibility for my behaviour' (2002: 224). Being challenged, being asked to account for one's behaviour, to take responsibility for oneself among others: this is what constitutes moral character – a character implicitly denied in the diagnosis of madness. But being able to speak as a moral person is surely basic in any narrative account.

All narratives are, in a fundamental sense, co-constructed. The audience, whether physically present or not, exerts a crucial influence on what can and cannot be said, how things should be expressed, what can be taken for granted, what needs explaining, and so on. We now recognize that the personal account, in research interviews, which has traditionally been seen as the expression of a single subjectivity, is in fact always a co-construction. Interviewers now routinely seek reflexively to trace how, often in the most subtle ways, they have jointly acted to construct the narrative which has emerged from the encounter. And perhaps the efforts at storytelling by 'disturbed' people or very young children offer a specially valuable research situation because there the active involvement of listeners is obvious and explicit.

The methods called for in situations such as these may perhaps be rather different from those used by most narrative researchers. Since in both cases non-verbal aspects may play a large part, video as well as audio recording might be important. In studying what is essentially 'joint action', it could potentially be useful to adopt the methods adopted by Colin Trevarthen (1988) and others. Using frame-by-frame analysis, these researchers illuminated the ways in which, within wordless 'conversations' between infants and their caretakers, human meaning comes to be accorded to initially random utterances.

Another method which might prove fruitful in these kinds of research situations is Interpersonal Process Analysis. Here, the participants in an encounter view retrospectively a video recording of their interaction, and talk from their point of view about each moment involved. This allows a deeper understanding of the whole complicated process of communication, its ambiguities, misunderstandings, nuances and moments of illumination. These factors seem particularly important in situations like these, because the speakers involved come from markedly different subject positions, and speak in clearly different terms.

Here is where Phil Salmon left off with this piece in 2004. For more of her thoughts on the challenges of working to create and sustain a sense of personhood through narrative, see her article 'The Schizococcus: An Interpersonal Personal Perspective' http://www.pcp-net. org/journal/pctp04/salmon04.html

Part II: Catherine Kohler Riessman

'To live means to participate in dialogue: to ask questions, to heed, to respond, to agree...'

(Bakhtin, 1981).

I pick up in this essay where Phil Salmon left off. In the spirit of a dialogic process, I comment on her comments, extending them with thoughts of my own. Her essay ends abruptly, but it contains a deep understanding of the complexities of narrative, and it anticipates developments in the field that came after her untimely death.

My friendship with Phil was short but precious. When she was diagnosed with advanced cancer and hospitalized, the lively conversation we had begun several years earlier came to an abrupt halt. We had met at a conference at Cambridge University, sponsored by the Centre for Narrative Research. Invited as senior women (how we laughed at that description!), the organizers imagined perhaps how we could comment wisely on the work of younger scholars (and we learnt they were doing ground-breaking research). The next day at a long and memorable breakfast conversation at the high table of Sydney Sussex College, we cemented our friendship, beginning a dialogue about narrative research (and life) that continued in emails and over dinners whenever I got to the UK. I felt I had located an intellectual 'soul mate' that transcended geography, academic discipline and even my specific orientation to narrative analysis.

When Phil got her terminal diagnosis and began a rapid decline, the dialogue stopped in one sense, though it continues in my mind and heart to this day. However, threads of the piece we had begun to craft together were left hanging. There is further irony: the perspective Phil took in the piece is fixed and cannot be changed. She made that clear to me during her stay in the palliative care unit: I was not to alter its coherence. Had she lived, I suspect her positioning and writing about narrative research in the piece would have changed. Mine certainly has changed in the time since I prepared a draft of my section. With the accident of time on my side, I could rework my part, changing it to reflect shifts in thinking about narrative, and developments in the field. Although Phil's words are fixed in time, they remain my starting point.

Note how she uses the brief unconnected fragments of Percy's speech – a participant in a research project on schizophrenic thought disorder – to open up the central question that all students of communication must grapple with: what do we mean when we use the word narrative? Is narrative discourse different and, if so, what distinguishes it from other discourse forms? Obviously, there are many ways to speak and write, including rapid question and answer exchanges, chronicles and lists. Oral narrative requires a longer turn at talk and 'contingency … a consequential linking of events or ideas'. A narrator constructs an order (often called plot) from random happenings. Scholars debate whether there is such a thing as pre-narrative experience or whether, on the other hand, experience is organized from the beginning. Is 'raw' experience formless, without plot, a series of isolated actions, images and sensations that are then 'cooked', that is placed in memory in meaningful temporal sequences?

As Phil notes, storytelling happens relationally, collaboratively between speaker and listener in a cultural context where at least some meanings and conventions are shared. Without some degree of ordering work on the part of the narrator, a listener or reader cannot begin to make sense of another's words. Evaluation, too, is essential; when a narrator simply reports events, feelings or experiences without commentary or reflection (as Percy did), even with 'generous listening' the joint narrative process fails. Hinchman and Hinchman (1997) provide a formal narrative definition: events are perceived as important, selected, organized, connected and evaluated as meaningful for a particular audience. Too often in the current wave of popularity of 'stories', these distinctive features are erased; narrative has come to mean anything and everything beyond a few bullet points – a trend that fails to honour the uniqueness and power of the narrative form (Riessman, 2007). I know Phil would agree that there must be some boundaries around the concept of narrative, even as rigid criteria must give way.

Some have argued that coherence should be the criterion – the narrative must hang together – but what does this mean? Does coherence depend on temporal ordering, or can a narrative be organized in other ways? Must there be a neat beginning, middle and end? As narrative researchers, we can limit our interpretive horizons when we carry the criterion of logical consistency too far. The 'chaos narrative' that Arthur Frank (1995) identified in written accounts of illness can be understood even though such accounts lack closure; the form conveyed the very uncertainty and 'wreckage' illness had brought to lives.

In my early writing about narrative methods, text-based coherence formed a central place, but now I am less sure (how I wish I could discuss this with Phil). The shift was influenced by reading Lawrence Langer's (1991) analytic work with Holocaust testimonies, and by scholarship questioning the idea of a coherent or unitary 'self' expressed in a life story. Langer viewed videotaped interviews of Holocaust witnesses at the Yale Video Archive and, in some cases, participated in interviews that included family members. He writes about incoherence in the testimonies, reflecting fragmented lives. Survivors spoke about events and experiences before the camps, memories from the time in Auschwitz, and some spoke about their lives since. But these are 'disrupted narratives … that do not function in time like other[s]' (p. xi). Speakers struggled with 'the impossible task of making their recollections of the camp experience coalesce with the rest of their lives…[there is] temporal rupture…a double existence' (pp. 3–5). It was the 'needful ears' of interviewers and the survivors' children who sought to connect the fragments, perhaps to mediate the atrocities survivors spoke about. (One interviewer interrupted a survivor to ask about whether a particular moral idea 'got you through to the end?' (p. 15). Others asked similar questions that 'simplified closure'.) Langer's important work suggests it may be listeners' (and investigators') need for continuity and meaning – our needful ears – that has elevated the significance of narrative coherence. I know Phil would have a great deal to add to this point.

I wish I could talk to Phil about children's narrative development. The excerpt she presents of the four-year-old boy illustrates well the word-finding problems young children have as they learn to narrate for adults who must 'listen generously'. Children's speech, even in the school years, is full of false starts, self-corrections and disfluencies. Phil writes that 'expressive capacity is fostered by adults who respond to what the child is trying to say'. I would add that children aid each other's expressive development. Children teach children how to narrate; in subtle ways they instruct each other, especially the need to take the audience's position into account. Karen Gallas (1994) makes detailed transcripts of her classroom practice, and displays how the narrative capacities of children in her first grade classroom shift over an academic year. Children learnt from one another various narrative styles and developed competencies in several over time. One African American girl initiated collaborative storytelling that the white children imitated and made their own. The classroom became a more inclusive place with many voices and subjectivities. Children became multilingual storytellers. The research vivifies the dialogic process, particularly the active involvement of the listener in the co-construction of narrative, which Phil writes about so eloquently.

Finally, as she ends her piece, Phil anticipates an idea that since her death has become a major trend in narrative studies. I read her 'wordless conversation' as part of the larger visual turn in narrative research, which attends to gesture, the unspoken and the image. I'm sure she would agree that the field has relied too long on the spoken word, represented so carefully in our holy transcripts. Many experiences cannot be spoken; others are communicated more easily with images. The challenge for narrative research is the development of a set of methods to reflexively interrogate visual data in dialogue with participants' spoken (or written) words. I wish Phil were here to carry the move forward. She would be excited by some contemporary visual narrative research (see suggested readings below).

The death of a person, however final, invites the living into a dialogue. The written words of the person are fixed in time, but their meanings are read in the present from current positionings. A speaker (or writer's) intent is met with the analyst's interpretation, which in turn is situated in shifting discourses, history, politics and culture. As the literary scholar, Wolfgang Iser (1989/1993) argues we bring current sensibilities and positionings into reading, adding new voices to interpretation. He describes the process:

> '[Innovating readings] would, of course, be impossible if the text itself was not to some degree, indeterminate, leaving room for a change of vision…Texts with…minimal indeterminacy tend to be tedious, for it is only when the reader is given the chance to participate actively that he [sic] will regard the text, whose intention he himself [sic] has helped to compose, as real'. (p. 10)

These ideas extend Phil's words about co-construction in spoken narratives into the reading process. The papers to follow take up these layers of narrative interpretation.

Suggestions for further reading

- Bell, S.E. (2002) Photo images: Jo Spence's narratives of living with illness. *Health* 6: 5–30.

  A sociologist interprets as visual narrative a sequence of three photographs of the British feminist photographer, Jo Spence. The images are interpreted in the context of the artist's writings about her illness experience (she lived for ten years with breast cancer). The research is an excellent example of working narratively with archival images alongside the image-maker's words.

- Luttrell, W. (2003) *Pregnant Bodies, Fertile Minds: Gender, Race and the Schooling of Pregnant Teens.* New York: Routledge.

An ethnography of a classroom for pregnant teens that includes images the girls make. The spoken and written words of the image maker about each image are set alongside lively classroom discussions about them, conversations that include the ethnographer. The research provides an excellent model of working ethnographically with visual data.

* Rose, G. (2001) *Visual Methodologies: An Introduction to the Interpretation of Visual Materials*. Thousand Oaks, CA: Sage.

An extensive discussion of methods for interrogating visual data. The author distinguishes three sites for interpretative enquiry: production of the image, the image itself, and the audiencing process (response of viewers). Application to narrative research projects can be made by readers.

* Tamboukou, M. (2007) Interior styles/extravagant lives: gendered narratives of sensi/able spaces. In E. H. Huijbens and Ó P. Jónsson (eds) *Sensi/able Spaces: Space, Art and the Environment*. Newcastle-upon-Tyne: Cambridge Scholars Press pp. 186–204.

Written by one of the co-editors of the present book, the study provides a compelling narrative analysis of the multiple identities of a visual artist, Gwen John. Her paintings are set alongside her letters; interpretation of the links among them uncovers the complex subjectivity of a woman artist living in *fin de siecle* Paris.

References

Bakhtin, M.M. (1981) *The Dialogic Imagination: Four Essays*. Translated by C. Emerson and M. Holquist. Austin, TX: University of Texas Press.

Berger, Peter L. and Luckmann, T. (1966) *The Social Construction of Reality: A Treatise in The Sociology of Knowledge*. New York: Doubleday.

Barham, Peter and Hayward, Robert (1991) *From the Mental Patient to the Person*. London: Routledge.

Dunn, Judy (1990) *Separate Lives: Why Siblings Are so Different*. New York: Basic Books.

Frank, Arthur (1995) *The Wounded Storyteller: Body, Illness, and Ethics*. Chicago: University of Chicago Press.

Gallas, Karen (1994) *The Languages of Learning: How Children Talk, Write, Dance, Draw, and Sing their Understanding of the World*. New York: Teachers College Press.

Hickmann, M. (1985) The implications of discourse skills in Vygotsky's developmental theory. In James V. Wertsch (ed.) *Culture, Communication, and Cognition: Vygotskian Perspectives*. Cambridge University Press.

Hinchman, L.P. and Hinchman, S.K. (eds) (1997) *Memory, Identity, Community: The Idea of Narrative in the Human Sciences*. Albany, NY: State University of New York Press.

Iser, W. (1989/1993) *Prospecting: From Reader Response to Literary Anthropology*. Baltimore: Johns Hopkins University Press.

Langer, Lawrence L. (1991) *Holocaust Testimonies: The Ruins of Memory.* New Haven, London: Yale University Press.

May, Rufus. (2002) The experience of madness. *Journal of Critical Psychology, Counselling and Psychotherapy* 2: 220–27

Riessman, C.K. (2007) *Narrative Methods for the Human Sciences.* Thousand Oaks, CA: Sage Publications.

Trevarthen, C. (1988) Universal co-operative motives: How infants begin to know the language and culture of their parents. In G. Jahoda and I.M. Lewis (eds) *Acquiring Culture: Cross Cultural Studies in Child Development.* London: Croom Helm.

Chapter 5

Never the last word: Revisiting data[1]

Molly Andrews

Renato Rosaldo opens *Culture and Truth* with these stark words: 'If you ask an older Ilongot man of northern Luzon, Philippines, why he cuts off human heads, his answer is brief ... He says that rage, born of grief, impels him to kill his fellow human beings ... he needs a place "to carry his anger"' (1989: 1). Though Rosaldo, with his wife and collaborator, lived amongst the Ilongots, studying their way of life, still he could not conceive of 'the force of anger in grief' (3). He explains that his life experience 'had not as yet provided the means to imagine the rage that can come with devastating loss' (4). Then, through a tragic accident, his wife died. He experienced, in his words, 'the deep cutting pain of sorrow almost beyond endurance' (9); with the intensity of this agony came a deeper comprehension of the Ilongot headhunters. Rosaldo explains: 'All interpretations are provisional; they are made by positioned subjects who are prepared to know certain things and not others ... analyses are always incomplete' (1989: 8).

Rosaldo's account of the effect of his wife's death on his ability to understand the previously incomprehensible is not only emotionally compelling; it illuminates a fundamental principle of the analytic process. All of us bring to our research knowledge which we have acquired through our life's experiences, and indeed how we make sense of what we observe and hear is very much influenced by that framework of understanding. This positioning is not static, but evolves over the course of our lives. New experiences, and new understanding of old experiences, bring with them a new perspective not only on our own lives – our present, as well as our pasts – but on the way in which we make sense of the lives of others. As many philosophers have argued, and Rosaldo's narrative illustrates, human reality is always the reality of interpretation.

The implications of this for qualitative narrative researchers are clear: our interpretations of our data are always, and can only ever be, connected to the vantage point from which we view the world. But we, and the world around us, are forever changing. Nor does the data we collect remain constant. Rather, our transcriptions of interviews represent choices we have made at a particular moment, and these choices might well alter over time. Similarly, our field notes are but interpreted observations; they are intimately part of the person we were when we wrote them. Still, many if not most researchers tell ourselves that our data are more or less constant, even while we accept that our interpretations of these data might be, as Rosaldo observes, provisional. Herein lies the impetus to return to data: the more vantage points from which we view phenomena, the richer and more complex our understanding of that which we observe.

'Seeing the paths you've taken'

Twenty years ago, I conducted a study on British lifetime socialist activists, which involved life history research with 15 women and men who had been politically active in left-wing politics for 50 years or longer. At the time of data gathering, the respondents ranged between seventy-five and ninety years of age. I spent many hours with each of them, asking them to recount the experiences of their lives, and to explain to me how it happened that they had sustained their high level of commitment to their political principles over such a long period of time. One of the respondents, Elizabeth, eloquently described to me this process of looking back:

> when you look back, you see the path or paths that you've taken. The path would obviously not be so clear when you're groping up and finding it, would it? I mean it's rather like going up a mountain, you're sort of looking that way and that track and it looks too steep and you're going round another one. Whereas when you're high up you can look back and see and it sort of stands out much more clearly, things you didn't realize at the time.

(Andrews, 1991: 176–7)

The analogy which Elizabeth constructs here is very powerful. Being in the midst of life, it is sometimes difficult to have a perspective of where we have been and where we are going. But as we ascend the mountain – and near the close of our life's journey – the path or paths that we have taken become visible. One of the most engaging aspects of Elizabeth's metaphor is the movement which lies at its heart: walking and climbing, the protagonist is forever coming to new vantage points from which to view what she/he has passed through. There is never a final stopping point in this journey, with the possible exception of death itself. Even here, however, our lives are never only our own; others interpret and re-interpret the meaning (or lack thereof) contained within them, and they are likely to do so even after we are no longer here. Our deaths thus become part of our life narratives, epitomized by Shakespeare's 'nothing in his life became him like the leaving of it' (*Macbeth* Act I Scene IV).

Elizabeth offers her description of the mountain climb as a way of explaining the multiple perspectives with which we look back on our lives. But there is much in this metaphor for researchers as well. While we may embark on our projects with a particular sense of what it is we wish to explore, very often this is transformed over time. When I conducted the research into lifetime socialist activism, I had a very clear idea of the focus of my project. However, as I sat with these men and women over many cups of tea and we talked about the rich lives they had led, they spoke to me about many things, including their relationships with their families – both the families they had been born into and those they had created. I listened attentively, but my orientation was almost entirely directed towards those aspects of these accounts which were relevant to my interest in sustained political commitment. Elizabeth, for instance, told me 'I'm not very conscious of being a woman … I'm just a human being' and yet she also elaborated on the very different opportunities that she and her husband had for pursuing interests outside the family. For her, it was only once her children were no longer small that she could engage in political activities which had the risk of taking her away from home. (Once she ended up in a maximum security prison for three weeks because of her protesting.) At the time of my original analysis, I made a mental note to myself that I needed to explore more fully the salience of gender identity and its relationship to the experience of ageing. Ten years later, I received a grant to explore this topic, and so it was that I returned to this set of data. What I found was something quite different from what I had expected.

As I re-read the transcripts, hundreds and hundreds of pages, I was absorbed by the accounts that my respondents told me about their relationships with their parents. How was it that I had side-stepped this before, when it was clearly of such importance to so many of them? This, more than anything else, was now the story that called out to me. So what had changed in this time? The transcripts were as they always had been, but the same could not be said of me. In the intervening decade, I had had two children, and this had changed me not only personally but professionally. This new aspect of my identity brought with it an enhanced perspective on life; as I reviewed these transcripts, I saw and heard new meanings and new nuances from those which I had observed earlier in my life. Thus it was that I came to write an article focusing on the maternal narratives contained in these interviews. I later reflected upon on the inspiration for writing this article:

> It is not a coincidence that the first time I returned to this set of data after more than a decade it was to explore how respondents recalled their early childhood. My two small children have enriched my life – and challenged me – in many ways, but it was an unexpected gift that my relationship with them would afford me a new perspective into conversations I had had long before they were born. What I saw, and perhaps wanted to see, in the four cases I presented in my paper, gives me personally, as a mother, hope for my children; despite how imperfectly we may parent, they – and we, as adult children – still have within them the ability to overcome whatever blows we may deal them, however inadvertently. The accounts of the narrators serve as an antidote to the stories of those adults who continue to see their parents as the ultimate arbitrators of the individuals they have become. We can shape our lives, but not in circumstances of our own choosing.

> (Andrews, 2004: 58)

But this was not the only time that I returned to this data set and found in it new meanings. Approaching my fortieth birthday and on maternity leave, I wrote an article on successful ageing. Re-reading the transcripts helped me to think through what kind of an old person I wanted to become. I described this process in the following way:

> Looking back on those transcripts, there was a lesson for me of how to resist the generally available social construction of what it means for a woman to turn forty (or fifty, or sixty …) These were not to me ageless voices, but rather voices which pointed to what aging could mean, what years ahead could hold. This message was one which I was particularly open to hearing at that moment in my life…. But as my interpretation of the stories changes over time, so does their function in my life. In some sense, the narratives which I collected for my PhD have served as a blueprint for me. The exercise of having spent so much time with others engaged in life review has produced in me a consciousness of the temporal aspects of my own life. In future years, what kinds of stories will I want to be able to tell myself about who I have been, based on what I have done? What can I do now that will make me feel fulfilled then?

> (Andrews, 2003b)

My changed circumstances, be it as a mother, or as a woman who was older than the one who had conducted the original research, had provided me with new ways in which to make sense of the accounts of those who participated in my research. To re-read transcripts of one's earlier career is also to look into the mirror of one's own professional identity.

Revisiting one's own data is not so much a journey back into that time, as much as an exploration of that moment from the perspective of the present, with all of the knowledge and experience that one has accumulated in the intervening time since the original data analysis. But the original analysis remains important; it represents the self of the interviewer and of the interviewee as they were perceived to be at that moment. As Brockmeier (2006) observes:

> there is no a priori privileged moment in time in which we can gain a deeper, more profound, truer insight than in any other moment. A secondary analysis can offer more, but it also can offer less than a third or even the first analysis.

Riessman, in her analysis of a 'thrice told tale' echoes this sentiment:

> I am not arguing that my third reading is 'truer' than my first or second; they are, simply different. Although I think the thrice-told tale illuminates a layered complexity rather well, I am sure other readings from other historical and dispositional standpoints can illuminate the material in other ways. There is never a single authorised meaning. (2004: 321)

The statements of Brockmeier and Reissman contrast with a growing tendency amongst some researchers returning to old data to construct their newly revised interpretations in the genre of a progress narrative. Communicating a sense of 'I was blind, but now I see' they are condescending towards the 'I' who they once were, their confidence expressed through a denigration of the self who asked those questions, wrote those things, and interpreted those passages in that way. Is it not possible for these different viewpoints, the past and the now-present, to co-exist?

Using Elizabeth's metaphor, one can argue that while a climber might obtain a more sweeping view of the vista below from the top of the mountain, equally, from this vantage point, some of the detail of the ascent will have been lost. Indeed, it is the multiple viewpoints, taken together, which are the most illuminating (Mishler, 2004). Thus it is in our research: subsequent readings of material we, or others, have gathered invariably bring with them a new layer of understanding. But no interpretation is ever final; our current framework is itself one which will change over time.

Debating the use of secondary-analysis in qualitative methodology

Historically, secondary analysis of data within the social sciences has not enjoyed a very hospitable welcome in the metaphorical homes of many qualitative researchers. The reverse has been true of quantitative data, which enjoys a 'well established tradition' (Corti and Thompson, 2004) of re-analysing data. However, the tide is turning, and in the past five years, qualitative researchers in general, and qualitative narrative researchers in particular, have begun to be much more interested in this process of 'looking back'. Indeed, some of the most compelling and reflexive pieces which explore the heart of narrative research have been written as a response to revisiting 'old data' (e.g. Riessman, 2002; Sparks, 2002).

Writing in 2004, Louise Corti and Paul Thompson describe a 'new culture of the secondary use of qualitative data' which had emerged over the previous five years (2004: 341), and Heaton (2004) describes qualitative secondary analysis as 'a new and emerging methodology' (2004: 35). In Britain, one key example of this lies in the proliferation of 'data sharing' policies, such as the requirement of the Economic and Social Research Council (ESRC), that all potential recipients of grants agree to archive their materials with Qualidata, 'a proactive service for the location, documentation and preservation of qualitative social science research data' (Corti and Backhouse, 2005). Other examples include the number of special issues of journals within recent years devoted to this topic, as well as the increasing number of self-reflective articles written by narrative researchers as they 'think again' about research they have conducted in the past.

Corti and Thompson identify four key arguments for the re-use of qualitative data:

(1)   it is resource efficient, optimizing the use of pre-existing material;
(2)   it creates the opportunity to generate new perspectives on the data;
(3)   it enhances the possibility of comparative research;
(4)   it allows for verification of the original study. (2004: 341)

Bornat (2003, 2005, 2006) has also made a significant contribution to this debate. In addition to the benefits listed by Corti and Thompson, she also mentions a few more, of which one is particularly important: 'Going back involves recognition of the significance of time in the creation of and life of a data set as well as those who contributed to its making' (2006: 3).

There are, however, passionate arguments which have been made against the recycling of old data (eg. Hammersley, 1997 and Mauthner et al., 1998). Chief amongst the concerns which are raised by these critics is that qualitative data is co-constructed, it is the product of human interaction and it cannot be fully understood outside of the conditions within which it was produced. Vital to what an interviewee says on tape is the person to whom they perceive themselves to be saying it, how they 'read' them as a person and how they evaluate the work they think they are contributing to. Important, too, is how the speaker feels on the day of the meeting, and what other 4pending concerns are (pre)occupying them while they talk. All of this is well travelled ground in the literature on interview practices, but its implication for secondary analysis of data is a less explored dimension of the same issue.

The public debate around the recycling of data tends to focus on a (re)interpretive process in which the social science analyst is someone other than the person who originally collected the data. This is true both for those who argue in favour of data sharing and for those who rally against it. Mauthner et al., for instance, raises concerns about 'fundamental epistemological issues which need to be acknowledged' surrounding the re-use of qualitative material (1998: 735). Data, they argue, are 'socially constructed' and 'meanings in data are not to be found in the data, but to be made by those doing the interpreting … findings are not in the data but created through the interaction of particular … researchers with particular respondents in particular locations and at particular historical junctures' (1998: 735).

But this argument against the re-use of data by others would seem to apply equally to the revisiting of one's own data, and would point to the near impossibility of ever making sense of data outside of the moment in which it is gathered. What is at issue here is not only the otherness of others, but also the otherness of ourselves to ourselves, for analysis of data is always carried out by someone other than the 'me-in-the-moment' who conducted the interview; interviewing and analysing data do not happen concurrently. As Brockmeier (2006) states:

> …we are never in the moment of gathering data, and … we are always in the moment of gathering data …. The observing, analyzing, and narrating 'I' always remains an unstable, provisional, and troubled vantage point … [Moreover] every 'secondary analysis' can be (and in real life, is) the subject of another 'secondary analysis'… we don't have any independent criterion to judge an autobiographical story as final and conclusive … all 'data' only live and breathe in the present, a present which they are delivering themselves.

The term 'secondary analysis' is elusive and opaque, referring to a process, with flexible and sometimes indecipherable boundaries. What is the relationship in time between the primary and secondary analysis? When does each begin and end, and how are they positioned in relation to each other? Despite our best efforts to construct these categories as absolutes, the more we begin to think about their meaning, we see that they exist on a continuum.

Moreover, some of the key epistemological issues surrounding the re-interpretation of data pertain to whether one is referring to the analysis of one's own data, or that of others. Bornat (2006) in her comparison between these processes, concludes that

> going back is very much the same process for both. Each can lead to reconceptualization, each enables new questions and interpretations and each results in new appreciations of temporality … in both cases, secondary analysis involves stepping into someone else's shoes, an earlier self or another self entirely. (2006: 10–11)

Bornat found that an important potential difference between revisiting one's own data and someone else's was not methodological or epistemological, but rather ethical. Research participants give their informed consent to a particular person, guided by a particular understanding of the goals of the research. If and when that researcher chooses to return to the data to explore a different focus to that of the original project, often it is possible to contact participants and to verify that this is okay with them. Even when this is not possible, the original researcher will have some sense of the participants, and can take this into consideration when assessing whether or not it is ethically defensible to pursue a new line of analysis. The same is not true when researchers wish to re-analyse data of others: unless research participants have given permission for the material to be held at a public archive with open access, it is very difficult to know if they would have agreed to be part of the research as it is newly reconfigured.

If there is never a definitive interpretation of data, how can we best assess competing interpretations? We, as members of the academic community and thereby as both producers of, and audience for, research, must ask ourselves how much consistency across interpretations is important to us, in other words, how much agreement must there be between different observers for their findings to be believable to us? Is there not much food to be found in the inconsistencies between these? What do we need to be convinced of the veracity of an interpretation? Freeman (2005) addresses this issue, arguing for the primacy of 'fidelity to the phenomena', and in narrative research, this phenomenon is very often 'the living, loving, suffering, dying human being' (Freeman, 1997: 171). The most believable interpretation of data about human beings is thus one which follows as closely as possible all of the twists and turns of what it means to be human – a meaning which is neither absolute nor enduring.

Whose story is it, anyway? Problematizing the authoritative voice

The implications of this are that not only are we very likely to view our own data differently over time, but equally, we are bound to see things differently from one another. This in turn invites the question, which interpretation is the most true, the most authentic? And by what criteria do we judge this – proximity to the moment of data collection? What then of the historical perspective which only time can provide? Equally, are we always the best listeners to stories which those who participate in our research tell us? How many times have we heard colleagues presenting papers at conferences, complete with long extracts of their data, and felt that those words do not speak to us in the same way that they do to the person who is presenting the work? Do we have a right to protest 'No, your respondent is trying to tell you something else. You have missed something important here'? And how would we ourselves respond were someone to say that to us? This is 'our' data – we have had an important role to play in the inscription of the words of respondents. Does that give us a privileged insight into the interpretations we offer?

Miguel del Unamuno famously protested that Cervantes was not capable of understanding the complexity of his two most celebrated creations, Don Quixote and his faithful manservant, Sancho. Rallying against Cervantes, Unomuno confessed 'I attempt to free Don Quixote from Cervantes himself, permitting myself on occasion to go so far as to disagree with the manner in which Cervantes understood and dealt with his two heroes' (1967: 4). Unamuno regarded himself as a freedom fighter, dedicated to liberating these two characters who had been so misunderstood over the centuries. He felt that he alone understood them; he alone was their champion.

Unamuno's 'most influential disciple' (Bradatan, 2004: 465), Jorge Luis Borges, resumed the freedom battle of Don Quixote. In 'Pierre Menard, Author of Don Quixote' – described by The Oxford Book of Latin American Essays (Stavans, 1998) as 'the most influential essay ever written in Latin America' – Borges (1964) creates a protagonist who recounts the efforts of Pierre Menard to rewrite Don Quixote. This essay, written while Borges was recovering from a head injury, was something of a task he set himself to test the functioning of his mind. (Amongst other ailments, he had been suffering from hallucinations.) Menard, our protagonist tells us, 'did not want to compose another Don Quixote – which would be easy – but *the* Don Quixote ... His admirable ambition was to produce pages which would coincide – word for word and line for line – with those of Miguel de Cervantes.' The end product of his efforts is to the uninformed eye an exact replica of Cervantes' original work. However, our narrator finds the two compositions utterly incomparable. For Cervantes to create this work when he did was 'reasonable, necessary and perhaps inevitable.' But for Menard to arrive at the same words 300 years later was evidence of nothing short of creative genius.

It is altogether an enchanting story. The historical context in which we produce our work not only frames its meaning, but is not replicable in other places and times. Even the very same words carry different meanings when they are authored – or read – in different places and times. Here Borges (1964) forces his reader to contemplate the ephemeral nature of meaning and its movement over time. Meaning is not something that, once extracted, can be contained in a pure, undiluted form, bottled as it were.

The applicability of Borge's theme to the present discussion is demonstrated in Riessman's (2004) discussion of reworking data which she had collected 20 years earlier. Riessman sensitively addresses her changing understanding of her interview with 'Burt', a man with advanced multiple sclerosis (MS) whom

Riessman had originally interviewed for her project on gender and divorce. On two subsequent occasions Riessman returned to Burt's narrative, and each time her own understanding of what he was saying to her changed. Riessman entitles her article 'A thrice-told tale: new readings of an old story.' It is, however, perhaps significant that the term 'thrice told' refers to Riessman's own tale, about Burt. He in fact only told her his story once; it is her reading and recounting of his narrative which changes over time.

And here lies the rub. We researchers ourselves do change over time. To use Borges' metaphor, the same words do not carry with them the same significance as our understanding of our own lives and the world around us changes. And if the meaning of the words changes, are they really the same words? If the meaning of the data changes, are they the same data? Meaning is variable not only because it is always in the eyes of the beholder, but, equally, the beholder never occupies a static position. Moreover, if views of 'time' and of 'temporal change' are themselves subject to change, all of this feeds back into the dynamics of the interpretation, and re-interpretation.

Narrative and time

Thus far, the issues which have been discussed are not particular to narrative research, but have a wider application. However, I wish now to make the case that the consideration of the issues surrounding the use of secondary analysis have a particular relevance for narrative researchers.

That considerations of time and narrative are closely, even inextricably, bound together is something which has received considerable deliberation (Brockmeier, 2000; Freeman, 1993; Ricoeur, 1984, 1985, 1988). Freeman claims that time lies at the heart of narrative thinking (2005), and Brockmeier asserts that 'we can neither think ourselves without thinking time, nor think time without thinking ourselves'(2001: 286). The implications of this for the present discussion are far-reaching.

As humans, we make meaning through and with time. But time itself proves to be a rather elusive entity. Autobiographical narratives, Brockmeier writes, are constructions which are

> not so much about time but about times. They encompass and evoke a number of different forms and orders of time, creating a multi-layered weave of human temporality ... But the different modalities [past, present, and future] also are inextricably interwoven among each other ... every narrative about my past is always also a story told in, and about, the present as well as a story about the future. This all ... is much like the temporal structure of human life itself, which is essentially a multi-layered and many-centred fabric of different orders of time. (2000: 57)

From this it follows that 'understanding a life is understanding the continuous oscillating of the different orders of past, present and future' (Brockmeier, 2000: 59). Invariably, the stories that we tell about ourselves, as well as those to which we attend as audience, are always and invariably anchored on shifting ground. As Kierkegaard (1843) commented:

> ... life must be understood backwards. But ... it must be lived forwards. And if one thinks over that proposition it becomes more and more evident that life can never really be understood in time simply because at no particular moment can I find the necessary resting place from which to understand it – backwards.

(cited in Brockmeier, 2000: 51–62)

Kierkegaard's observation here is reminiscent of Elizabeth's metaphor of mountain climbing. The autobiographical process itself is an 'interplay of positioning possible pasts and possible beginnings in the light of an end, that is the present of the story at the time, and in the context, of its telling' (Brockmeier, 2000: 55). Autobiographical narratives are always, and can only ever be, recounted from the present perspective, a position which is characterized by, amongst other things, its incompleteness. Freeman (2003) observes that the challenge of the moral life is 'to live mindfully enough of the limits of one's present perspective as to bring into view other, potentially more adequate or comprehensive perspectives' (2000: 72). This is a challenge that ultimately all of us fail at one point or another; 'try as we may, we can never wholly anticipate the memory that will eventually put this present into perspective'(2003: 54).

Thus we are forever re-scripting our pasts, making sense of the things that happened in light of subsequent events. This is true not only as narrators of our own lives, but also as narrators of the lives of others. This process of reinterpretation of events is one which is ongoing throughout our lives, as different parts of our pasts reveal themselves to hold increased importance, or to be void of meaning, depending not only on who we are, but critically, on whom we wish to become. The narration of the self occurs through an ongoing creation and re-creation of 'possible pasts and possible beginnings in the light of ... the present' (Brockmeier, 2000: 55).

'If I had known then what I know now': history, time and personal narratives

We come to see and understand the world, and our experiences within it, in new ways not only because we have changed, but because the world has changed too. Indeed, psychological transformation and political change are often closely connected, as much of my own work has documented (Andrews, 1991, 1997, 1999, 2003a, 2003b, 2007).

Sometimes when people talk about the lives they have lived, they convey a sense of a sudden and unexpected interference of historical forces, and the determining influence this has on their own biography. Shortly after the fall of the Berlin Wall, I conducted a life history with an East German Jewish woman, Ursula. At the time of our interview, she was in her mid-seventies. She had been evacuated to Britain during the war, but some of her family stayed behind, and were murdered in the concentration camps. After the war, she had no wish to return to Germany, but she was convinced to do so in order to help build a new society.

> I found it very, very difficult emotionally to return to that country voluntarily. But on the other hand we were told by our comrades 'who else would be there to reshape Germany and rebuild Germany if it's not these few anti-fascists who survived or came out of concentration camps?' because a majority of the Germans had been with Hitler and supported him ... and for that reason I thought it was my duty to return to this country. So I returned ...

At the time of our interview, not only did East Germany no longer exist, but the socialism which was its trademark was generally regarded as morally bankrupt. She laments the decision which she took so many years ago: 'I spent fifty years of my life on the wrong horse ... [socialism] doesn't work the way I thought it would work, you see, it doesn't work, that's why I say I put myself on the wrong horse.' Addressing herself, she says 'you have wasted, absolutely wasted your whole life, fifty years of your life you could have done all sorts of things ...' For Ursula, the meaning, or lack of meaning, of her life has been determined by the verdict of history. The socialism to which she had dedicated her life turned out to be different from what she had believed, but this retrospective evaluation brings her no satisfaction. Her desperate feeling of having 'wasted, absolutely wasted' her life was palpable throughout our interview. And yet, that interview itself was historically positioned. I do not know if her feelings about her life would be the same today, more than 15 years after the fall of the Berlin Wall. Many East Germans with whom I spoke in the early 1990s shared Ursula's deep disappointment with the fate of their country. And yet, more recently there has been a resurgence of pride in East German identity (see Andrews, 2003). There is never a final analysis, only points along the way.

Freeman, describing the moral challenge to live mindfully of the limits of one's present perspective, writes:

> Oftentimes, human beings are only able to recognize and understand the meaning(s) of experience after it has occurred. This phenomenon is especially evident in the moral domain: the morality (or immorality) of an action (or inaction) is often gauged only after the action has been completed. As such, we are often, and tragically, too late in our arrival on the moral scene. (2003: 54)

At the time that Ursula was persuaded to return to Germany, she did not know what the future of East Germany would be. During our interview, she tells me 'Now, now I have some ideas' but she does not elaborate on these. Instead, she says: 'I can't see a role for myself much really ... I am seventy years old now ... I'm glad I'm old now, I wouldn't like to be young again ... Enough is enough.' Time and timing, or more accurately missed timing, lie at the heart of this most poignant life narrative.

Freeman's haunting words, that 'we are often, and tragically, too late in our arrival' brings to mind Gorbachev's perspicacious warning, delivered at the celebrations marking the fortieth anniversary of the German Democratic Republic, weeks before its downfall: 'History will punish those who arrive too late.' No one, not even Gorbachev himself, could have anticipated the events that his words foreshadowed. And yet looking back to that moment in history, we can see a most poignant example of what Freeman describes as 'the dilemma of time'. It is hard to put ourselves back into that earlier time when we did not know what we know now.

As my research over the years has been largely focused on the relationship between personal and political narratives, it is not surprising that I have amassed a considerable amount of data whose historical relevance I could not have known at the time I gathered them. Indeed, some of these data only became significant in light of subsequent events.

The tumultuous events of 1989, for instance, forced me to revisit the data I had collected on the roots of sustained commitment to socialism during the previous years. When the events of that now-famous year began to unfold, it was difficult for me not to experience this with a mixture of excitement and frustration; excitement, because of the spreading of political ferment; but frustration because I knew I would need to analyse my data with a new lens. In this sense, my 'secondary analysis' was carried out on the heels of my original analysis, and illustrates the fluidity of boundaries between these supposed separate moments in time. Most of the 15 respondents in my study had identified 1956 – Khrushev's acknowledgement of the excesses of Stalinism which he delivered at the Twentieth Party Congress – and 1968 – the Prague Spring – as the most challenging times in their decades of commitment. As the events of 1989 unfolded, I knew I must return to my respondents to gain a perspective on the data which I had gathered in the previous few years. I wrote to all of them, and their responses were rich and varied, with one participant suggesting that we should 'toast the future together in champagne' while another described it as 'a huge setback'. History had intervened most dramatically in my research, and my ongoing analysis of my subject demanded that I re-examine the data I had collected.

From a post-1989 perspective, the transcripts of the interviews, conducted before the demise of socialism in Eastern and Central Europe, contain fascinating passages. In one interview, for instance, one of the respondents spoke for an exceptionally long time about the importance of Hungary (and the events of 1956) to her political biography. Neither of us were to know then the critical role that Hungary would play in the events which were to follow. I look back on those passages now with a strange feeling – in time, the words were spoken much closer to the events of 1989 than to 1956, and yet they are wholly ignorant of the future significance they will contain. As Freeman remarks, it is only with hindsight that we can detect the foreshadowing.

The research I conducted on patriotism in the United States as a response to the Gulf War in 1992 presents another example of the impact of a shifting historical lens. None of us were to know then that this war would later be known not as the Gulf War, but as the first Gulf War. And it is difficult, if not impossible, to take one's mind back to the time before 9/11. But looking back on those transcripts with the knowledge of what was to come is a most illuminating exercise. One of the dominant discourses which followed in the wake of 9/11 is that the world is now a different place. The arguments made for enhanced militarism, which is sometimes accompanied by enthusiastic waving of the flag, directly place the events of that fateful day at their centre. Re-reading these transcripts, however, I am struck by the resonance they have with this discourse – despite the fact that the events of 9/11 were nearly ten years after these interviews were conducted. Elsewhere I have written about this deja vue experience:

> I feel now when I look back on the research I conducted in Colorado Springs that it contains far more than I could ever have realized at the time. Now, when I read both the transcripts of my interviews, as well as reviewing the materials written by others and myself at the time regarding the issues addressed in the interviews, I am overcome by a seemingly contradictory set of reactions. On the one hand, the project is marked by the absence of 9/11, an innocence of events and their fall-out which were still to happen; on the other hand, the arguments made at the anti-war vigil and at the anti-anti-war vigil mirror those which would dominate our post 9/11 world.

(Andrews, 2007: 112)

Revisiting these transcripts invites the insight that while 9/11 may have increased the susceptibility of the US population to arguments supporting military engagement in the Gulf region, the groundwork for these arguments was well in place more than a decade earlier. On 20 March, 2003, the day the war in Iraq commenced, I had organized a workshop on Narrative and Politics. At the last minute, one of our speakers had to withdraw, and I found myself having to prepare a presentation with one day's notice. I chose to talk about the study I had done in 1992. I could not have known at the time of gathering the original data how current it would seem more than ten years later, in the context of the events of March 2003.

Conclusion

This chapter has explored the particular relevance of secondary analysis for narrative research. Using examples from my work, I have argued that historical changes, as well as changes in our individual life circumstances, provide us with opportunities to see new layers of meaning in our data. These subsequent interpretations and re-interpretations should not always be regarded as supplanting earlier understandings, but rather as possibly complementing them, a picture taken from a different angle as it were. Seen in this light, we come to more fully appreciate that our conclusions are always and only provisional, that they will be forever subject to new readings. Far from being problematic, this characteristic of narrative data is evidence of its resilience and vitality, and of its infinite ability to yield more layers of meaning when examined from yet another lens, as we explore the ongoing changes of the world within and around us.

Note

1   I would like to thank Jens Brockmeier for his very thoughtful feedback on earlier versions of this chapter.

Suggestions for further reading

- *Forum: Qualitative Social Research* 6(1) January 2005 Special Issue: Secondary Analysis of Qualitative Data http://www.qualitative-research.net/fqs/fqs-e/inhalt1-05-e.htm
- *Forum: Qualitative Social Research* 1(3) December 2000 Special Issue: Text. Archive. Reanalysis. (Especially the section 'Re-use and secondary analysis). http://www.qualitative-research.net/fqs/ fqs-e/inhalt3-00-e.htm
- *Forum: Qualitative Social Research*, the online journal of qualitative research, has dedicated two special issues to the issue of secondary analysis. Some of the articles have been cited in this chapter. However, it is advisable for readers who wish to become familiar with the current debates regarding secondary analysis to visit these issues of the journal, as the articles taken together represent a wide range of work in this area, including, for instance, life history work in the Czech Republic, the problems of revisiting oral histories contained in 'German Memory' Archives, and the use of qualitative software in secondary analysis of archives.
- Riessman, C.K. (2002) Doing justice: Positioning the interpreter in narrative work. In W. Patterson (ed.) *Strategic Narrative: New Perspectives on the Power of Personal and Cultural Stories.* Boston: Lexington Books.
  Through a detailed discussion of one of her own case studies, Riessman addresses the general issue of the shifting standpoint of the analyst/interpreter. The article articulates some difficult questions which researchers revisiting data should ask themselves, and it has a very thorough bibliography.
- Rosaldo, R. (1989) *Culture and Truth: The Remaking of Social Analysis.* London: Routledge.
  The first chapter of this book provides an exceptionally moving account of the effect of the change in personal circumstance on the interpretive lens we bring to our work. Here, Rosaldo describes the process by which he came to understand the deep experience of grief which had led to the tribal practice of headhunting.
- Sparks, R. (2002) Out of the 'Digger': The warrior's honour and the guilty observer. *Ethnography* 3(4): 556–81
  This article provides a very thoughtful discussion on retrospective evaluation of decisions made in the original research context. Sparks conducted fieldwork in the Barlinnie Special Unit in the early 1990s. In this article, written from the perspective of a decade's insight, he discusses the extent to which his research might have unintentionally been implicated in the decision to close the Special Unit.

References

Andrews, M. (1991) *Lifetimes of Commitment: Aging, Politics, Psychology*. Cambridge: Cambridge University Press.

Andrews, M. (1997) Life review in the context of acute social transition: The case of East Germany. *British Journal of Social Psychology* 36: 273–90.

Andrews, M. (1999) Truth-telling, justice, and forgiveness: A study of East Germany's 'Truth Commission.' *International Journal of Politics, Culture and Society* 13(1): 103–20.

Andrews, M. (2003a) Continuity and discontinuity of East German identity following the fall of the Berlin Wall: A case study. In Paul Gready (ed.) *Cultures of Political Transition: Memory, Identity and Voice*. London: Pluto Press.

Andrews, M. (2003b) Conversations through the years: Reflections on age and meaning' 4th International Symposium on Cultural Gerontology; Tampere, Finland, Conference Proceedings.

Andrews, M. (2004) Response to commentaries. In M. Bamberg and M. Andrews (eds) *Considering Counter-narratives: Narration and Resistance*. Amsterdam: John Benjamins.

Andrews, M. (2007) *Shaping History: Narratives of Political Change*. Cambridge: Cambridge University Press.

Borges, J.L. (1964) Pierre Menard, Author of the Quixote. Translated by James E. Irby. In James E. Irby and Donald A. Yates (eds) *Labyrinths*. New York: New Directions.

Bornat, J. (2003) A second take: Revisiting interviews with a different purpose. *Oral History* 31(1):47–53.

Bornat, J. (January 2005). Recycling the evidence: Different approaches to the reanalysis of gerontological data [37 paragraphs]. *Forum Qualitative Sozialforschung/Forum: Qualitative Social Research* [On-line Journal] 6(1): Art.42. Available at: http://qualitative-research.net/fqs-eng-texte/1-05/05-1-42-e.htm [Accessed 30 January, 2005]

Bornat, J. (January 2006) Secondary analysis of one's own and others' data. Paper delivered to the Practice and Ethics in Qualitative Longitudinal Research Seminar, University of Leeds.

Bradatan, C. (2004) 'God is dreaming you': Narrative as Imitatio Dei in Miguel de Unamuno *Janus Head* 7(2): 453–67.

Brockmeier, J. (2000) Autobiographical time. *Narrative Inquiry* 10(1): 51–73.

Brockmeier, J. (2001) Time. *Encyclopedia of Life Writing: Autobiographical and Biographical Forms* 2: 876–77. London: Fitzroy Dearborn.

Brockmeier, J. (2006) Personal communication. 16 March, 2006.

Corti, L., and Thompson, P. (2004) Secondary analysis of archived data. In C. Seale, G. Giampietro, J. F. Gubrium and D. Silverman (eds) *Qualitative Research Practice*. London: Sage.

Corti, L. and Backhouse, G. (2005, May) Acquiring qualitative data for secondary analysis [31 paragraphs]. *Forum Qualitative Sozialforschung/Forum: Qualitative Social Research* [On-line Journal] 6(2): Art. 36. Available at: http://qualitative-research.net/fqs-eng-texte/2-05/05-2-36-e.htm [Accessed 11 January, 2006]

de Unamuno, M. (1967) *Selected works of Miguel de Unamuno, Vol. 3 Our Lord Don Quixote. The life of Don Quixote and Sancho with Related Essays*. (Translated by A. Kerrigan) Princeton: Princeton University Press.

Freeman, M. (1993) *Rewriting the Self: History, Memory, Narrative*. London: Routledge.

Freeman, M. (1997) Why narrative? Hermeneutics, historical understanding, and the significance of stories. *Narrative Inquiry*, 7: 169–76.

Freeman, M. (2003) Too late: The temporality of memory and the challenge of moral life. *Journal fur Psychologie* 11(1):54–74.

Freeman, M. (2005) Science and Story. Paper delivered to the ESRC Methods in Dialogue Seminar Series.

Hammersley, M. (1997) Qualitative data archiving: some reflections on its prospects and problems. *Sociology* 31(1): 131–42.

Heaton, Janet (2004) *Reworking Qualitative Data*. London: Sage.

Mauthner, N.S., Parry, O., and Backett-Milburn, K. (1998) The data are out there, or are they? Implications for archiving and revisiting qualitative data. *Sociology* 32: 733–45.

Mishler, E. (2004) Historians of the self: Restorying lives, revising identities. *Research in Human Development* 1(1 & 2): 101–21.

Ricoeur, P. (1984) *Time and narrative Vol. 1*. Chicago: University of Chicago Press.

Ricoeur, P. (1985) *Time and narrative Vol. 2*. Chicago: University of Chicago Press.

Ricoeur, P. (1988) *Time and narrative Vol. 3*. Chicago: University of Chicago Press.

Riessman, C.K. (2002) Doing justice: Positioning the interpreter in narrative work. In W. Patterson (ed.) *Strategic Narrative: New Perspectives on the Power of Personal and Cultural Stories*. Boston: Lexington.

Riessman, C. (2004) A thrice-told tale: New readings of an old story. In B. Hurwitz, T. Greenhalgh, V. Skultans (eds) *Narrative Research in Health and Illness* Oxford: Blackwell Publishing.

Rosaldo, R. (1989) *Culture and Truth: The Remaking of Social Analysis*. London: Routledge.

Sparks, R. (2002) Out of the 'Digger': The warrior's honour and the guilty observer. *Ethnography* 3(4): 556–81

Stavans, I. (ed.) (1997) *Oxford Book of Latin American Essays*. Oxford: Oxford University Press.

Chapter 6

A Foucauldian approach to narratives

Maria Tamboukou

In this chapter I want to explore research strategies for a Foucauldian approach to narratives. In doing this I am taking the perspectives of the previous chapter into the field of feminist research. Here, narrative is understood through the structures and forces of discourse, power and history that are the focus of the work of Michel Foucault. In this context I shall be looking back into the ways I have deployed genealogical strategies as research tools that have opened up analytical paths in the reading of women's auto/biographical narratives (Tamboukou, 2003a).

Over the last fifteen years, my research has been focusing on the constitution of the female self, tracing its genealogical emergence in the social, political and cultural milieu of the turn of the nineteenth century. But – the question might come: what is genealogy and how can it make connections with narratives? Genealogy as a Nietzschean concept redeployed in Foucault's work is, put very simply, the art of archival research, the patience to work meticulously with grey dusty documents, looking for insignificant details, bringing into light unthought-of contours of various ways, discourses and practices that human beings have used to make sense of themselves and the world. Instead of setting itself the task of reaching the ultimate and hidden truth, genealogy offers archaeological journeys with no final destinations. Working in parallel with archaeology, it keeps uncovering layers of distortions/constructions and is directed to the future rather than to the past. How has our present been constituted in ways that seem natural and undisputable to us, but are only the effects of certain historical, social, cultural, political and economic configurations? By revealing this contingency we become freer to imagine other ways of being.[1]

Doing genealogy involves focusing on insignificant details, searching in the maze of dispersed dusty documents to trace discontinuities, recurrences and play where traditional research sees continuous development, progress and seriousness. In the process of my enquiries, I have therefore wondered where I should look for those traces, those 'grey meticulous details' (Foucault, 1986: 76), the forgotten documents genealogy is after: this is how I have become interested in auto/biographical narratives as sources revealing how human subjects constitute themselves through writing practices interwoven with power/knowledge relations.

Since my work has always been situated within a feminist theoretical and political plane, it is no wonder that my interest has been directed into tracing other possible ways of being or rather of becoming a woman. In doing this I am rather interested in excavating marginal practices in the constitution of the female self, practices that have remained obscured, but which can help us imagine different futures. My book, *Women Education and the Self: A Foucauldian Perspective* (Tamboukou, 2003a) has focused on the area of education in fin de siècle Britain as a social field opening up possibilities for unruly female subjects to emerge. Foucault's genealogies of the subject and particularly his notion of the *technologies of the self* – cultural practices that human beings have historically used to constitute themselves as subjects – have been central in the theoretical framework within which I have worked. My current project, entitled *In the fold between life and art* attempts once again to become a genealogy of women artists.

Looking back into how I have worked, I have therefore identified a list of research strategies that I now want to deploy and discuss. In doing this, it is important to note that I am aware of the fact that the classification to follow is indeed a heuristic device that will enable the particular aims of this chapter as a primary navigator in the deep grey sea of genealogical analyses of narratives. It is by no means presenting a closed methodological framework; it should rather be taken as a map charting genealogical trails and at the same time inviting the researcher to follow these lines, but also to bend them, erase them or add his/her own. Such an approach seems to come closer to what Foucault has suggested about his work:

> Still I could claim that after all, these were only trails to be followed, it mattered little where they led; indeed it was important that they did not have a predetermined starting point and destination. They were merely lines laid down for you to pursue or to divert elsewhere for me to extend upon or redesign as the case might be. They are in the final analysis, just fragments and it is up to you or me to see what we can make of them.
>
> (Foucault, 1980b: 79)

Let us therefore see what we can make of them and let us start with the art of cartography – mapping a range of Foucauldian research strategies in ways that can make multifarious connections with narrative analysis. In making this cartography, I will discuss a number of genealogical problematics, methodological movements and emerging themes of the genealogical approach. In deploying genealogical research strategies I will use aspects of my own research to illustrate the cartography I am attempting to draw.

Genealogical problematics, strategies and themes

Genealogy involves and demands that we struggle against our own way of reasoning. Within the genealogical framework, there is a decisive challenge for the researcher to become more sceptical about what s/he thinks s/he can 'read' in the narratives under investigation. In this light a genealogical approach to narratives will be attentive to a number of themes that will emerge in the process, stripping away as it were the veils that cover narrative practices, by simply showing how they have been mere discursive constructs of historical contingencies and in this vein how they can be interrogated and reversed. As I have written elsewhere, stripping away the veils that cover people's practices is a specific strategy of doing genealogies (Tamboukou, 2003a: 12). I have used this strategy in my work to problematize practices and discourses that constitute woman as a subject, gendering as it were the seemingly neutral context of Foucauldian analytics. A genealogical reading of narratives will therefore raise a range of problems, questions and tactics to which I am now turning.

Narrative modalities of how power operates as productive

A key insight of the genealogical approach is that truth cannot be separated from the procedures of its production. Consequently genealogy is concerned with the processes, procedures and apparatuses, whereby truth and knowledge are produced as power effects. A genealogical analysis of narratives will thus pose the question of which kinds of practices, linked to which kinds of external conditions determine the discursive production of narratives under investigation. What is at stake here is the way power intervenes in creating conditions of possibility for specific narratives to emerge as dominant and for others to be marginalized. What has to be remembered here, however, is that power should not be seen in its negative dimension – as a force imposing and sustaining domination – but rather in its Foucauldian reconfiguration as producing truth, knowledge and ultimately the subject.

In writing the genealogy of women in education (Tamboukou, 2003a), I have therefore traced narrative modalities of truth production through which women teachers were constituted as subjects in the interface of discourses around the private and the public. There were three interconnected planes wherein the private/public discursive regime was explored and interrogated: first, women's auto/biographical narratives inscribing experiences of living within and striving against the constraints of the private; second, the dominant public narratives constructing the image of the Woman in the late nineteenth, early twentieth centuries; finally, the interface of private and public narratives, an antagonistic field of power/knowledge relations at play.

In taking women's autobiographical narratives as effects of power/knowledge relations, I have therefore followed a genealogy of conflicting episodes and paradoxes in the discursive constitution of the persona of the woman teacher. It goes without saying that women teachers fought hard to escape domesticity and enter the public space through education. Indeed the desire to go away from familiar places and spaces was a common theme of their autobiographical narratives. Contemplating her decision to leave London and go to Leicester to work as an assistant teacher Clara Collet[2] was writing in her diary in 1876: 'Next Saturday I am going to Leicester; I am not sure whether I shall like it; but I do know I shall like it better than being at home (unpublished, p. 2). Eight years later however, school life had imposed new regimes of spatial suffocation for the young assistant teacher, who would once again take the decision to leave teaching:

> 20-10-1884: My diary makes no reference to my decision to go into residence at College Hall, London in October 1885, to study at University College and take my MA degree in Moral and Political Philosophy [which included Psychology and Economics], nor does it mention that I told Miss Leicester I was giving up my post in July 1885.

> (Collet, unpublished, p.75)

Clara Collet became a social researcher and worked with Charles Booth. Her own experiences would later inform her research on the lives of educated working women:

> The result is that we see girls following the stream and entering the teaching profession; after a few years, growing weary and sick of it, tired of training intellects, and doubtful about the practical value of the training, or altogether careless of it; discontented with a life for which they are naturally unsuited, and seeing no other career before them.

> (Collet, 1902: 140)

Literary work would further depict how some women teachers felt trapped within the public spaces of the teaching profession they had so hard fought to enter. In her autobiographical novel *Pilgrimage,* Dorothy Richardson (1995) has most forcefully expressed women teachers' spatial suffocation within the school classroom:

> The sunlight in this little schoolroom was telling her of other sunlights, vast and unbroken, somewhere-coming, her own sunlights, when she should have wrenched herself away [...] The girls did not know where she belonged. They were holding her. But she would go away, to some huge open space.

> (Richardson, 1995: 287–8)

Narratives emerging from Collet's diary, the book she wrote on the lives of the first women who entered the professions as well as novels of the period, illustrate my threefold approach to the analysis of narratives delineated above. In drawing on these narratives interwoven around the private/public dichotomy, I have therefore asked: what were the conditions of possibility for narratives to emerge depicting women teachers' suffocation within the public sphere? What were the power/knowledge relations at play in the way stories of 'getting away from home' would be redeployed as those of 'getting away from school'? How did it come that 'the angel in the classroom' would feel as constrained and unhappy as 'the angel in the house'? How did women teachers' auto/biographical narratives unfold within the discursive constraints of the private/public dichotomy but ultimately work towards undoing the dualistic opposition within which they were formed?

How in short did the paradox of being a woman teacher emerge and what were its narrative tropes (Tamboukou, 2000)?

What I have discussed in this section is that narratives always emerge in contexts, saturated by power/knowledge relations that keep destabilizing their meanings and characters. It is thus considering narratives within the polyvalence of discourses and power relations to which I now turn for discussion.

How apparatuses of power function through narratives and counter-narratives

Moving within, but also beyond, the narrative realm of public and personal narratives, genealogy places the auto/biographical practices of writing the self in a cartography of polyvalent and multifarious historical transformations, depicting the conditions of possibility for the 'figure' of the woman to emerge. This self is a discursive formation, emerging from the margins of hegemonic discourses, in what can be represented, but also in what is left without or beyond representation (de Lauretis, 1987). Auto/biographical narratives thus constitute a discursive regime creating the conditions of possibility for counter-discourses to arise and unruly subjects to emerge.

In this context I have explored narratives and counter-narratives revolving around gender and travelling. The following extract from a letter written in August 1902 by Winifred Mercier[3] to a friend and fellow teacher exemplary demonstrates how women teachers' narratives have inscribed their attempts to rearrange the space/power relations permeating their lives:

> Donald, wouldn't you like to go to America, Canada or the great wide west? Where perhaps there might be more chance of finding out what manner of being you were? – where there is more room, more freedom, and one is not so hide-bound by conventions – where you could get nearer the soil, and as I said before not be stifled by artificialities and habits and conventions, your own and other people's. Oh wouldn't you like it, wouldn't you? Wouldn't you?

(Mercier cited in Grier, 1937: 34)

Mercier's narrative forcefully expresses the passionate desire of an early pioneer in women's education to go away in search of more freedom. Her narratives counterpoise dominant Victorian perceptions around the role of the woman, particularly challenging patriarchal restrictions upon her mobility. In considering what Molly Andrews has theorized as 'counter-narratives' (2002), I have further suggested that women teachers' travel narratives bring forward a significant bending in the colonial practices and ideologies underpinning travel discourses. I have particularly referred to travel narratives exploring the multiple meanings and effects of crossing borders and transgressing boundaries. In this context, I have seen travelling constituting an interesting set of *technologies of the self* and becoming an exemplary case of how narratives, heavily invested by notions of patriarchy and colonialism – as indeed is the case with travelling – can be appropriated, bent, reversed. In making the argument of travel narratives being constituted as *technologies of the self*, I am therefore moving to the next problematic.

Narratives as technologies of power and as technologies of the self

Following the discussions above, I have therefore identified narratives as carrying out a twofold functioning: first, as technologies of power, 'which determine the conduct of individuals and submit them to certain ends or domination, an objectivizing of the subject' according to Foucault (1988: 18) and second as *technologies of the self*, active practices of self-formation. Auto/biographical narratives are therefore theorized as a discursive regime wherein the female self is being constituted through procedures of objectification – wherein she is categorized, distributed and manipulated – and procedures of subjectification – ways she actively turns herself into a subject.

In thus focusing on the stories of the first university-associated women's colleges, I wanted to show how women's personal narratives interwoven around their daily practices undermined spatial and hierarchical boundaries of their educational institutions and created a particular set of technologies in the constitution of the female self, what I have called *technologies of space* (Tamboukou, 2003a). The genealogical analysis of women's narratives has further traced complex and antagonistic discourses at play within these colleges. This discursive struggle over space underlines the fact that women's colleges at the turn of the century were indeed contested, multiple, and highly unstable places, and these contradictions were forcefully expressed in women's personal narratives:

> The Mistress's sitting-room and the library, where lectures were given and which was also our common room, were on the ground floor, and the dining-room was in the basement, a bare ugly room with two tables, at one of which we students sat, while the Mistress and her friends sat at the 'High table' alongside. It was at first expected that we should sit in a formal row down one side of our table, lest we should be guilty of the discourtesy of turning our backs upon the 'High'. But this was too much and we rebelled, quietly ignored rule and insisted upon comfortably facing each other. So academically formal was the order imposed from the first at Hitchin, small as our numbers were.

> (Lumsden, 1933: 47)

As the above extract from Lumsden's[4] autobiography demonstrates, while women in colleges were resisting patriarchal domination by claiming their right to education and to the public sphere, they replaced it with a patriarchal structure (albeit with a matriarchal name and body) in the organization of college life. Yet, what became of more importance in the genealogical analysis of women's narratives were not so much the effects of power, but the subjective capacities that were being developed in the attempt to resist the power that had made women what they were. It was through these *technologies of resistance,* as I have called them (Tamboukou, 2003a), that women began to fashion new forms of subjectivity. By thus focusing on questions of power and resistance in the constitution of the self, I can make a link to a crucial question that a genealogical approach to narratives keeps raising.

Who speaks or writes?

Writing has been a preoccupation for Foucault. In the writing of genealogy, questions arise about how under what conditions and in what forms the author appears in the 'order of discourse'; how she reveals herself in the discursive context of her narrative; which institutional constraints she accepts and what rules she has to obey. For Foucault, authorship is a problem; we must, he argues, 'locate the space left empty by the author's disappearance, follow the distribution of gaps and breaches, and watch for the opening this disappearance uncovers' (Foucault, 1998: 209). Foucault wanted to displace or desacralize the 'author-function' as a convention of discourse. The author-function distinguishes certain discourses from others, privileges them, in effect. Authorship is also an appropriation of discourse and Foucault challenges the unity of the 'I' represented within the text: 'I am no doubt not the only one who writes in order to have no face', he was writing in the introduction to the *Archaeology of Knowledge* (1989: 17). One might wonder then, how 'the author's disappearance' in Foucault's genealogies could be compatible with the autobiographical project, which has been dominated by Lejeune's (1989) notion of 'the autobiographical pact', an implied contract existing between authors and readers validating as it were the truth of the authorial signature. To put it bluntly: when analysing women's narratives did it matter who spoke or wrote and from which position? It is in working out this problematic that the notion of *technologies of autobiography* arises (Gillmore, 1994).

In writing the genealogy of women in education, I have considered the author's disappearance as an immensely thrilling and exciting theme that has been radically reworked in the narratives revolving around the construction of female subjectivities. These autobiographical narratives, I have argued, have constructed a space 'in the margins of hegemonic discourses' (de Lauretis, 1987: 18) for the female self in education to emerge rather than disappear. This emergence however, has not constituted a unitary core self, but rather a matrix of subject positions for women 'writing themselves' to inhabit, not in a permanent way, but rather temporarily, as points of departure for going elsewhere, becoming other. In this light, women's signature has indeed become important in forging new and unthought-of identities at the dawn of the twentieth century. In writing and signing themselves, these 'new women', however, were constructing fragmented subjectivities: they were charting cartographies of often inconsistent subject positions, ultimately having nothing else but 'only paradoxes to offer' (see Scott, 1996). Indeed, a feeling of living in existential transit is a recurring theme in women teachers' auto/biographical narratives. This is Clara Collet in transition, at a critical point in her life as a teacher, where she is very close to abandoning teaching for good:

> I think I am leaving off being a girl; the future does not look very bright and that is a pretty sure sign with me that I am losing the power of building castles in the air

which has been my chief delight until now. I am almost coming to a turning point in life I think and how I shall turn out I don't know. I have no particular ambition have no special power and neither my religious nor social views suggest my clear aim is to be followed. I don't feel exactly unhappy while I am writing this; I only feel emotionless. Tomorrow I shall enjoy life as much as ever and laugh at what I have written; but today's frame of mind seems to me to be the one which will take hold of me more and more because it is the result of racing facts. If coming events cast their shadow before I am just in the frame of mind to hear bad news as though I expected it or to bind myself to some decisive course of action.

(Collet, unpublished, pp.70, 71)

In the above narrative, Clara Collet expresses her frustration for lacking all the characteristics that would constitute a coherent, determined (male) identity. In addition she cannot discern emotions: 'female gifts' have flown away as well. What is this creature then? Where can she find a place for herself? In distancing herself from her gloomy thoughts, she attempts to slide towards the light side of being. Life can be both unbearably heavy and/or unbearably light, Milan Kundera (1984) reminds us, and writing her diary becomes for Collet a means of holding together the multiple selves she lives with, a *technology of the self* (Foucault, 1988) she draws upon in making sense of herself and the world.

Having explored some of the problems emerging from a genealogical approach to narratives, what I want to do now is to consider some methodological tactics that arise in the research praxis.

Charting the narrative grid of intelligibility, making narrative cartographies, remaining on the surface of narrative analysis

Foucault has seen his genealogical project as 'ontology of the present' (Dean, 1994: 50), a history of the present. Calling into question self-evidences of the present by exposing the various ways they were constructed in the past, such histories shatter certain stabilities and help us detach ourselves from our 'truths' and seek alternative ways of existence. To write 'a history of the present', as Foucault suggests, it is necessary to distance ourselves from this present of ours, objectify ourselves and pose practical questions about life. In this light, I have argued that the genealogical approach scrutinizes both personal and public narratives for the excavation of distortions and discursively constructed regimes of truth. The focus on narratives is thus inserted in the genealogical project of promoting 'a logic for thinking not in terms of generalities and particularities, but rather in terms of singular ideas, complications and complex themes' (Rajchman, 2000: 53).

In the genealogical literature, the starting point of a genealogy is the construction of the *dispositif*, a grid of intelligibility wherein power relations, knowledges, discourses and practices cross each other and make connections. As Foucault sees it, a *dispositif* is a system of relations that can be established between heterogeneous elements, discursive and non-discursive practices, 'the said as well as the unsaid' (1980a: 194). A *dispositif* can include 'discourses, institutions, architectural arrangements, regulations, laws, administrative measures, scientific

statements, philosophic propositions, morality, philanthropy, etc.' (1980a: 194).
Given the heterogeneity and multiplicity of any *dispositif*, the genealogist can
indeed draw on an immense variety of data and approaches in the process of
its construction. What is particularly interesting however is what I have called
a focus on narrative modalities in the construction of the *dispositif*, in other
words an exploration of how narratives – both public and personal – become the
medium through which connections are made and regimes of truth are established.
Following the construction of her *dispositif* the genealogist puts together the
different elements that concerned him/her in sketching out the diagram of his/her
enquiries and in turning his/her attention to narratives, s/he raises the question:
'How has the subject been compelled to decipher herself in regard to what was
forbidden? It is a question of the relation between asceticism and truth' (see
Foucault, 1988: 17). It is significant that a genealogical approach to narratives
should interrogate what has been accepted as the 'truth', any truth concerning the
ways individuals understand and indeed narrate themselves as subjects of this world.
The genealogist endeavours to trace the emergence and development of narrative
practices of self-formation. S/he paints the historical as well as the philosophical
background of these practices and starts to weave the nexus of texts, where the
self is being spoken of and/or written about.

In thus analysing women teachers' narratives around their sexuality, I created
a cartography of the multiple and contradictory discourses and practices of the
Victorian era, the sociohistorical and cultural milieu within which these narratives
emerged and unfolded. What their narratives most forcefully expressed was that in
their struggle to make sense of their sex, acknowledge their desires and make life
choices, women teachers sought to imagine themselves as equal partners in sexual
relationships within and beyond the institution of marriage, as in the following
extract from Collet's unpublished diary where she reflects on her decision to turn
down a marriage proposal:

> 10-5-1885: E.W. The little momentary weakness I had for him was the result of much
> thinking and has died out completely. I hope sincerely that if he ever does as he said
> he would do and ask me again, he won't do so when I am in low spirits. It is just
> because I often meet men for whom I have a strong attraction that makes me like
> them in spite of faults that I feel sure that if in a moment of depression, I imagined
> I liked him because he was worthy of being loved for his virtues and married him,
> I should grow to hate him and perhaps fall wildly in love with someone else, or feel
> that I liked a dozen other men better than I did him. It is much better to live an old
> maid and get a little honey from the short real friendships I can have with men for
> whom I care myself than to be bound for life to a man just because he thinks he cares
> for me.

> (Collet, unpublished, p.81)

Women teachers' narratives criticized marriage on many levels and from
different perspectives: as a crude commercialization of women's bodies, as a pretext
to a double-standard sexual morality and therefore immoral, as an institution constraining nature, but also intellectual independence and freedom; even the idealized

image of marriage in a romantic love context was problematized as a human relationship inevitably leading to emotional stagnancy and boredom. Escaping from the discourses of sexual subjection through marriage, women teachers' narratives were nevertheless entangled with other discourses, those of love, care, and personal sacrifice to sometimes unreal, idealized, spiritual relationships, raising walls between bodily and spiritual needs, and thus perpetuating the constraining mind/body dichotomy. Circulating among the polyvalent discourses of marriage, love and sexuality, what those women teachers attempted to do through the narration of their stories, amongst other things, was to negate their fate and try to imagine a different sexuality. This imagination of the new or improbable is, I have suggested, of significant importance in the way their narratives were charted and analysed.

Within the genealogical framework, the archive of women teachers' autobiographical narratives around sexuality has been explored not in terms of hidden meanings, the search for truth about what these women 'really' thought or felt about love, marriage and sexual relationships but rather in terms of how what they wrote made connections and sometimes created oppositions with the polyvalent Victorian discourses of marriage, love and sexuality. This is the point of remaining on the surface of narrative analysis: it is the act of treating narratives as multiplicities of meanings and creating a map of how different stories connect with other stories, discourses and practices in shaping meanings and perceptions and in constituting the real and ultimately the subject herself.

Tracing the non-linear order of discourse, points of limits, reversals and juxtapositions

Genealogy, notes Foucault, 'requires patience and knowledge of details' (1986: 76). In analyzing narratives, the genealogist is careful with minor textual details; s/he scrupulously cites her examples, commenting on their structure. S/he further follows the 'order of discourse' of the texts she cites; she compares them, juxtaposes them and traces their repetition, recurrence or even disappearance. In working with narratives, the genealogist is careful enough to discern subtle variations and systematize her conclusions. S/he weaves the nexus of the power relations, the historical and cultural conditions and the practices under scrutiny, by drawing new lines and making interconnections among the different points of his/her narratives. Being sensitive to the uniqueness of the self, the genealogist is very much interested in wider biographical elements of the subjects whose narratives are under scrutiny. These biographical details however are read in a way that deconstructs their coherence and reveals contradictions, gaps and broken narrative lines, fragmented and incomplete sketches of the self.

Finally, the genealogical approach to narrative analysis stresses the limits imposed by the historical and social conditions within which narratives are produced. The genealogist is particularly attentive to what is left unsaid, the noisy silences of the grey documents s/he is working with. S/he is further tracing points of limits, narrative moments when discourses are contested or juxtaposed by counter discourses, reach the limits of their possibility to function 'in the truth' and are thus bent or reversed towards different planes of consistency. It is in the process of tracing narrative moments marking discursive boundaries, limitations, constraints and even reversals that the genealogist is charting transformations of old narrative themes or the emergence of new ones. In the process of such discussion the 'conclusions' seem to emerge naturally, like the subtle drawing of a veil, so easy and simple to uncover but at the same time, so difficult to imagine uncovering.

In tracing narrative moments in the constitution of the persona of the woman teacher I have therefore revealed quite a rich and complex archive of private and public narratives constituting the woman teacher as the educated working woman, the mother/angel of the classroom, the passionless spinster and/or neurotic flapper exercising bad influences on girls, the married woman neglecting both her family and her classroom, the sexually promiscuous teacher. The following extracts from contemporary women teachers' narratives convey an image of the complexity and incompleteness of the female self in education and I have drawn on them in raising the genealogical task of interrogating the present:

> I was a teacher. I never wanted to be, and now that I've stopped, I never will be again, but for several years it took my heart. I entered a place of darkness, a long tunnel of days: retreat from the world. I want to explain, to tell what it is I know. Teaching young children must always be, in some way or other, a retreat from general social life and from fully adult relationships, a way of becoming Lucy Snowe's dormouse, rolled up in the prisonhouse, the schoolroom.
>
> (Steedman, 1992: 52)

> The staffroom is full of women eating cottage cheese or grapefruit. Each of them knows about diet and eating and sexuality. They are willing and happy to talk about these, caught inside what they are: the unique combination of worker and woman, dependent and independent, free and trapped.
>
> (Walkerdine, 1990: 28)

> At the end of August in 1987 I sat on the floor in my bedroom and I cried. I had spent the whole summer finishing my dissertation and had left myself only four days in which to get ready for the examinations which were to follow. And I didn't know a thing. I couldn't remember anything I had ever read … At the end of August I had been teaching for seventeen years and I had been a college lecturer for the last three of these years. I already had an MA … And yet here I was sitting on the floor and crying … One year after the MA I was suffering from withdrawal symptoms. I honestly believe that you are a better teacher if you are also a student at the same time … So I registered for a PhD exactly one year later and I am going to finish this year. I will never do another course again, I have really had enough this time. Or have I?
>
> (Holding On diaries, 1994)[5]

Different as they are in their perspectives and problematics, the above extracts bring forward a number of interesting dualities: 'worker and woman', 'mother and teacher', 'teacher and student', 'dependent and independent' 'free and trapped' interwoven in the construction of the self of the woman teacher. In working with these narratives I have therefore attempted to trace the formation of discourses around the persona of the woman teacher: identify different moments of its emergence, follow continuities and discontinuities of its deployment, trace recurrences or sudden eruptions.

One of the questions that have kept coming up in relation to the rationale of a genealogical take on narratives has been about the specific intellectual insights that such an approach has offered. In therefore reflecting on my genealogical practice, I have identified a range of issues, which I believe came up as 'research effects' of the genealogical research strategies I have followed and it is to these that I now turn.

Unveiling the materiality of narratives: questions of space

Rossi Braidotti (1991) has identified two major areas of interest that have been opened up by the French philosophical school and especially by Foucault and Deleuze: the corporeality of subjectivity and the materiality of ideas, 'the fact that they [ideas] exist in an in-between space caught in a network of material and symbolic conditions, between the text and history, between theory and practice, and never in any one of these poles' (Braidotti, 1991: 126).

I have followed Braidotti's critical observation in suggesting that a genealogical approach unveils the materiality of narratives exposing as it were not only specific historical and cultural conditions in their constitution, but also spatial and therefore social relations interfering in their production; the fact for example that women needed a sort of private space, 'a room of their own' wherein to reflect upon their experiences and narrativize them, make them into meaningful stories. In this light, the genealogical approach opened up a rich archive of spatial narratives expressing women teachers' discursive and non-discursive practices in repositioning themselves in the spaces of modernity and moving beyond the private/public dichotomy. In the extract below, Molly Hughes,[6] a young woman in a new teachers' training college at Cambridge, gives a colourful topoanalysis of her room and her narrative most forcefully illustrates the power of space in opening up new ways of re-imagining the self within the Woolfian room of one's own:

> With the new curtains the Growlery had a gay aspect, even in the dreariest weather. This was as well, for otherwise the room looked very bare. While the others had been buying little ornaments and framed views of the colleges, my limited pocket-money kept me to the barest necessities. So I made a bold move by adopting the role of a hermit, and telling everyone that I preferred my room to be severely plain, that this indeed was the latest fashion among people who really counted. Pictures I maintained distracted thought, an ornament merely for the sake of ornaments was démodé. On a piece of cardboard I illuminated the words 'Thou shall think', and hung it over my mantelpiece. That would set the tone and prevent any tiresome remarks.

> (Hughes, 1946: 123)

Women teachers wrote extensively about their rooms as places to hide, disengage themselves from the world and reflect upon themselves. As already discussed above they also wrote about their travelling and their desire to get away from home. This spatial interaction between the microcosm of the room and the macrocosm of the new worlds opening up to them, constituted the material conditions for repositioning themselves as subjects in space and were vividly expressed in their narratives.

Beyond space, but related to it, the genealogical approach was most critical in recovering the body as a spatial site of interaction of material and symbolic forces, a battlefield of power relations and antagonistic discourses and it is by way of the body that I explored auto/biographical narratives of/on sexuality.

Narratives of/on the body

The genealogical approach has identified narratives as a site for embodied knowledges to be deployed. Memory itself is embodied and in this light my analysis has focused on narratives of sexuality in the constitution of the female self in education and has unearthed marginalized experiences of passionate relationships, both real and fictional:

> Louisa caught me one day by the shoulders and said half in play, but shaking her head safely, 'I wish I were that poor man for an hour! I believe I could win you yet' Win me? Of course she could and long before the hour had run out too! … Oh dear, let him speak with the musical voice she does, let him look at me with her eyes, let his manner be compact of noble confidence and the most endearing, reverent attention as hers at times can be and every possible disadvantage is outweighed and I am his forever. Yet who am I that should let not the feeling, but nearly the expression of it, thus turn the scale? I can only suppose that the want of the electric spark on my side is the symptom of some real hindrance to unity, however fine and firm the spiritual foundations of such unity may be.

> (Maynard, unpublished, ch. 33, p.308)

In 1879, this is how the strict Evangelical Constance Maynard[7] lets her body speak, while she compares her feelings for a man she has just rejected, with Louisa Lumsden, her old fellow student at Girton, who was at the time headmistress at St. Leonard's – the school in which Constance Maynard worked for three years, at the beginning of her career in education. In Maynard's view, 'the want of the electric spark' can even overcome 'the fine and firm spiritual foundations of a unity'. Maynard's reference to the need to feel the electric spark in her body is a rare verbal reference to bodily needs and feelings and it is persistent in her narratives about love and eros:

> I really wished I could love him, but that would have been a mockery. My hands I remember were lying on my knees and when he spoke of the honour and deference and faithful affection that awaited me, if only I could trust myself to his keeping, he very gently laid one of his hands over mine. I drew mine hastily away and put them both behind my back.

> (Maynard, unpublished, ch. 33, p. 299)

Hands moving, even if they do so to touch or avoid contact, paint rare pictures of body language in women teachers' auto/biographical narratives. Bodies are usually absent from the classrooms as well as from women's lives, 'erased from the blackboard' (Tamboukou, 2003a). It is only through relevant, but not directly 'bodily' occasions, that women teachers refer to their bodies. These counter-narratives of the body counterpoise the discourses of frigidity and passionlesness constructed by the sexologists in the context of medicalization of sexuality and the construction of the hysteric woman (Foucault, 1990). What the genealogical turn unearthed in women's narratives was a multiplicity of embodied images and subject positions, creating a much more complex picture around their persona and their lives, putting 'differences together in open or complex wholes' (Rajchman, 2000: 57).

Problematizing experience

As already stated one of the key processes in genealogy is its focusing on insignificant details, on what has been sidelined or kept silent. Seen therefore from a genealogical perspective, women's auto/biographical narratives emerge from the grey spheres of history to give voice to experiences long unattended and discredited. However, the feminist project of drawing on and validating women's experiences, has been critically interrogated in light of the problematization of the very notion of experience and its supposed privileged explanatory capacity. Joan Scott has argued that women's experiences should be considered as discursive constructs, rather than indisputable points of reference.

> Experience is at once always already an interpretation and something that needs to be interpreted. What counts as experience is neither self-evident nor straightforward; it is always contested, and always therefore political … Experience is in this approach, not the origin of our explanation, but that which we want to explain.

(Scott, 1991: 797)

What is mostly highlighted in this extract from Scott's influential essay is the theoretical and political need for experience to be deconstructed and for the analyst to be situated. In the light of these problematics, women teachers' practices of self-representation, be they autobiographies, memoirs, diaries, journals or letters cannot be taken as indisputable documents of life, but rather as discursively constructed narratives, which however, have recorded and revealed various and significant processes in the constitution of the female self.

Multiple stories, narrative archives

I have already discussed how a genealogical approach to narratives problematizes and indeed multiplies the meaning of stories and decentres the author. In my work with women teachers' autobiographical narratives I have mapped an extremely divided and contested field opened up by women narrating their stories of becoming a subject. These narratives were multiple and often contradictory; I have not read them in terms of what they 'really' meant or in terms of the narrative identities they were constructing. In reading women's autobiographical narratives alongside other public narratives, be they fictional, philosophical or scientific I have been creating an archive of stories, an assemblage of textual practices around the constitution of the female self. Rather than focusing on the meaning of stories I was more interested in exploring their connections and interaction in the production of truth and knowledge about the female self in education. I have therefore seen these narratives both as discursive effects and as sites for the production of meaning. What I suggest is that narrative research creates a rich archive for understanding how 'realities' – be they social or personal, past or present – are being constructed.

Conclusion

Narratives, genealogy, history

In this chapter I have suggested that studying women's autobiographical narratives can be an ongoing genealogical exercise, towards a revaluation and reorganization of the historicity of women's actuality. Clearly, giving women a genealogical history does not claim to reconstruct their past 'as it really was'. It is rather an attempt to reveal the temporality and contingency of contemporary 'truths' by tracing how they were constructed in certain historical periods. As Gillmore (1994: 86) has put it:

> Autobiography demonstrates that we can never recover the past, only represent it; yet it encodes the possibility of recovery as desire and the possibility of representation as its mode of production. The autobiographical I is at home in both history and narrative because it is produced by the action that draws those fields together.

It is the Foucauldian idea of a history starting from the present and aspiring to the future that has inspired my interest in using narratives to write genealogies of the female self. Perceiving the contingency of discourses and practices that construct contemporary 'realities' seems a useful way of distancing ourselves from certain self-models socially imposed and highly restrictive today.

In navigating the sea of Foucauldian analytics, I have charted a map of genealogical problematics, research strategies and themes emerging from a Foucauldian approach to narratives. I have attempted this systematization being aware that Foucault's work has been criticized for failing to employ recognizable methodologies. As I have written elsewhere, 'rather than following [a priori] methodological principles, Foucault's genealogies create a methodological rhythm of their own, weaving around a set of crucial questions […] questions which create unexplored and even unthought-of areas of investigation. Foucault's genealogies do not offer methodological "certainties"; they persistently evade classification, but they do encourage and inspire the making of new questions to interrogate the truths of our world.' (Tamboukou, 1999: 215)

Notes

1 It goes without saying that Foucault's conceptualization of power and his genealogical approach to history has received severe criticism, and the debate between Foucault and Habermas over the meaning of Enlightenment and Modernity is still going on (see Ashenden and Owen, 1999). More specifically and addressing some of the criticisms on his theorization of power, Foucault has argued that within relations of power, individuals and groups can find space to resist domination, exercise freedom and pursue their interests. He has thus drawn a significant line of distinction between relations of power, as fields of games where freedom can be exercised, and relations of domination, which need resisting. While this distinction overturns arguments that his theorization of power leaves no possibility of freedom, it is however a blurring distinction that has created certain tensions in genealogical research that seeks to trace specific 'drawings' of this line. As has been suggested: 'where do the various medical, psychiatric and carceral systems of surveillance and discipline, detailed in *Discipline and Punish* and elsewhere, stand in relation to that distinction?' (Maggil, 1997: 66). As I have argued elsewhere (Tamboukou, 1999) such theoretical and political questions, raised by the use of genealogy, are more effectively worked out in the actual 'writing' of specific genealogies. Whether they are 'solved' or surpassed, becomes a task and a challenge for the genealogist.

2 Clara Collet (1860–1948) was a student at the North London Collegiate School. At the age of seventeen she left London to become an Assistant Schoolmistress in a girls' high-school in Leicester. While teaching there, she studied for both an external London BA and a teaching qualification. She later left teaching to study for an MA in Moral and Political Philosophy at University College London and became a social researcher.

3 Winifred Mercier (1878–1934) became a pioneer in the reform of teacher training colleges and later in her life a Girton College don.

4 Louisa Lumsden (1840–1935) came from Scotland and was one of the five Girton pioneers. In *Yellow Leaves,* her autobiography, she bitterly criticizes many aspects of Girton life, which as a student she had persistently resisted (Lumsden, 1933). She became a tutor at Girton, then a teacher at Cheltenham Ladies' College and finally headmistress of St. Leonard's public school for girls.

5 'Holding On' was a group of women teachers that was formed at the end of an MA in Urban Education course. We came from different sectors of education, had different life patterns, different stories and even different countries behind us. The group kept us together for almost two years, between 1992 and 1994. During this period we had meetings, followed by social outings, discussed our readings of books and papers, wrote a paper in collaboration; we kept a diary for the same day and then for the same week, to share our experiences.

6 Molly Vivian Hughes (1866–1956) came from a family from the lower middle classes, attended the North London Collegiate School and trained as a teacher in Cambridge. Hughe's autobiography follows her adventures in several educational institutions both as a pupil and teacher.

7 Constance Maynard (1849–1935) was an early Girtonian student. She came from a strict Evangelical family and had to overcome many difficulties, before she was allowed to sit in the examinations to enter Girton College. She later founded Westfield College. She was a prolific writer and produced volumes of diaries, an autobiography and books drawing on autobiographical aspects of her life.

Suggestions for further reading

- Deleuze, G. (1992) What is a dispositif? In T. J. Armstrong (trans.) *Michel Foucault, Philosopher: Essays Translated from the French and German,* London: Harvester Wheatsheaf.

(Constructing a dispositif is a fundamental stage of the genealogical approach. Please read this paper in relation to Tamboukou (2003b), where the construction of a particular 'dispositif' is being discussed.)

- Foucault, M. (1988) Technologies of the self. In L. Martin, H. Gutman and P. Hutton (eds) *Technologies of the Self*. London: Tavistock.

(This is the paper where Foucault clearly articulates the importance of auto/biographical writing in the constitution of the subject.)

- Gillmore, L. (1994) *Autobiographics: A Feminist Theory of Women's Self-Representation*. Ithaca and London: Cornell University Press.

(This book is a Foucauldian approach to the analysis of women's auto/biographical writings.)

- Scott, J.W. (1991) The evidence of experience. *Critical Inquiry* 17 (Summer 1991): 773–97.

(A very important paper problematizing experience as an analytic strategy of life narratives.)

- Tamboukou, M. (1999) Writing genealogies: an exploration of Foucault's strategies for doing research. *Discourse* 20(2): 201–18.

(A more detailed theoretical articulation of genealogy as a set of research strategies.)

- Tamboukou, M. (2003a) *Women, Education and the Self: A Foucauldian Perspective*. Basingstoke: Palgrave Macmillan.

(A book constituting an example of what a genealogical approach to narratives could offer.)

- Tamboukou, M. (2003b) Genealogy and ethnography: finding the rhythm. In M. Tamboukou and S. J. Ball (eds) *Dangerous Encounters: Genealogy and Ethnography*. New York: Peter Lang.

(A step by step scrutiny of working genealogically.)

References

Andrews, M. (2002) Counter-narratives and the power to oppose. *Narrative Inquiry* 12(1): 1–6.

Ashenden, S. and Owen, D. (1999) *Foucault contra Habermas*. London: Sage.

Braidotti, R. (1991) *Patterns of Dissonance*. Cambrigde: Polity Press.

Collet, C.E. The Diary of a Young Assistant mistress (unpublished). In The Modern Records Centre, University of Warwick.

Collet, C.E. (1902) *Educated Working Women: Essays on the Economic Position of Women Workers in the Middle Classes*. London: P. S. King.

de Lauretis, T. (1987) *Technologies of Gender: Essays on Theory, Film and Fiction*. Basingstoke: Macmillan.

Dean, M. (1994) *Critical and Effective Histories: Foucault's Methods and Historical Sociology*. London: Routledge.

Foucault, M. (1980a) The confession of the flesh: a conversation. In C. Gordon (ed.) *Power/Knowledge: Selected Interviews and Other Writings 1972–1977*. London: Harvester Wheatsheaf.

Foucault, M. (1980b) Truth and power: an interview. In C. Gordon (ed.) *Power/Knowledge: Selected Interviews and Other Writings 1972–1977*. London: Harvester Wheatsheaf.

Foucault, M. (1986) Nietzsche, Genealogy, History. In P. Rabinow (ed.) *The Foucault Reader*. Harmondsworth: Peregrine.

Foucault, M. (1988) Technologies of the self. In L. Martin, H. Gutman and P. Hutton (eds) *Technologies of the Self*. London: Tavistock.

Foucault, M. (1989) *The Archaeology of Knowledge*. London: Routledge.

Foucault, M. (1990) *The History of Sexuality, An Introduction, vol. 1*. Harmondsworth: Penguin.

Foucault, M. (1998) What is an author? In P. Rabinow (ed.) *Michel Foucault, Aesthetics, Method and Epistemology, the Essential Works of Michel Foucault, 1954–1984, Vol. II*. Harmondsworth: Penguin.

Gillmore, L. (1994) *Autobiographics: A Feminist Theory of Women's Self-Representation*. Ithaca and London: Cornell University Press.

Grier, L. (1937) *The Life of Winifred Mercier*. Oxford: Oxford University Press.

Hughes, M.V. (1946) *A London Girl of the 1880s*. Oxford: Oxford University Press.

Kundera, M. (1984) *The Unbearable Lightness of Being*. London: Faber and Faber.

Lejeune, P. (1989) The Autobiographical Pact. In Paul John Eakin (ed.) *On Autobiography*, translated Katherine Leary. Minneapolis, MN: University of Minessota Press.

Lumsden, L. (1933) *Yellow Leaves: Memories of a Long Life*. Edinburgh: William Blackwood.

Maggil, K. (1997) Surveillance-Free-Subjects. In M. Lloyd and A. Thacker. *The Impact of Michel Foucault on the Social Sciences and Humanities*. Basingstoke: Macmillan.

Maynard, C. Unpublished Autobiography. Queen Mary and Westfield College, Archives.

Richardson, D. (1995) *Pilgrimage 1*. London: Virago Press.

Rajchman, J. (2000) *The Deleuze Connections*. London: The MIT Press.

Scott, J.W. (1991) The evidence of experience. *Critical Inquiry* 17 (Summer 1991): 773–97.

Scott, J.W. (1996) *Only Paradoxes to Offer: French Feminists and the Rights of Man*. Cambridge, MA: Harvard University Press.

Steedman, C. (1992) *Past Tenses: Essays on Writing, Autobiography and History*. London: River Oram Press.

Tamboukou, M. (1999) Writing genealogies: an exploration of Foucault's strategies for doing research. *Discourse* 20(2): 201–18.

Tamboukou, M. (2000) The paradox of being a woman teacher. *Gender and Education* 12(4): 463–78.

Tamboukou, M. (2003a) *Women, Education and the Self: A Foucauldian Perspective.* Basingstoke: Palgrave Macmillan.

Tamboukou, M. (2003b) Genealogy and ethography: finding the rhythm. In M. Tamboukou and S. J. Ball (eds) *Dangerous Encounters: Genealogy and Ethnography.* New York: Peter Lang.

Walkerdine, V. (1990) *Schoolgirl Fictions.* London: Verso.

Chapter 7

Narrating sensitive topics

Margareta Hydén

Introduction

I can still recall the scent of dry heat that so intensively flavored that day in July 1971 when I first met Maria.[1] I can hardly think of an encounter more embedded in incongruence. I was a very inexperienced social work student of 23 years, working for the summer at a shelter for homeless women with drug problems. She was a 26-year-old experienced sex worker. She was nine months pregnant with her second child and seeking refuge because she needed a safe place to stay awaiting the delivery of her child. Her plan was to give the baby up for adoption immediately after its birth. I had no children, lived in a cozy little apartment with my husband and spent my days at Stockholm University. The streets of Stockholm and a van were her regular working sites.

Maria and I spent a great deal of time alone over the following days. Everyone but us seemed to be on vacation, staff and guests alike. We had time to talk. Maria gave me detailed accounts of the kind of work she did, emphasizing that she was a 'real professional'. Sex did not seem to be a sensitive topic for her. She invited me to join her in talking about sex and to share my best sexual experiences. Her invitation made me very embarrassed: Such private, sensitive issues – should I talk about them with a stranger? No way. I do not remember her showing any signs of understanding or sensitivity toward my embarrassment. She simply continued. I tried to introduce some more neutral topics into our conversation, like 'Where did you grow up?' or 'A new episode of the TV-series everybody talks about is coming on, maybe we should watch it'. I had no success in my efforts, however. Topics like those I picked only seemed to irritate and almost embarrass her. 'My childhood wouldn't interest you a bit and I don't watch TV in the van', she snapped.

Maybe she wanted to talk more about her children. I deliberately avoided the topic. I found it heartbreaking that in a few days she would give birth to the child she had carried for nine months and immediately give him or her up for adoption. I could not think of a more sensitive topic. Finally, I reluctantly brought it up – 'You are giving your child up for adoption?' – and got a prompt answer. 'I already have a son', she said, 'so I'd like a girl this time. I want my children to have good homes, good upbringings. I am definitely not the right person to give them good lives. You know, I don't know who their fathers are and I live in a van. What kind of life is that for a child? By the way, do you have any idea how difficult it is to be approved as an adoptive parent? First they have to fill in all kinds of forms and then they're interviewed. Even if they're really good, they can't be sure of being chosen – there are so many to choose among. It's great, I mean, anyone can fuck and get pregnant – but these people are the chosen ones, they're the best. I want them for my children.'

One night she knocked on the door – 'It's time, I'm off' – and left. Two days later the telephone rang and a man told me that Maria wanted to talk to me. She was so under the influence of heroin that I could barely hear her. 'I had a girl', she said. The man came back on the line. 'She isn't feeling very well', he said. I asked him to bring her to the shelter. They came. I took care of her, washed her, gave her something to drink, put her to bed. She slept for about 24 hours and then left the shelter. I never saw her again.

Maria taught me, a young, inexperienced and childless social worker, a great deal. First and foremost, I learned about the ways in which maternal love can be manifested and what it takes to live accordingly. Just as important, she also gave me insight into the complexities of identifying the meaning of the term 'sensitive topic'. Before I met her, I generally considered a person's sexual life as private and a potentially sensitive issue for a researcher. I think this notion was very much in line with my middle-class, Lutheran upbringing. I thought of sensitive topics as established facts. I considered questions like 'Which part of the country do you come from?' or 'Do you like the new TV series?' classic examples of non-sensitive topics, and therefore well suited to serve as an invitation to small talk and at the same time indicate an interest in the other person. Maria taught me that it could be quite the reverse; what is sensitive to one person might not be the same for another. All of a sudden, it seemed to me that *any* topic might be a sensitive one.

Content of the chapter

So, what is a sensitive topic? That this question might not have a simple answer is, in fact, the main point of this chapter. I will make the claim that what is a sensitive topic and what is not is due mainly to *relational* circumstances, that is, the relationships between the teller and the listener. In the opening story about my encounter with Maria, I have already introduced some of the main factors that such a relationship includes, such as *cultural* and *contextual* circumstances and the *personal* views held by the people involved. During the course of this chapter I will focus on factors such as *power* and *space* and I hope to be able to provide some insight into why these concepts play such a profound role in shaping the relational circumstances for research on sensitive topics.

In the second part of the chapter I will raise the question: 'What kind of methodological steps do we as narrative researchers have to take when dealing with sensitive issues?' Since I have relied mainly on interviews throughout my work, I will focus on the research interview and include some examples from my research on domestic violence. As a point of departure I will present my idea of the ideal interviewer. In my opinion, he or she is more a *listener* than a *questioner*. Correspondingly, my ideal interviewee is a person who is a good narrator. My ideal interviewer – and also my ideal narrative researcher – is a person equipped with the essential skills to assist the interviewee in his or her efforts to narrate.

The first point I want to make is that as a researcher dealing with sensitive topics you are always at risk of your interviewees positioning you as superior to them. This is due mainly to the fact that they might be telling you about issues they are ashamed of, issues that might be rated culturally low, or events that have left them vulnerable. A researcher explicitly positioned as superior is at risk of meeting resistance from an interviewee that is manifested in various ways of avoidance. This will seriously limit your research.

My second point is that as a researcher of sensitive topics – and this is very true if you are a researcher of domestic violence – you are always at risk of being so preoccupied with the sensitive and painful that you more or less conceal your interviewees in their suffering. That is, the interview focuses entirely on the dark side of your interviewee's life, which may cause suffering and seriously limit your research.

I will end the second part of the chapter by expanding my analysis to the potential harm the *circulation* of narratives on sensitive topics may cause the involved, since they might be reinterpreted beyond the narrator's control.

In the third and final part of the chapter, I will emphasize the importance of making *physical* and *discursive space* for sensitive topics to evolve in narrative research.

What is a sensitive topic?

Before I continue, I think it is important to emphasize the difference between an *event* that involves sensitive, even traumatic, experiences and a sensitive *topic*. An event is something you experience and a topic is something that appears in a discussion and is dealt with discursively. An event that involves a traumatic experience has the potential to form a sensitive topic, without necessarily doing so. Talk about a traumatic experience, for example, has the potential to pose a threat and even has the potential to re-traumatize the traumatized, but such talk can just as well have the potential to heal. This chapter deals with sensitive topics that may appear and need to be dealt within the context of research.

Textbooks on research methods rarely deal explicitly with the issue of researching sensitive topics. There are no entries for 'sensitive' or 'sensitive topics' in commonly used textbooks such as *Handbook of Interview Research* (Gubrium and Holstein, 2002) or *The Sage Handbook of Qualitative Research* (Denzin and Lincoln, 2005). When the question of sensitivity is considered, it is often approached from the perspective of ethics (e.g. Johnson, 2002). *The Oxford Dictionary of English* (2005) entry for 'sensitive' reads: 'easily damaged, injured, or distressed by slight changes, having or displaying a quick and delicate appreciation of others' feelings, easily offended or upset'; thus, 'sensitive' has to do with personal characteristics rather than certain topics.

One of the few books on research methodology that explicitly deals with sensitivity is *Researching Sensitive Topics,* by Renzetti and Lee (1993). The authors define a sensitive topic as 'one that potentially poses for those involved a substantial threat, the emergence of which renders problematic for the researcher and/or the researched the collection, holding, and/or dissemination of research data' (1993: 5). They bring up the issue of whether all topics could carry sensitivity, and come to the conclusion that 'it is probably possible for any topic, depending on context, to be a sensitive one' (6). Renzetti and Lee continue:

> Experience suggests, however, that there are a number of areas in which research is more likely to be more threatening than in others. These include (a) where research intrudes into the private sphere or delves into some deeply personal experience, (b) where the study is concerned with deviance and social control, (c) where it impinges on the vested interests of powerful persons or the exercise of coercion or domination, and (d) where it deals with things sacred to those being studied that they do not wish profaned (1993: 6).

Renzetti and Lee indicate that sensitive topics basically have to do with *personal* circumstances. My alternative understanding is that sensitive topics basically have to do with *relational* circumstances.

Sensitive topics as relationally defined

Throughout my professional life I have been involved in conversations about sensitive topics. As a social worker I have listened to all kinds of socially embarrassing problems and dilemmas. As a researcher on domestic violence I have dealt with criminal and morally reprehensible deeds, potentially harmful to discuss for victims as well as for perpetrators. Spending my professional life in these two discursive domains has given me numerous occasions to reflect on the decisive influence of the outcome of the conversation, the multilayered power relations within and outside the conversation, as well as to consider what kind of discursive and psychical space they were embedded in. Since I have relied on interviews throughout my research work, I have given the relationship between interviewer and interviewee some thought over the years.

If I had to identify a single factor that has been significant to success in gaining access to narratives on sensitive topics, I would mention my growing insight that the process of interviewing can be a jointly conducted enterprise between interviewer and interviewee (see further Bruner, 1990; Mishler, 1986; Riessman, 2002). Accordingly, during the course of several studies based on interviews, I have allowed my interviewees and myself together to actively shape the form of the interviews in a joint process. In such a process, the concepts of 'question' and 'answer' are to be thought of as a part of a circular process, with my informants and I trying to make continuing sense of what we were talking about. This way of conducting interviews differs from standard interviewing, according to which a question with a predetermined meaning serves as a stimulus, intended to elicit a certain response (Mishler, 1986).

If I had conducted my interviews along the lines of standard interviewing, I would most likely have faced considerable difficulties in researching domestic violence, for various reasons. Domestic violence meets several of the criteria identified by Renzetti and Lee (1993) as characterizing topics 'that potentially [pose] for those involved a substantial threat', that is, a sensitive topic. Research on domestic violence (a) is research that intrudes into the private sphere and delves into deeply personal experience and (b) could be concerned with deviance and social control. Another reason why the stimulus–response metaphor would not have served well as a model for conducting my interviews was that they were essentially 'untold stories', stories that had not been told before. Stories of this type are not well suited to a format of pre-prepared questions followed by brief answers – they may fall short entirely and never be articulated. Or, as one man responded to my request for his participation in a study I was conducting on abusive men and battered women:

> Yeah, I can be part of your study, I guess. I mean, I have been through a lot, I really have. If you think someone else can be helped by what I have been through, that's good. But I am not sure you will get anything good out of talking with me. The fact is that I don't *know* anything about what happened.

> (Hydén, 1994: 53)

Despite all the differences that exist between the interviews with the abusive men and abused women I spoke with, they were similar in the sense that in most cases what I asked them concerned previously 'untold stories' and something they 'did not know anything about'. The significance of the difference between 'having been through a lot' and 'knowing about' what happened is that of reflection and giving meaning to an experience. This difference is decisive when it comes to research interviewing: Without having experienced the cognitive process of 'having been through' an experience and rendering it some meaning so you 'know about it', it is difficult to discuss the experience.

Sensitive topics as culturally defined

My introductory story reflects my understanding of the relationship between teller and listener as the defining factor for what is a sensitive topic and what is not. It also reflects the culturally situatedness of this relationship; the sensitive topics were brought into our conversation as Maria violated a series of culturally defined norms. First, sensitive topics in the capacity of intimate topics should not be discussed in public, or with unknown persons. They can be discussed in intimate relationships such as between a couple, within the family, or with a close friend – this type of talk even defines such relationships. Second, sensitive topics can be discussed in special relationships using special discourses that strip the topics of their intimacy, like doctor–patient discourses (see further Mishler, 1984).

Sex can be linked to intimacy, when a person has learned to feel sexy only when they feel close to someone. The converse is a learned separation between sex and intimacy such that knowing and feeling close to someone makes them sexually uninteresting (Jamieson, 1988). 'A question to ask is whether sex is becoming more or less tied to intimacy, as are questions around gender differences. Are we witnessing the decline of macho-male masculinity with its predatory sexuality that ritually denies intimacy?' Lynn Jamieson (1988: 107) asks, as she traces personal relationships in modern societies.

Prostitution is a form of sexual behavior in which sex is separated from intimacy. According to prevailing cultural norms, this separation is taken too far. The dominant discourses deprive a narrator like Maria of the possibility of positioning herself as a responsible person who consciously condemns her actions. Predominant discourses position her as a prostitute, a vocation imposed on her from outside: She is the victim of patriarchy; she might have been victimized by men who sexually abused her in her childhood; she might be the victim of her addiction to drugs which works in two directions – she might be in need of money to finance her drug use and she might be able to sell sex because she is under the influence of drugs. These discourses make her one of us: She connects sex and intimacy, as the norms prescribe, but she cannot live accordingly for reasons beyond her control.

Maria did not speak within these discourses at all, instead violating a series of culturally established norms in her talk.

Sensitive topics defined by power relations

The interpretations of cultural norms play profound roles in shaping not only the relationship between teller and listener, but also the power relation between the two. Social work practice exemplifies this distinctly.

As a social worker, I was involved in conversations concerning a range of sensitive topics. Sometimes I met people because of their requests for state support, or because they had been reported on suspicion of having neglected their children. Sometimes I met young people because they had been reported for various kinds of misconduct, such as drug use, or different types of destructive behavior. In these conversations I was explicitly involved in a power relation that put me in the dominant position and the help-seeking or reported person in a subordinate role.

In the context of social work practice, everything can be sensitive due to this pattern of the distribution of power. At a meeting with the powerful and repressive state, a client may have reason to fear that everything he says or does can be held against him. What we social workers try to do is convince our clients that our main mission is not to be repressive, but helpful. As representatives of a welfare state with considerable resources, we definitely have the possibility to play a significant role in people's well-being. In this context, our authority can first and foremost be at our clients' disposal when it comes to matters such as providing counseling or furnishing them with financial support for realizing various needs. In most cases, it turns out well. In others it does not and we are turned away, left alone with our efforts to do good. From experiences like these I learned that power truly is relational. There I was with all the power the state had assigned me, and the presumed powerless client could just say 'no' to what I had to offer and I could do nothing. 'There are no relations of power without resistance', Foucault (1980) states – 'it exists all the more by being in the same place as power; hence like power, resistance is multiple and can be integrated in global strategies' (1980: 142). Foucault's insight can hardly be more clearly manifested than when the communication between social worker and client breaks down. However, as a young social worker, I struggled with the unequal distribution of power that permeates every part of social work practice. Little did I imagine at that time the even more complex kinds of power relations that characterize research on domestic violence.

Dealing with sensitive topics in narrative research

The research interview as a power relation

As a social worker, I became very well aware of the imbalance in power between my clients and myself. When I first reflected on the matter as a researcher on family violence, the case seemed to be quite the reverse: I was the dependent one. My informants were in the dominant position and I was the subordinate. I was the one who asked them for something that was valuable to me, i.e. their experiences. Later I came to understand that it was more complex than this. Since I as a researcher held a culturally highly valued position and they as battered women or abusive men were asked to tell me about self-experiences that were culturally of low value, our power relation was not as different from the one of social worker–client as I first thought. One woman vividly expressed her apprehension in seeing herself as culturally a woman of low value – as well as the reason for her evaluation:

> To think of yourself as a battered woman ... that is almost impossible. I feel so ashamed ... to me, a battered woman is an unloved woman. I think this is why a woman doesn't want to go to the grocery store with a black eye. She doesn't want people to think: 'See , there is a woman whose husband beats her'. It's simply a way to protect yourself.

> (Hydén, 1995: 131)

It was not the violence as such that placed her in a culturally low position but the message it carried: You are unloved.

Over and over, the battered women I have interviewed have taught me the significance of being involved in activities of culturally low value – even if you were forced into them, even if you were a victim of them:

> I don't like to talk about the fact that I have been beaten. You see, I haven't had a good childhood either. If you haven't had that, no one ever gives you a chance. I think one should look forward, but no one else seems to think so. If they find out that there is a lot of misery at

hand, they think they really know something about you. Just get down in all the old damned trash and stay there, that's what they want you to. I hate it when the decent and clever people feel sorry for you. They look as if no one has ever been awful to them. I can see immediately what they think: There's someone who is inferior to me.

(Hydén, 1995: 132)

These two women's words made a deep impression on me. I had a reason to recall them some years later when I was studying battered women's break-ups. My informants were a group of women I first met at the Women's Shelter in Stockholm, Sweden, and then on six separate occasions over a two-year period. I had reflected upon the fact that I as an academic researcher was probably quite highly ranked, and considered what this might mean in my encounters with these women. I had come to no significant conclusion, when one of the women approached me one day with some other women giggling behind her: 'May we ask you something?' 'Sure'. 'They say that you're divorced – is that true?' 'Yes it is'. This confirmation seemed to make everyone very happy! The giggling increased and I heard them say: 'So it's true that Margareta Hydén is divorced! Amazing! She seems so competent and clever, but she's also a failure when it comes to marriage! She's just like us!'

Over the years, I let the two women's words and similar words from other women encourage me to take my research in a direction that not many had taken before me. It occurred to me that I was in the danger zone of being just another person, luring the women to 'get down in all the old damned trash and stay there', or as bel hooks (1999) so vividly puts it, I was at risk 'of concealing the woman into her suffering'. In a series of articles (Hydén, 1999; 2005; forthcoming), I have traced the women's suffering as well as their strategies of resistance, including what I have called 'the process of leaving'. What is important in these studies, which include sensitive topics, is the focus on what has *not* been said and *why,* as well as on what *has* been said. The two women taught me that if interviews that include sensitive topics deal principally with 'damned old trash' they are potentially harmful, and a basic feature of the sensitive topic of being the victim of domestic violence, for example. strategies of resistance, is left out.

Circulation of narratives on sensitive topics as potentially harmful

Having reflected on the power relation that constitutes the interview setting, we must now consider the wider context of the interview and the power relations it carries. The aim of all research is to circulate its results to audiences often far from the interviewees, but it is important to remember that audiences close to them may also pay attention. In order to protect the interviewees, basic methodological and ethical codes require the alteration of names and other circumstances that may make identification possible. The circumstances of research results being circulated to an audience far 'out there' have been quite uncomplicated for most of my interviewees. In fact, it has been one of the main reasons for their participation. Like the man I interviewed in a study on abusive men and battered women put it: 'If you think someone else can be helped by what I have been through, that's good' (Hydén, 1994: 53). More problematic was the imaginable audience close to him, like the police. Most of the abusive men I interviewed were under investigation by the local police and wanted to know if they could under any circumstance demand access to my files.

Other researchers have had similar experiences. In her study of marital rape, Diana Russell (1990) found that many women were hesitant to disclose information to her for fear that their husbands might read her work. John Brewer (1993) received a positive response from the authorities, but a quite hostile response from his intended informants, when he implemented his ethnographic study of routine police work by the Royal Ulster Constabulary in East Belfast, Northern Ireland. The policemen and women were afraid that Brewer's writings could harm them, if used by the IRA or the authorities. Brewer concluded that 'the issue of sensitivity needs to emerge from the shadows and be recognized as an important problem in research, so that social researchers can give more attention to its negative effects' (Brewer, 1993: 143). Narratives are always open to reinterpretation. By passing them on to new audiences, we pave the way for possible new meanings – and as they are passed on, they make entrance into new power relations.

A tragic outcome of such a transference was related to me in a study I conducted, entitled 'To talk about sexual abuse and other difficult experiences', concerning the treatment of young girls in compulsory youth care. At the institution, there was a general agreement among the staff that if memories of sexual abuse were repressed and never came out into the open, the young women would become self-destructive and, for instance, injure themselves. Untold, the story was seen as dangerous in that although it was not verbalized, it was nevertheless presented in a fragmented form *inside* the young woman, casting her in her own eyes as someone repulsive and worthless, responsible for her own victimization. Consequently, the staff tried to trace signs of suspicious sexual abuse, thereafter allowing and encouraging talk about the sexual abuse. The main purpose of this was not to circulate the story – quite the contrary – it was told under professional secrecy. But the message was quite clear. Stories of sexual abuse must be told, or they will harm you. The following story demonstrates how problematic this message can be, due to the lack of control over the wider circulation of the story and the reinterpretations it may undergo. The teller is a female staff member at the institution:

> And she [a 15-year-old girl at the institution] said things like in the end she wanted to have a pregnancy test after she'd been at home. We knew she'd just been home with mum and dad and not gone out or anything. So it was … well it was like that.
>
> When she got home, her dad would send her mum out to walk the dog. And he'd take her down to the root cellar and abuse her sexually. So it was under pretty grotesque conditions you know. It had been going on for a number of years and all that kind of stuff, yeah, so I think …
>
> When she told and there was a trial and all that but then she got she got completely you know … disowned by her family, you know, her brothers and sisters refused to

have any contact and she ended up in the mental hospital. I think now she's committed suicide.

It's really difficult.

It's really difficult.

(Överlien and Hydén, 2003: 231)

What was supposed to be a healing narrative turned out to be a harmful one. It moved away from the closed space of the institution and reached the powerful space of the courtroom, was retold and reinterpreted and in its new form reached the private family sphere it once came from – in a different form. From the family's perspective, the narrative was never meant to leave the private sphere and be transformed in the courtroom.

Making space for sensitive topics

The very sad story about the young woman who committed suicide after disclosing her father's sexual abuse and being disowned by her family can serve as one of many illustrations in this chapter of the complex power relations in research on sensitive topics. It may also serve as an illustration of the second factor, that is, *space,* which in close relation to power, plays such a profound role in shaping research that includes sensitive topics. The story told in the courtroom is never the same as the one told in the family.

My second more comprehensive study on domestic violence concerned women who had left their violent husbands (e.g. Hydén, 1999; 2005; forthcoming). From that study, among other things, I learned the profound importance of space in narrative studies on sensitive topics.

Offering physical space

Generally speaking, breaking up is about difference and movement. When you break up, you stage discontinuity in time and location/physical space. You leave, you depart from something or someone. When a battered woman leaves her husband, she leaves their joint home. At the same time as she changes her *physical space*, she changes her *discursive space*. This self-inflicted disruption, this difference she has administered to herself, gives her an opportunity to (re)form her life history.

The Battered Women's Shelter in Stockholm, Sweden, is a special place in that it offers housing and support to women in exile after they leave abusive relationships. In doing so, it offers physical space for all kinds of practices aimed at liberating women from an oppressive man and a patriarchal society. In this, it also offers a discursive space for all kinds of conversations about what happened in the past and wishes for the future. For many women, their time at the shelter represents a turning point, well suited for reflection, creating an ideal space for research based on interviews.

The Youth Detention Home for Girls did not offer a similar ideal space. The girls were incarcerated in a disciplinary space and much of their energy was aimed at maintaining distance and acquiring some degree of freedom and control. In this setting I focused mainly on the staff, trying to understand how they attempted to create a space aimed at healing within the institution. However, something unexpected happened when my doctoral student, Carolina Överlien, and I had been present for some time; the girls became increasingly curious and irritated because we only paid attention to the staff and not to them. Basically, to meet their wishes, we decided to include them in the research. This idea was not met with much enthusiasm by the staff. 'It will fail', they said. 'The girls don't want to sit down and talk, and even if they want to, they are not able to – too vulnerable, in too bad shape physically. In addition, they may be very violent, there is a security issue involved here'. Since the girls had more or less asked to be involved I decided to go ahead, at the same time taking the staff's worries into account. What I was aiming for was to transfer the disciplinary space into a physically and discursively more open space, where stories could be elicited.

Offering discursive space

I planned a series of focus groups under the heading 'To be a young woman in Sweden'. I asked Carolina to be the leader and to choose stimulus material from journals about all kinds of pleasure and problems that might constitute a young Swedish woman's life. I instructed her to be very liberal when it came to attendance – if a girl wanted to leave the group and return, this would be all right.

I chose a group format because personal interviews, especially when it comes to sensitive topics, can be quite intrusive. I chose the overall topic for the focus groups relevant to the study, but it was still open enough for the girls to shape the conversations as they wished. I chose the liberal come-and-go rules to offer them an additional opportunity to shape the situation along their own lines. I did this for methodological reasons – without the creation of an open discursive space I was convinced that the girls would not have been able to talk; I did it for ethical reasons as well – I did not want to harm the girls, I wanted to give them a good experience.

Following these procedures, one of the things the girls liked to talk about concerned themselves as future mothers. There was an obvious rift here between the discourses of the girls and the staff; the latter drew on discourses about sexuality in their interviews, discourses that were problem-oriented and failed to recognize the young women as future mothers. Although the girls were placed in custody because of drug problems and crime, their case notes focused on identified 'problems' – in particular their experiences of sexual abuse. As the prevailing problem-oriented sexual abuse discourse did not regard women's sexuality as active and consensual, childbearing and motherhood were not discussed. Thus, the *risk* of pregnancy was discussed by the staff and treated as a problem with a solution; the staff administered birth control pills and condoms. In the focus group sessions, the question of childbearing and motherhood took up a considerable amount of time, since the girls wanted to discuss things like their emotional longing for children, what is needed to take care of them, and how to handle demands from children with their own wishes 'to explore life and have fun' – topics most young women are concerned with (Överlien and Hydén, 2004).

Offering discursive space by challenging the narrative performance
In my first study on domestic violence (see for example Hydén, 1994) I sometimes tried to open up a discursive space by challenging versions of the abuse story that I found too narrow, or too lacking in coherence and logic. In most cases I did this by quietly calling into question what had been said and suggesting further exploration. In some cases I did not act that quietly, but rather showed my non-acceptance in a more direct way. I must admit that when I first acted in this straightforward way, I had not devoted myself to much reflection on whether or not this was in accordance with my idea of the ideal interviewer I was very eager to become. My straightforwardness simply came to me after I had experienced an increased state of irritation at listening to the abusive men's stories that I came to think of in terms of 'rhetoric of exculpation or narratives of disclaimed actions' or, 'the story of how someone else beat my wife'. The storyline was something like 'My wife has been beaten (severely in most cases) and I am very sorry, but I cannot be responsible because …' One man often returned to his favorite story:

IP: You see, in our heads there is a place with two poles. There has to be a certain distance between them. When you get angry, you get close to one of the poles. In my head, the poles are too close together, so that when I get angry, they crash into each other. I can see on your face that you don't believe me, but it is in fact true. A doctor himself told me this. I think it was caused by a motorcycle accident I was in.
M: How can you tell when this happens?
IP: I simply have a total blackout. I get mad and then BANG, it crashes and I am not aware of anything for a long time. When I come to again, I have often done something violent. Hit Pia (his wife) or trashed the apartment.

Then I posed the question that made his story follow another direction:

M: Then it must be unbelievable luck that Pia is still alive.
IP: What do you mean?
M: I mean that when you get mad at her and it short-circuits in your head, your body takes on a life of its own and becomes violent. It's lucky that you haven't stuck the bread knife in her, or scissors, or hit her even worse than you have.
IP: Are you crazy or something??!! Do you really think I could do such a thing? I would never hurt her that bad. (Hydén, 1995: 58)

After he was confronted in this way, his account became more detailed. By challenging his narrative and drawing it to its extremes, I created the possibility for other narratives to be told about the violent events. These narratives were much more complex and also included his responsibility.

Offering discursive space by empowering the narrator

I cannot claim that my repertoire for opening discursive space is generally characterized by a confrontational style – quite the contrary. My years of studying sensitive topics have rather given me a constantly growing repertoire of ways to support and empower my interviewees – for methodological, ethical and humane reasons – and not challenge them. Presently, I am working on a study of children who have witnessed violence in their home. This study is one of the most difficult studies I have ever worked with, and has given me reason to further develop my repertoire of supportive attitudes. What these children are going through and the straightforward way they talk about it is very difficult to listen to. I chose 'empowerment' as my closing remark, not only because it is an important topic for the informants, but also because it is important for me and my fellow researchers who study sensitive topics. Studying sensitive topics is a relational state of affairs in more ways than one. It emotionally affects the informant as well as the researcher. They both need to be empowered from time to time, or they risk 'getting down in all the old damned trash and staying there'. My last example, taken from the study of children who have witnessed violence in their home, aims at illustrating how such an empowerment can be manifested.

The excerpt is taken from an interview with Christine. She is 15 years old and has experienced her stepfather's severe violence toward her mother and sometimes toward herself. She has had a hard time at school and has been bullied. These living conditions brought her to the brink of suicide, but she was saved at the last minute. She is very emotionally affected during the interview and I stop her at several points, asking her if it is OK, if she really wishes to continue, and she says she does. I become more and more worried, however, that she is 'getting down there' a bit too deep. So I decide to intervene and open the space for another story to be elicited, a story that might empower her a bit more:

M: Have you ever thought that there are other children who have been exposed to almost the same as you, do you know that?

C: Yes, it's a lot actually

M: Mmm

C: When I think of it … it's almost fun, that so many have the same problem, it's less lonesome

M: Just think of what a huge political party you and the others could start

C: Mmm

M: Then one becomes a bit happier

C: Then you think that you're not alone. When you're deep down there you think you're totally alone, but then … I wonder how many it actually is?

M: You can think of it when you take the bus from school

C: Today it was nice weather, I was thinking about that and was happy But when it snows or rains, I hate it

M: Next time it rains and you're on the bus, think of it then

C: (smiling) Yeah, and if you count every seat in the whole bus, I think it might be 15%

M: (smiling) Yeah, and then you can count the next bus, and the next and the next …

My intervention is quite powerful. I interrupt Christine's talk by introducing a new topic. The interruption is deliberate, as is the choice of topic. From several years of researching domestic violence I have learned that exposure to violence is embedded in feelings of vulnerability and powerlessness, due to the fact that neither the victim nor anyone else has been able to offer protection. The feelings of vulnerability and powerlessness are therefore closely linked to feelings of loneliness, which is further stressed because it is not culturally acceptable to be exposed to domestic violence.

What I acted on in the interview with Christine was my apprehension at her increasing vulnerability and suffering. I also understood her as someone who was not very good at taking care of herself and stopping before our conversation became too painful – and this for many reasons: she was young and inexperienced; she had not had much assistance during her childhood in supporting herself; she was very ambitious and wanted to give a good interview; and she had not had many encounters with people who truly wanted to listen to her, so she wanted to use this chance to talk. I acted because I wanted to save Christine from another painful experience. I decided to 'rewind the tape backward' and try to substitute loneliness with belongingness and thus provide her with the empowering strength that a group of people with similar experience have to offer each other. Christine's story illustrates how empowering a disruption of feelings of loneliness can be. The group of people she felt kinship with did not even have to be identified; the very notion of their existence was enough to give her – and me – strength and energy. The latter is not the least important to emphasize; for me, the content of what Christine had to tell me was difficult to listen to. I felt I somehow needed to compensate her for the obvious emotional strain I had caused her, and finding a way for her to tell new stories that brought new energy to her, and to me as well.

Conclusion

During the course of this chapter, I hope I have made my main point quite clear. There is no simple answer to the question 'What is a sensitive topic?' Consequently, my concluding remarks will not offer a definite summary and suggest that the work is finished and complete. Quite the contrary; I would like this conclusion to serve as an opening for others to enter into a dialogue on narrative research and sensitive topics.

I have emphasized that as in all relationships, the relation between teller and listener in narrative research is a power relation. This feature appears particularly distinctly when sensitive topics are involved. Throughout my research, I have dealt with the sometimes extreme incongruence between a victimized and vulnerable woman and myself, a female, well-off, academic researcher. I have not tried to hide the obvious, but have rather stressed the *similarities* as well as the *differences* between us. In the divorce example the similarity between myself and the women at the Battered Women's Shelter was emphasized – although I had not been exposed to violence, we were 'all failures when it came to marriage'. In the example of the young Christine the differences between us were emphasized. I used my experience and authority to introduce a new topic.

Throughout this chapter I have argued that what is a sensitive topic and what is not is mainly dependent on relational circumstances, that is, it has to do with the relationship between the teller and the listener as well as the personal, cultural and contextual circumstances of that relationship. My opening story aimed to illustrate the different values of what is sensitive and what is not that two young women of almost the same age living in the same city can hold, basically because of different personal experiences and different interpretations of cultural norms. The story also illustrated the significance of contextual circumstances for narrative on sensitive topics to evolve. The shimmering heat of the urban Swedish high summer and the isolation at the place emptied for the holiday season, hosted the encounter between the two young women who embraced a great number of 'sensitive topics' in their conversations.

Different physical spaces offer different discursive spaces. What could not be said at a battered woman's home could be said at the Battered Women's Shelter, and vice versa. What could not be said in the family could be said in the courtroom, and vice versa. I call upon the narrative researcher's interest for further examination of the relational aspects of their work, especially when it includes sensitive issues.

Note

1   All names have been altered for reasons of anonymity.

Suggestions for further reading

- For a review of definitions of narrative and the criteria for what can be seen as 'good enough' narrative research in social work, we recommend Riessman, C.K. (2005) Narrative in social work. *Qualitative Social Work* 4(4): 391–412.
- Students who wish to clarify and grasp the understanding of the interview as culturally and contextually grounded discourse between speakers are advised to start with *Research Interviewing: Context and Narrative,* by E. Mishler (1986).
- For a good and thorough discussion of sensitive subjects and research, see Lee (1993).

References

Brewer, J. (1993) Sensitivity as a problem in field research: A study of routine policing in Northern Ireland. In M. Renzetti and R. Lee (eds) (1993) *Researching Sensitive Topics.* Newbury Park: Sage.

Bruner, J. (1990) *Acts of Meaning.* Cambridge, MA: Harvard University Press.

Denzin, N. and Lincoln, Y. (eds) (2005) *The Sage Handbook of Qualitative Research.* Thousand Oaks, CA: Sage.

Foucault, M. (1980) Power and strategies. In Gordon Collin (ed.) *Power/Knowledge: Selected interviews and other writings 1972–1977 by Michel Foucault.* London: Harvester Wheatsheaf.

Gubrium, J. and Holstein, J. (eds) (2002) *Handbook of Interview Research: Context and Method.* Thousand Oaks, CA: Sage.

hooks, b. (1999) *Remembered Rapture. the Writer at Work.* New York: Henry Holt.

Hydén, M. (1994) *Woman Battering as Marital Act: The Construction of a Violent Marriage.* Oslo: Scandinavian University Press.

Hydén, M. (1995) *Kvinnomisshandel inom äktenskapet. Mellan det omöjliga och det möjliga.* Stockholm: Liber.

Hydén, M. (1999) The world of the fearful: battered women's narratives of leaving abusive husbands. *Feminism & Psychology* 9(4): 449–69.

Hydén, M. (2005) 'I must have been an idiot to let it go on': Agency and positioning in battered women's narratives of leaving. *Feminism & Psychology* 15(2): 169–88.

Hydén, M. (forthcoming) Break up narratives. In L-C Hydén and J. Brockmeier (eds) *Health, Illness and Culture: Broken Narratives.* New York: Routledge.

Jamieson, L. (1988) *Intimacy: Personal Relationships in Modern Societies.* Cambridge: Polity Press.

Johnson, J. (2002) In-depth interviewing. In J. Gubrium and J. Holstein (eds) *Handbook of Interview Research: Context and Method.* Thousand Oaks, CA: Sage.

Mishler, E. (1984) *The Discourse of Medicine: Dialectics of Medical Interviews.* Norwood, NJ: Ablex.

Mishler, E. (1986) *Research Interviewing: Context and Narrative.* Cambridge, MA: Harvard University Press.

Renzetti, M. and Lee, R. (eds) (1993) *Researching Sensitive Topics.* Newbury Park: Sage.

Riessman, C. (2002). Analysis of Personal Narratives. In J. Gubrium and J. Holstein (eds) *Handbook of Interview Research: Context and Method.* Thousand Oaks, CA: Sage.

Riessman, C.K. (2005) Narrative in Social Work. *Qualitative Social Work* 4(4): 391–412.

Russell, D. (1990) *Rape in Marriage.* New York: Macmillan.

Överlien, C. and Hydén, M. (2003) Work identity at stake: the power of sexual abuse: Stories in the world of compulsory youth care. *Narrative Inquiry* 13(1): 217–42.

Överlien, C. and Hydén, M. (2004) 'You want to have done your living if you know what I mean': Young incarcerated Swedish women speak about motherhood. *Feminism and Psychology* 14(2): 226–30.

Chapter 8

The public life of narratives: Ethics, politics, methods

Paul Gready

Self narration offers what Isabel Hofmeyr calls 'transitory forms of power' (1988: 4); it allows the narrator to relive, control, transform, (re-) imagine events, to reclaim and construct chosen identities, social interactions and communities. Enormous expectations are placed on testimony, both oral and written, in the contexts of political resistance and transition. From truth commissions, to the courtroom, to trauma counseling, to collaborative narratives such as *testimonio* – all of which are considered as forms of narrative in this chapter – these potentials are often seen as empowering, cathartic, as heralding the arrival of a new 'regime of truth' (Foucault, 1991: 73). The purpose of this chapter is to ask some questions about the ethical, political and methodological implications for narrative and narration when they take place in or enter public fora and an increasingly globalized public sphere: what happens when testimony, often initially embedded in relationships of immediacy and even intimacy, goes public and global?

A number of themes raised in earlier chapters of the book – including the exploration of narratives as co-constructed within research and audience–response relationships, and narratives as structures of power, forged at the interface with a variety of external contexts – are revisited. The particular issue addressed in what follows has both a broad context and a more proximate set of implications. Contextually, narrative in the form of first person testimony has become central to new forms of activism, politics and history-making from below. Such trends have been driven by the media and information technology. A rapidly changing context of testimonial circulation means that at a more proximate level our modes of self-reflection and behaviour as researchers or activists also have to adjust to an altered environment, over which we often have incomplete control. Questions about the relationship between the articulation of voice and representation, or the ownership and control of testimony, need to be re-visited. This chapter examines certain ethical, political and methodological challenges facing narrative work entering a brave new world, now often spanning the intimate, interpersonal and the abstract, global.

Ownership and control

The argument put forward in this chapter is that the marginalized and subaltern increasingly have a voice, but little or no control over representation, interpretation and dissemination (Spivak, 1988). To speak or be spoken for is not a one-off event but a process spanning various narrations, interpretations and reinterpretations, the telling and the representation and reception of the telling. The highly selective nature of this process, or why some testimonies get taken up and resonate publicly and others do not, is also an issue with profound political and ethical dimensions. Testimony is spoken, written, translated into visual images by the media; moves between the private and the public, memory and history, the personal and the political; between south and north, and different cultures; between an original context of performance and subsequent (re-) performances. In this movement across and between, testimony retains the highly suggestive capacity to be in both places at once.

> Testimony is where the public and the secret ... intersect. To be immersed in testimony means to reside in both places at once – navigating by two sets of landmarks, trying to fathom two sets of codes, and two different, but interconnected, cultures.

> (Feitlowitz, 1998: 16)

It is in part these journeys, simultaneities and translations in an emerging global public sphere that make public testimony so suggestive and complex.

But there is a price to pay too. A central concern in the discussion that follows is who owns and controls testimony within the increasingly globalized public sphere. This is a common problem, posing challenges for research and advocacy undertaken by individuals, organizations or official institutions. The 1990s saw the interconnected rise of globalization, human rights and testimony or personal narrative, and specifically such narratives as a potent vehicle for advancing global human rights claims (Schaffer and Smith, 2004). A tension between the global and the local is often now manifest in the circulations and uses of narrative. One example will suffice. Keck and Sikkink in the context of the work of transnational advocacy networks and particularly the mobilizing potential of testimony, write:

> Information flows in advocacy networks provide not only facts but testimony – stories told by people whose lives have been affected. Moreover, activists interpret facts and testimony, usually framing issues simply, in terms of right and wrong, because their purpose is to persuade people and stimulate them to act ... however, we have to recognize the mediations involved ... [t]here is frequently a huge gap between the story's original telling and the retellings – in its sociocultural context, its instrumental meaning, and even its language. Local people, in other words, sometimes lose control over their stories in a transnational campaign. How this process of mediation/translation occurs is a particularly interesting facet of network politics. (1998: 19)

The issues of ownership and control of testimony in a globalized public sphere raise important ethical, political and methodological questions that need to be addressed by academics and activists alike. 'Transcription, translation, entextualization, interpretation, analysis, dissemination … As scholars, we need to develop a critical ethical theory of risk and vulnerability in relation to subjectivities forged in and inhabiting globalized linguistic forms' (Ross, 2003c: 337).

What follows looks at the work of and research on the South African Truth and Reconciliation Commission (TRC) as a case study of the challenges posed by the public life of testimony.[1] An examination of problematic aspects of institutional practice and narrative circulation is followed by an exploration of some of the ways in which individuals and organizations in South Africa are reclaiming control and ownership over their own life stories, and of some possible components of methodological ethics and politics for contemporary testimonial practice. This chapter draws on my own research in South Africa on the TRC, and material from the forthcoming book is called *Aftermaths: Truth, Justice and Reconciliation in Post Apartheid South Africa*. What this case study confirms is that: 'The right to narration is not merely the right to tell one's story, it is the right to control representation' (Slaughter, 1997: 430).

Problems[2]

Alex Boraine, deputy chairperson of the TRC, has described the victims' hearings of the South African TRC as a 'liberated zone' (2000: 99). Although this is not an uncontested framing of the hearings, it provides a useful way of distinguishing between the locations of testimonial delivery and subsequent circulation. Several circulatory problems will be detailed briefly below: hearability or narrative inequality; the reification of victimhood; women's experience reduced to sexual abuse; disseminatory patterns in communities and national politics; and narrative appropriation by the media, academics and others.

One problem arose from what Blommaert et al. (2000) describe as 'narrative inequality and the problem of hearability' with regard to the public victim hearings. Echoing Boraine, these authors depict the hearings as spaces of intended equality, 'a format of power and prestige [was] offered to the powerless' (5), while acknowledging that '[p]eople don't enter the public forum as equals' (2–3). Inherited, structural inequalities percolated into the hearings. Impacting on the who, what and how of 'hearability' were factors such as the testifier's communicative skills, understandings of and ability to adapt to the requirements of the hearings (logical consistency, linearity), and awareness of the immediate and more distant audiences. These relate to what Young (2002: 53–7) calls internal rather than external patterns of exclusion from political discussion and decision-making. Among the commentaries Blommaert et al. provide on these inequalities are commissioner elicitation and co-authorship as an attempt to bridge the communicative divide and improve the discursive 'fit', and the clash of discourses in the testimony of Colin de Souza[3] that, despite commissioner interventions, stressed resistance rather than suffering. The issue of 'hearability', or '([h]ow) can the subaltern be heard?' augments questions about whether the subaltern has a voice and control over representation, interpretation and dissemination both within the TRC and beyond: 'The challenge … is for the privileged audience to hear the subaltern without duplicating a hegemony which renders the marginalized speechless yet again' (Libin, 2003: 124, 126).

Other concerns also emerged from within the immediate contexts of institutional narration and documentation. Ross (2003a, 2003b), for example, details how, the TRC circumscribed and misrepresented the lives and concerns of women. In particular, she argues that the emergence of 'women' as a category in the Commission's work carried with it assumptions about the nature and severity of particular harms, notably privileging sexual violence while silencing other kinds of experience:

> diverse identities, activities and experiences were obscured through the emphasis on sexual difference and harm. The result is an overemphasis on the similarity of bodily experience at the expense of an understanding of the subjectivities produced through apartheid and resistance to it.

> (Ross, 2003b: 175)

Yvonne Khutwane's[4] experience (Ross, 2003a: 80–93) exemplifies these patterns, demonstrating 'the elicitation, condensation and crystallization of testi-monies in circulation' (93). Khutwane was the first woman to include a description of sexual violation in her public testimony. During her testimony at the victim hearings in Worcester in the Western Cape during June 1996 she spoke about her experience of abuse, including solitary confinement, torture, sexual molestation and the petrol bombing of her house and alienation by her political community due to rumours that she was an informer. Sexual violation in the form narrated at the hearing was not part of Khutwane's written statement (in which a threat of rape was mentioned, not actual sexual molestation), and despite her reticence at the hearing the new revelations were both solicited and returned to by the persistent interventions of Human Rights Violations Committee member and psychologist, Pumla Gobodo-Madikizela (see Gobodo-Madikizela, 2003: 90–4). In the end, one third of the time was taken up by questions and answers about an event of sexual violation that Khutwane had not intended to narrate. In the collaborative testimonial narration, media reports, the TRC report (in four separate entries) and academic studies, sexual violence is represented as the primary violation. The narrative Khutwane wanted to tell was thus displaced; certain kinds of violence and her political activism were downplayed as she was reduced to a victim of sexual abuse.

Reification of victimhood could also be a characteristic of reception in the media and academic commentaries. In one of the three Blommaert et al. (2000) commentaries cited above, de Souza, having resisted the imposition of victimhood at the hearing, is reinscribed as victim as the authors read for the 'deeply hidden transcript' of suffering and victimhood, arguing that this is its 'real' nature. While de Souza clearly suffered, and the reading is subtle, de Souza himself sought to frame his life as one of struggle and resistance. Surely this self-framing is what the TRC should have been about? If he did not see himself as a victim should others seek to so label him? In my own research, reacting against the reification of suffering and victimhood I found myself privileging agency and resistance – but this of course is simply another form of selective listening and rendering the marginalized speechless. People may not see themselves as victims/survivors or heroes; resistance comes in many guises. Experience and identities are nuanced, changing over time, often directly influenced by narrative episodes.

TRC testimony also inserted itself into, and became the subject of debate and contestation within, national and community politics. Truth claims accepted in one site can be questioned elsewhere. The concerns of the TRC were not necessarily those of other constituencies, as illustrated by the reception of Khutwane's testimony in her home community, Zwelethemba. The reception of Khutwane's testimony included public responses to her account of sexual violation – 'I didn't know it would be like this' she comments (Ross, 2003a: 86) – but also discussion and disputes about the political strand of her narrative, specifically allegations of betrayal and the arson attack on her home as issues germane to local politics (93–102). Within the community the story, locally embedded and interpreted, provides a commentary on a complex intersection of personal and political concerns: the late 1980s political repression and the deep damage done by real and rumoured informing; political cleavages and fragility within the community, including Khutwane's affair with the ex-boyfriend of a powerful female comrade; and intergenerational tensions with activist youths. The politics of the past continues to shape the present, resulting in the reassertion of a broader political agenda in relation to testimonial interpretation in this context. As Ross suggests (100–2), the reassessments of testimony in different locations and over time, 'the contingency of interpretation and the unevenness of reception', matter in relation to claims that truth produces healing and reconciliation.

Elsewhere, and I would suggest more frequently, the problem was that the TRC's work and testimony failed to resonate within communities. I have followed a post-TRC victim–offender mediation intervention by the Centre for the Study of Violence and Reconciliation (CSVR). I attended a mediation involving the Bonteheuwel Military Wing (BMW), and more specifically the allegation that one member (W) was an informer who had been a state witness against another member (S) in a court case; S had subsequently attacked and attempted to kill W. While members of the BMW approached the TRC – 12 statements were made to the TRC by BMW members – much was left unresolved. Both W and S made victim/survivor statements to the TRC; S testified at a victims' hearing and applied for amnesty, and apologized, for the attack on W. And yet the TRC failed to resolve the relational rift, and more generally only scratched the surface of complex, community specific dynamics. In this case, personal testimony in the context of a restorative justice intervention and face-to-face meeting augmented the work of the TRC.

Testimony also circulated beyond communities in the broader public sphere. Here, as well as needing to revisit inequality and hearability ('celebrity victims') and the imposition and adoption of victim status as almost a condition of hearability in the transitional era, a range of new concerns arise. One such concern is the commercialization of testimony, by both testifiers themselves and others. I can recount a personal experience in this regard. In early 2005 I sought to meet a victim/survivor I had first interviewed in 1998, to see whether her reflections on the TRC had changed over time. My first port of call was my intermediary and translator in Cape Town. We had worked together before, and he readily agreed to try and set up the interviews. He joked that people were charging now for interviews – people's lives had not changed, they were tired of telling their stories – but did not specify what the fee might be. Shortly thereafter, he texted me saying that the prospective interviewee wanted a fee of R2,000 (£200) for a one-hour interview; his fee would have been extra. The figures I had envisaged were nothing like as much as this. I contacted him and said that I would not pay such a sum and he then asked me to propose a fee, in effect to bargain over the price. At this point I withdrew from the discussions feeling thoroughly compromised. Was this the right thing to do? Later discussions with support group members about this incident indicated that they were against such high fees being paid to select individuals, preferring a policy of more modest amounts being paid to organizational support structures.

Yazir Henri's[5] experience with the TRC and beyond offers a final set of insights into testimonial circulations in the public sphere. He has stated that the opportunity to testify before the TRC provided a previously lacking space to speak out in his own voice, to tell his story and officially reappear, to confront his past and reclaim his dignity. Reasserting his solidarity with the struggle, he contested a narrative of betrayal, contextualizing his story within layers of compromise and complicity: 'I have a question: where does culpability rest? ... I wish to be recognized for who and what I am so that the falsification of my history be rectified'.[6] To speak, while itself not uncomplicated, was on balance a positive experience. Beyond the public hearing, and in a manner that can be said to be characteristic of the TRC's charismatic narrators, Henri's story ceased to be his, took on a life of its own as it was variously appropriated, edited, (re-)interpreted, retold, sold by others (the media, individual commentators [Krog, 1998: 50–5], the TRC report [1998 Vol. 3: 458–9]) in a way that impacted profoundly on his life.

> Since testifying ... I have been called many names, placed within several stories, given several histories and the most harmful of narratives ... have now become a part of my public face ... the agonized confessor ... the betrayer ...
>
> (Henri, 2003: 266)

Henri has written: 'At the time of my testimony I had no idea what the consequences of "public" could have meant in the context of public hearings' (2003: 266). His attempt to reclaim and recontextualize himself and his voice were undermined by public processes of dissemination and commentary. For the speaker, a violation of the narrative became a violation of the self. Ross asks: 'If selfhood and "story" come to be experienced as congruent ... then what happens to the sense of self when "experience" is traced through the processes of entextualization in which "testimony" becomes "text" and is re-embedded in diverse products?' (2003c: 333). While, of course, outcomes of such processes can be both positive (fresh perspectives, deeper understandings) as well as negative, a prevailing complaint is that of appropriation (the de Souza case is an example of both). It must also be noted that Henri is unusual in that he both testified before the TRC and, as indicated above, subsequently produced commentary on his testimony and its public life.

In circulations and appropriations expanding outwards into the global public sphere TRC testimonies were de/recontextualized in arenas ranging from written texts to community politics. Initial and intended sites of delivery, objectives, audiences and importantly, benefits, could be effectively erased (or augmented). Facilitating linkages between truth, dignity, healing and reconciliation requires greater control for the testifier in the realms of representation, interpretation and dissemination.

Responses

One outcome of these problems of testimonial reception is that some victims and survivors in South Africa reinhabit a narrative space all too reminiscent of the past, characterized by a sense of disempowerment, a loss of agency, re-traumatization, a distrust of research relationships lacking reciprocity, and a reluctance to retell stories that appear to benefit others while their lives remain unchanged. Appropriation has not, however, been a one-way process. The struggle to establish control over narrated and lived life continues, but elsewhere. This section reflects a shift in my own research, as I was challenged on whether I was myself not part of the problem, from an exclusive focus on eliciting testimony to an additional examination of subaltern methods.

Shirley Gunn, a former member of Umkhonto we Sizwe and now Director of the Human Rights Media Centre (HRMC) in Cape Town, uses the terms 'plundering' and 'rape' to describe the testimonial research attention and processes around the TRC South Africa – she also testified before the TRC and her story acquired a high public profile.[7] The HRMC uses forms such as books of collected interviews, exhibitions and films, advocating a distinctive ethics, politics and methodology. Projects have included the film *We Never Give Up*, made with the Western Cape branch of the Khulumani Support Group as part of the reparations campaign. This was followed by an exhibition of memory and healing work entitled 'Breaking the Silence: *A luta continua*', again involving Khulumani members and including scrapbooks and body maps as autobiographical forms. When work enters the public sphere under the HRMC's auspices, participation and consultation underpin interview/transcript finalization, product choices, editing and consent and release agreements.

Further, the Centre offers oral history and media training, and has so far trained 28 people from 17 organizations. Training includes the development of skills in areas such as oral history interviewing and the rights of subjects, research methodology and ethics, computing and media training, and encompasses radio, film and print dissemination. Instructively, a guide for practitioners on how to do oral history projects covers three phases: pre-production, production and post-production.[8] Thembi Mgonjeni (telephone interview: 29 April 2005), formerly of the HIV/AIDS social movement, Treatment Action Campaign (TAC), who participated in an HRMC training programme credited an increased use of oral histories in the TAC newsletter, and more ethically sensitive practice, to the training. In short, the HRMC seeks to enable people and organizations to take ownership of their stories – 'there is a lot of power in that, it is often all people have got' – in an attempt to free them from the agendas of outsiders.

The District Six Museum provides a second, less directly TRC-inspired, example of alternative and innovative research practice. District Six was a diverse, inner-city community in Cape Town which was subject to forced removal under apartheid. It now houses a museum, opened officially in 1994, that while in some ways set in deliberate contrast to the TRC's spectacle and concerns (for example it addresses forced removals and structural violence), is also influenced by the TRC-informed discourse of the era (linking truth-telling to reconciliation).[9] Its former Director, Valmont Layne's characterization of the role of the museum – in the service of a social cause (land restitution and the return of former residents to the area, social justice in the city); collecting 'exchanges, dialogues, narratives'; insider oral history telling an unfinished story, rather than seeking a linear narrative or to close off discussion – is an important starting point for understanding its life history work.

Stories, the location of people in relationships, time and place, are inscribed in diverse ways and through methodologies and aesthetics that are accessible, interactive and participatory. Exhibits have been designed to become generators of cycles of telling. Launching the museum, the exhibit *Streets: Retracing District Six* (1994) encouraged visitor inscription of fragments of personal pasts onto a hand painted map of District Six on the museum floor and into a name cloth, now embroidered and several kilometres long. Such history-making, often in itself an act of reclamation and return (the marking of a residential address and former home; the identification of neighbours) is not fixed by official commissions or academics but continually forged by visitors, and in particular by ex-residents and those subject to forced removals:

> An essential concern …is to open up opportunities for individuals in different arenas of life to move beyond the boundaries where *others* write their histories for them and instead *themselves* interpret their own experiences … *Streets: Retracing District Six* acknowledges the crucial role many individuals have played in being the guardians and interpreters of their own historical experience, and the material selected for the exhibition honours this role.
>
> (Delport, 2001: 43)

A second major exhibition in 2000, *Digging Deeper* (*deeper* implying other places of removal, to interior and private spaces, into personal self-reflection and examination, beyond the comfortable and familiar) uses the concept of the 'memory room' (Layne and Rassool, 2001). Such rooms use recorded voice to provided insights into working class lived experience (for example in Nomvuyo's room) and offer access to a memory room for the sound archive ('a place where the individual is encouraged to take on a confessional mode, to be vulnerable in a secure environment': Layne and Rassool, 2001: 152). As part of a broader strategy to challenge hierarchical relationships of knowledge and research (oral/written, public history/the academy), and echoing the Delport quotation above, 'the erstwhile "informant" becomes simultaneously subject and author of oral history, and researchers or public scholars in their own right' (2001: 149). Voices are heard on their own terms, rather than being subordinated to writing or to the agendas of others. Residues of these exhibitions remain as the museum has begun to develop its own layered archaeology of lives told, and methods and forms used. One outcome is a set of very diverse archives of testimony, voice, music and photography.

Methodologically, the museum foregrounds community-based research and forging relationships. 'Guerrilla tactics', quick in and out raids by external researchers, are not supported, and researchers seeking to access people through the museum have to commit to a process of at least six weeks to two months. Insider oral history raises methodological issues beyond on what terms to let outsiders in, such as when not to record compromising or embarrassing information. It easily blurs conversation/interview boundaries, and given the community setting, inappropriate material, from personal gossip to questioning the status of people as claimants in the restitution programme, is edited out of public transcripts. Again, Bennett notes that 'people do not know what moving from the private to the public means'.

As a form of commentary and political intervention, those who testified before the TRC or whose work was more indirectly affected by its aura, have entered the debate about research ethics and dissemination. Theirs is a subaltern method to complement the subaltern voice. In conclusion: when placed alongside one another, what do the problems raised by the TRC's testimonial practice and responses to them reveal about desirable institutional and individual researcher methods?

Methods

This chapter concludes by suggesting some signposts towards an alternative methodology, returning to the challenge of ownership and control in the global public sphere.

First, a broad range of local and international actors and fora must retain the capacity for analysis; such processes are an important safeguard against relativism. So many voices and a self-consciousness about which voices are listened to and privileged – yes; an absence of analysis and judgement – no. Here two distinctions are important. There is a difference, although clearly not an absolute one, between life story interviews/testimony that need to be respected as such, and event or issue driven interviews/testimony in which moments in a given life are of relevance to the extent that they converge with the event/issue in question, and this is made clear to the interviewee. The latter can be dissected as the prioritization of event/issue over individual life story has been made clear. There is also a crucial, related, distinction between using a text, which appropriates it to an agenda other than its author's, and interpreting it, which must respect its and its author's origins and intentions (see Eco, 1992: 68–9). The right to analyse and even criticize testimony and truths of all kinds can be combined with the right of each individual to tell his/her story in his/her own way and have the story retold in a way that respects its origins and intentions. If only life were always this simple! People do not always conceptualize their stories in neat categories, or want to tell the story you as a researcher want to hear – in my experience, a question about an event may elicit a life story. In terms of representation, however, I have found that self-recognition, which can take various forms, is often more important than a slavish adherence to full narration.

Further, research on testimony requires a sensitivity to testimonial journeys, translations and afterlives within the public sphere. An appropriate methodology needs increasingly to anticipate and communicate to all relevant parties both the reality and the unpredictability of the globalized public sphere, and discuss the possibility of the re-performance and reinterpretation of testimony as process breaching private/public and personal/political/community boundaries.

Research relationships based on collaboration or partnership and researcher reflexivity are also necessary. This approach would privilege giving process the same priority as product(s) beyond the moment of narration, and the spotlight of urgency, into subsequent analysis, documentations and disseminations. In my research I have engaged with the projects discussed in the *Responses* section several times, over a number of years and shared and discussed my research (including this chapter) with relevant personnel wherever possible. One practical means of implementing this agenda, is as part of agreeing the research 'contract' to negotiate the degree of control the interviewee has over the final results, on a continuum from no control (no sight of transcripts or control over published results) to commentary on the accuracy of the interview transcript, commentary on analyses and interpretations of their interviews, and commentary on research findings for publication (Miller, 2000: 83–5). The continuum marks a shift in participant role from source to analyst. There are a range of research methodologies – various collaborative arrangements, new forms of information ownership, action research, research for empowerment (Krulfeld and MacDonald, 1998; Smyth and Robinson, 2001) – that speak to this agenda, but difficult issues remain. For example, what is the degree of interviewee ownership (commentary or control? veto power? co-authorship? a share of royalties?). I have incorporated into this chapter suggestions made by participants, but ownership remained at the level of commentary.

Conclusion

From both local South African responses to the TRC and these methodological discussions a basic set of parameters for research emerges.

- Victims and survivors should sign a **research contract** that clearly specifies an agreement reached over the degree of control they have over their testimony and its proposed uses. Attempts should be made to enable the participant to shift along the continuum from source to analyst. Beyond this setting, control is more difficult to determine for either party. This too should be acknowledged.
- A range of **written documents** and **new representational forms** can be used to engage with research constituencies and build research capacity. Writing styles can be used that register differences of opinion and areas of debate.
- **Self-recognition**, for participants, is possible to achieve through naming, quotations, and longer narrations of life experiences in various research products.
- The **co-production of knowledge** and **development of local capacities for history-making** are more difficult. Using and training local interviewers and translators, as well as reporting back and discussing research processes, interpretations and findings, would be a positive starting-point.

However, I would argue that to place the emphasis solely on research strategies and power dynamics is to misidentify the problem. Control is situated not only, perhaps not even mainly, within immediate hierarchies of research and knowledge production and control (oral/written, public history/academy, interviewee/interviewer), but also within hierarchies of global dissemination over which neither the researcher, whether working as an individual or institutionally embedded, nor the researched, have very much control. Voice can no longer, if it ever really could, be considered a simplistic form of power. The struggle now is less over the articulation of the marginalized and subaltern voice than for greater control over voice, representation, interpretation and dissemination. Voice without control may be worse than silence; voice with control has the capacity to become a less perishable form of power because in essence it allows voice to enter into a more genuinely reciprocal dialogue. Such dialogue could provide a more enduring challenge to the power relations of research, knowledge production and the public sphere. To create the conditions for dialogue therefore implies a research agenda that both revisits research methods and ethics, but also unmasks and challenges the inequalities of the global public sphere.

Notes

1   Established by the Promotion of National Unity and Reconciliation Act of 1995, the TRC was an innovative mechanism, often characterized as a middle road between mass prosecutions and amnesia/impunity, designed to address the gross violations of human rights committed under apartheid. It had three committees, on amnesty (administering a conditional, individualized amnesty procedure), on human rights violations (which gave victims a platform to tell their stories) and on reparation and rehabilitation (to make recommendations to the government on these issues).
2   The discussion that follows under the subheadings 'problems', 'responses' and 'methods' owes a substantial debt to Fiona Ross (2003a, 2003b, 2003c, 2005). In relation to the TRC, it is Ross who has written most perceptively about the issues raised here, and many of the debates and examples featured overlap with those in her work.
3   De Souza was a member of Umkhonto we Sizwe, the military wing of the African National Congress (ANC), and the Bonteheuwel Military Wing, a group from an area north of

Cape Town with unclear and contested links to more formal oppositional groups such as the ANC.

4   Khutwane is a veteran political activist for the ANC.

5   Henri was a member of Umkhonto we Sizwe, and is now Director of the Direct Action Centre for Peace and Memory.

6   This reference is from the testimony of Yazir Henri to the TRC's Human Rights Violations Committee on 6 August 1996. The testimony is available on the TRC's website (http://www.doj.gov.za/trc/).

7   This section of the chapter is based on interviews conducted by the author with Shirley Gunn in Cape Town on 27 August 2002 and 5 April 2005.

8   *Three Phases of a Life History Project: A Model Developed by the Human Rights Media Centre*, November 2004 (unpublished document on file with the author).

9   This discussion is based in part on interviews with Valmont Layne, then Director of District Six Museum (8 April 2005) and Bonita Bennett, then Head of the Collections and Research Department (12 April 2005).

Suggestions for further reading

* The best book I know on the global circulation of human rights testimony is Schaffer and Smith (2004); also see Keck and Sikkink (1998). An emblematic case study is the Menchú-Stoll controversy (Arias, 2001; Menchú, 1984; Stoll, 1999).

* The kinds of methodologies advocated here are often traced to Paulo Freire's work on education (1970) and Augusto Boal's writings on theatre (1979). For other practical applications of relevant methodologies, see Chambers on Participatory Rural Appraisal (1994) and Penal Reform International's action research programme monitoring the gacaca courts set up in Rwanda to try to help process the enormous numbers of people held in connection with the 1994 genocide < http://www.penalreform.org/interim/>.

* There is little written on truth commission research methodologies. In relation to the TRC it has been argued that testimony was deconstructed and reduced to 'data' for the report: see Buur (2001, 2002) and Wilson (2001: 33–61). More generally on quantitative methodologies within truth commissions, see Ball et al. (2000) and Landman (2006: 107–25). More work needs to be done on how such commissions can sensitively handle and reproduce qualitative data. While the kinds of methodologies advocated here are difficult to institutionalize, there are case studies which illustrate that more can be done by large-scale human rights projects to sensitize their methodologies. In Guatemala, the unofficial Recovery of Historical Memory Project (REMHI), initiated by the Human Rights Office of the Archbishop of Guatemala in 1995, trained local people and facilitated a community statement taking process. In a context of widespread illiteracy, diverse media were used to disseminate the REMHI's work and report – theatre, radio, videos, public workshops, educational materials, rituals and ceremonies. Teams, based on the network of interviewers, worked on popularizing the report. Reflecting a research process driven by civil society, and concerned with participation, consultation and accessibility, Beristain, a member of the REMHI project team, describes it as a social movement seeking 'social reconstruction' and the return of memory to the communities (Beristain, 1998a, 1998b).

References

Arias, A. (ed.) (2001) *The Rigoberta Menchú Controversy*. Minneapolis, MN: University of Minnesota Press.

Ball, P., Spirer, H. and Spirer, L. (eds) (2000) *Making the Case: Investigating Large Scale Human Rights Violations using Information Systems and Data Analysis*. Washington, DC: American Association for the Advancement of Science.

Beristain, C.M. (1998a) The value of memory. *Forced Migration Review*, 2: 24–6.

Beristain, C.M. (1998b) Guatemala: *Nunca Más*. *Forced Migration Review*, 3: 23–6.

Blommaert, J., Bock, M. and McCormick, K. (2000) Narrative inequality and the problem of hearability in the TRC hearings. Gent: Working Papers on Language, Power and Identity No. 8.

Boal, A. (1979) *Theater of the Oppressed*. London: Pluto Press.

Boraine, A. (2000) *A Country Unmasked: Inside South Africa's Truth and Reconciliation Commission*. Oxford: Oxford University Press.

Buur, L. (2001) The South African Truth and Reconciliation Commission: A technique of nation-state formation. In T. Hansen and F. Stepputat (eds) *States of Imagination: Ethnographic Explorations of the Postcolonial State*. Durham: Duke University Press.

Burr, L. (2002) Monumental historical memory: Managing truth in the everyday work of the South African Truth and Reconciliation Commission. In D. Posel and G. Simpson (eds) *Commissioning the Past: Understanding South Africa's Truth and Reconciliation Commission*. Johannesburg: Witwatersrand University Press.

Chambers, R. (1994) The origins and practice of Participatory Rural Appraisal. *World Development* 22(7): 953–69.

Delport, P. (2001) Signposts for retrieval: A visual framework for enabling memory of place and time. In C. Rassool and S. Prosalendis (eds) *Recalling Community in Cape Town: Creating and Curating the District Six Museum*. Cape Town: District Six Museum.

Eco, U., with Rorty, R., Culler, J. and Brooke-Rose, C. (1992) *Interpretation and Overinterpretation*. S. Collini (ed.) Cambridge: Cambridge University Press.

Feitlowitz, M. (1998) *A Lexicon of Terror: Argentina and the Legacies of Torture*. Oxford: Oxford University Press.

Foucault, M. (1991) Truth and power. In P. Rabinow (ed.) *The Foucault Reader: An Introduction to Foucault's Thought*. London: Penguin.

Freire, P. (1970) *Pedagogy of the Oppressed*. London: Penguin.

Gobodo-Madikizela, P. (2003) *A Human Being Died that Night: A Story of Forgiveness*. Cape Town: David Philip.

Henri, Y. (2003) Reconciling reconciliation: A personal and public journey of testifying before the South African Truth and Reconciliation Commission. In P. Gready (ed.) *Political Transition: Politics and Cultures*. London: Pluto Press.

Hofmeyr, I. (1988) Introduction: Exploring experiential testimony – a selection of History Workshop papers. *Social Dynamics*, 14(2): 1–5.

Keck, M. and Sikkink, K. (1998) *Activists Beyond Borders: Advocacy Networks in International Politics*. Ithaca, NY: Cornell University Press.

Krog, A. (1998) *Country of My Skull*. Johannesburg: Random House.

Krulfeld, R. and MacDonald, J. (eds.) (1998) *Power, Ethics, and Human Rights: Anthropological Studies of Refugee Research and Action*. Lanham, MD: Rowman and Littlefield.

Landman, T. (2006) *Studying Human Rights*. London: Routledge.

Layne, V. and Rassool, C. (2001) Memory rooms: Oral history in the District Six Museum. In C. Rassool and S. Prosalendis (eds) *Recalling Community in Cape Town: Creating and Curating the District Six Museum*. Cape Town: District Six Museum.

Libin, M. (2003) Can the subaltern be heard? Response and responsibility in South Africa's Human Spirit. *Textual Practice* 17(1): 119–40.

Menchú, R. (1984) *I, Rigoberta Menchú: An Indian Woman in Guatemala*. Edited and introduced by Elizabeth Burgos-Debray; translated by Ann Wright. London: Verso.

Miller, R. (2000) *Researching Life Stories and Family Histories*. London: Sage Publications.

Ross, F. (2003a) *Bearing Witness: Women and the Truth and Reconciliation Commission in South Africa*. London: Pluto Press.

Ross, F. (2003b). The construction of voice and identity in the South African Truth and Reconciliation Commission. In P. Gready (ed.) *Political Transition: Politics and Cultures*. London: Pluto Press.

Ross, F. (2003c) On having voice and being heard: Some after-effects of testifying before the South African Truth and Reconciliation Commission. *Anthropological Theory* 3(3): 325–41.

Ross, F. (2005) Codes and dignity: Thinking about ethics in relation to research on violence. *Anthropology Southern Africa*.

Schaffer, K. and Smith, S. (2004) *Human Rights and Narrated Lives: The Ethics of Recognition*. New York: Palgrave Macmillan.

Slaughter, J. (1997) A question of narration: The voice in international human rights law. *Human Rights Quarterly* 19: 406–30.

Smyth, M. and Robinson, G. (eds) (2001) *Researching Violently Divided Societies: Ethical and Methodological Issues*. Tokyo; London: United Nations University Press/Pluto Press.

Spivak, G. (1988) Can the subaltern speak? In C. Nelson and L. Grossberg (eds) *Marxism and the Interpretation of Culture*. Chicago: University of Illinois Press.

Stoll, D. (1999) *Rigoberta Menchú and the Story of all Poor Guatemalans*. Boulder, CO: Westview Press.

Truth and Reconciliation Commission (TRC) (1998) *Truth and Reconciliation Commission of South Africa Report*. Volumes 1–5. Cape Town: Juta Press.

Young, I. (2002) *Inclusion and Democracy*. Oxford: Oxford University Press.

Wilson, R. (2001) *The Politics of Truth and Reconciliation in South Africa: Legitimizing the Post-apartheid State*. Cambridge: Cambridge University Press.

Concluding comments

Catherine Kohler Riessman

The editors of this volume invited me to contribute a conclusion to their book, a great honor. What follows is a little different than they requested, some observations and questions related to my understanding of their objective. The goal of the book was to illustrate applications of different methodological perspectives that fall under the broad rubric of narrative research. To focus on methodological aspects – *doing* the work rather than abstractly theorizing about narrative – inevitably invites us to think about interviewing practices, analytic methods, writing and dissemination.

As the editors note in the Introduction, the field of narrative studies is multivocal, cross disciplinary, and extremely diverse theoretically and methodologically – a real strength. The contributors have mapped a good portion of the diversity, although some omissions remain (noted below). I think of narrative analysis as a 'family' of analytic approaches to texts, only some of which take the traditional storied form. As in all families, there is conflict and disagreement among those holding different theoretical perspectives. Analysis of data is only one component of the broader field of narrative inquiry, a way of conducting case-centered research (Mishler, 1996).

The editors intend the book for students embarking on research careers. With this audience in mind, I draw some lines of contrast among the papers related to three questions I think are essential for investigators to consider; (see Riessman, 2007, for more on the questions and some applications). I hope students will interrogate the papers and their own projects in relation to the three questions.

First, how is the idea of narrative employed in a research project? Where in the broad range of definitions discussed in the Introduction is a particular piece of research located? Several chapters argue for key features that distinguish narrative (sequence, contingency, change through time, etc.), while others adopt commonsense understandings of the term. Phil Salmon and I argue for some boundaries in our chapter, a theme others pick up in theirs. Several contributors resist the limited definition from social linguistics, arguing instead for the inclusion of habitual and imaginary experience, as well as autobiographical accounts of entire lives. The breadth of applications of the narrative concept gives students freedom at the same time as it invites contemplation about where in the broad spectrum their research will be positioned. I urge students to resist the loose talk about narrative that is common these days. The term has come to mean anything beyond a few bullet points; when someone speaks or writes more than a few lines, the outcome is now called narrative by news anchors and even some qualitative investigators. Narrative runs the danger in this usage of becoming little more than a metaphor. Particularity – lives located in specific times and places – tends to get lost with such broad application. The contributors to this volume embrace a diversity of definitions while also holding to core components.

Related to the definitional question is kind of data. The majority of contributors to this volume examined spoken (first person) stories of experience, mirroring the pattern in the field of narrative research in general. Even here, however, investigators worked with an unusually wide range of empirical materials: brief bounded segments of research interviews and ongoing conversations (Patterson, Phoenix, Hydén); extended accounts and life stories collected in community and institutional settings (Squire, Andrews); and first person testimonies before truth commissions and other governmental bodies (Gready). Tamboukou's research departs from the pattern with her archival study of documents and other written autobiographical materials. Life writing in all its forms (biography, autobiography, memoir, diaries and journals and blogs) constitutes a growing area in narrative research. Here, of course, the written word replaces the spoken word but reliance on textual accounts remains, hinting at an untapped resource for future scholars.

Visual materials call for careful narrative study, and methodological guidance is available (Knowles and Sweetman, 2004; Pink, 2004; Rose, 2001). Some paintings and photographs tell stories, although not with clear beginnings or endings. An image depicts a moment, inviting us to speculate about what will happen next, or what transpired to bring the scene about. But some artists produce sequences of images that draw us into events and lives unfolding in particular times and places (the series of 60 paintings of Jacob Lawrence come to mind, which sequence the great migration of African Americans from the south to the north). Photographers and other visual artists sequence images in ways that invite narrative inquiry (see Bell, 2002; Radley and Bell, 2007). Then there are images produced with investigators in participatory research projects, where images are interrogated collaboratively by image-maker and researcher (Luttrell, 2003; Lykes, 1991). Although collaborative work and visual projects were not included in the volume, they represent a logical extension of perspectives that are included.

My second question for students returns to the typical data that researchers interrogate – oral and written accounts. To what degree does an investigation attend to narrative features? The Introduction observed that attention to language and form – the building blocks of narrative – is rare in the field outside of the social linguistics tradition. The editors caution against a 'fetishisation of narrative language in social research' at the same time as they do support a 'slower and more attentive reading of narrative language'. I find it curious that so few narrative scholars attend to language and form, given that narrative study originated in drama; ever since Aristotle literary scholars have drawn attention to *how* a story is composed, including the rhetorical devices employed. Squire does identify particular genres in the oral stories of South African HIV survivors, and how they resonate with broader cultural narratives in the region, but otherwise attention to language and form is largely missing from the papers. There are many ways to narrate an experience; how a speaker, writer or visual artist chooses to do it is significant, suggesting lines of inquiry that can be missed without focused inquiry.

Rita Charon (2006), writing from her dual position as physician/literary scholar, emphasizes the need for 'close reading' of texts:

> The kind of reading taught in graduate programs in literature in which the reader … pays attention not only to the words and the plot but to all aspects of the literary apparatus of a text … [including] ambiguity, irony, paradox, and 'tone' contained within the words themselves … [Recent literary criticism interrogates] those texts historically, politically, semiotically, economically, in terms of gender or sexuality or colonial status … [grounding] their critique in their own close readings of texts. What texts 'do', we all ultimately realize, they do in the resonance achieved between the words themselves and the worlds that surround them, elicit them, and are reflected and transformed by them. (2006: 113)

Narrative texts that social scientists collect require a similar level of close reading. As visual methods of data gathering are adopted to a greater degree (e.g. videotaping), researchers can interrogate paralinguistic features of communication as well, such as gaze and body positioning (for examples, see Mishler, 2004; Örulv and Hydén, 2006; Young, 2000).

My third and last question concerns the importance of context in the interpretive process. Exactly what constitutes context, as Phoenix notes, is subject to considerable debate. But extending the observations of Rita Charon (above), how do narrative analysts take into consideration the 'worlds' that surround a narrative text? Here I think the contributions to the volume are particularly strong, albeit in very different ways. All agree with Mishler's (1986) paradigmatic formulation of the interview as a conversation during which the parties engage in ongoing negotiation of meaning. Several authors focus on this local context: the interview itself or, put differently, the relational world telling and listening (Patterson, Phoenix, Hydén). Patterson correctly notes that the work of Labov, which was a watershed in the history of narrative research in the social sciences, implicitly approached stories as self-contained monologues with recurrent formal features, not influenced by the listener/questioner. Ironically, his interviewing team purposefully included black researchers 'who knew the culture of the inner city as full participants' (Labov, 1972: xiv). Yet the subtle ways they co-constructed stories with African American youth are ignored. Phoenix's contribution to the present volume illustrates how central the research relationship can be: racial and other commonalities shape how a story is told and heard. Hydén extends this line of argument with her years of experience in social work where, among other roles, she aided women in shelters as they struggled to leave violent marriages. Although the focus of her paper is on 'sensitive' topics (a topic she turns on its head), the data extracts vivify the importance of skilled interviewing.

We see, too, how different physical spaces can open up (or close down) discursive spaces.

Other papers in the collection dwell on broader contexts, and draw connections between 'personal' stories and social worlds. We may think that we are writing our private thoughts in a letter to a friend, but Tamboukou shows how power and space function in the construction of women subjectivities and the stories they develop in private correspondence. In the genealogical method she describes, interrogating minor textual detail – a hallmark of narrative research – uncovers contradictions and gaps. In Gready's paper where audience is dispersed and anonymous, personal experience gets severed from the context of production. As difficult moments of testimony before truth commissions begin to assume a public life, they are appropriated by powerful others for their ends, commercialized perhaps, and in other ways meanings are wrested from the control of narrators. Gready challenges us with his research materials to confront fundamental ethical questions in our own work, and search for ways to return authority to narrators. He proposes alternative history-making projects that take the form of exhibits and community-based research, where speakers can retain control over how their experiences are represented – a hallmark of the kinds of collaborative narrative projects cited above.

An often neglected aspect of context is identified by Andrews: our imprint as investigators on the narratives we collect and interpret. Andrews recontextualizes the work she did earlier in her career, providing a twist on the idea of the revisit (Burawoy, 2003). Our analytic stories are never fixed; meanings can shift with developments in methods, in our lives and social worlds. In my foray into the terrain that Andrews explores (see Riessman, 2002, 2004, 2005), I was inspired by Barbara Myerhoff's early 'conversion to reflexivity' (see Myerhoff and Ruby, 1992). Prescient comments about work she did in the 1970s in an essay published posthumously anticipate (and caution against) developments that were to follow among some anthropologists and sociologists, where 'the self' of the ethnographer becomes the center of the work. Andrews charts the preferred course that Myerhoff advocates; she includes relevant aspects of her biography without losing sight of the 'Other'. Her elegant and personal writing style also calls up Myerhoff's observation: 'It is difficult to express your self-awareness and reflexiveness to others without employing some first-person narrative' (1992: 322). To write a scholarly paper in the first person was more unusual in Myerhoff's time. Now we can and do use the rhetorical form, illustrated in many papers in this volume. Perhaps this is the best evidence of the narrative turn in contemporary social research.

In sum, the book will aid students at many levels. The contributors demonstrate that no story speaks for itself but instead requires interrogation and contextualization. As the Introduction notes, the narrative form is a universal form of human sense making. Individuals interpret events and experiences in the stories they construct collaboratively with listeners. As investigators we, in turn, interpret their interpretations, constructing analytic stories from (and ideally with) those we study. I hope the three broad questions I have posed about the 'theoretical bricolage' of narrative research will help future investigators think about their own work. Ours is a field characterized by extreme diversity and complexity. There is no single way to do narrative research, just as there is no single definition of narrative.

References

Bell, S.E. (2002) Photo images: Jo spence's narratives of living with illness. *health: An Interdisciplinary Journal for the Social Study of Health, Illness and Medicine* 6(1): 5–30.

Burawoy, M. (2003) Revisits: An outline of a theory of reflexive ethnography. *American Sociological Review* 68: 645–79.

Charon, R. (2006) *Narrative Medicine: Honoring the Stories of Illness.* New York: Oxford University Press.

Knowles, C. and Sweetman, P. (eds) (2004) *Picturing the Social Landscape: Visual Methods and the Sociological Imagination.* London and NY: Routledge.

Labov, W. (1972) *Language in the Inner City: Studies in the black English Venacular.* Philadelphia, PA: University of Pennsylvania Press.

Luttrell, W. (2003) *Pregnant Bodies, Fertile Minds: Gender, Race and the Schooling of Pregnant Teens.* New York: Routledge.

Lykes, M.B. (1991) Creative arts and photography in participatory action research in Guatemala. In P. Reason and H. Bradbury (eds) *Handbook of Action Research.* Thousand Oaks, CA: Sage.

Mishler, E.G. (1986) *Research Interviewing: Context and Narrative.* Cambridge: Harvard University Press.

Mishler, E.G. (1996) Missing persons: Recovering developmental stories/histories. In R. Jessor, A. Colby and R. A. Shweder (eds) *Ethnography and Human Development: Context and Meaning in Social Inquiry.* Chicago: University of Chicago.

Mishler, E.G. (2004) Historians of the self: Restorying lives, revising identities. *Research in Human Development* 1(1–2): 101–21.

Myerhoff, B. and Ruby, J. (1992) A crack in the mirror: Reflexive perspectives in anthropology. In B. Myerhoff, with D. Metzger, J. Ruby and V. Tufte (eds) *Remembered Lives: The Work of Ritual, Storytelling, and Growing Older.* Ann Arbor: University of Michigan Press.

Örulv, L. and Hydén, L.C. (2006) Confabulation: Sense-making, Self-marking and World-making in Dementia. *Discourse Studies* 8(5): 647–73.

Pink, S. (2004) Visual methods. In C. Seale, G. Gobo, J. F. Gubrium and D. Silverman (eds) *Qualitative Research Practice.* London: Sage.

Radley, A. and Bell, S.E. (2007) Artworks, collective experience and claims for social justice: The case of women living with breast cancer. *Sociology of Health & Illness* 29(3): 366–90.

Riessman, C.K. (2002) Doing justice: Positioning the interpreter in narrative work. In W. Patterson (ed.) *Strategic Narrative: New Perspectives on the Power of Personal and Cultural Storytelling.* Lanham, MD: Lexington Books.

Riessman, C.K. (2004) A thrice told tale: New readings of an old story. In B. B. Hurwitz, T. Greenhalgh and V. Skultans (eds) *Narrative Research in Health and Illness.* London: British Medical Journal Books/Blackwell.

Riessman, C.K. (2005) Exporting ethics: A narrative about narrative research in South India. *health: An Interdisciplinary Journal for the Social Study of Health, Illness and Medicine* 9(4): 473–90.

Riessman, C.K. (2007) *Narrative Methods for the Human Sciences*. Thousand Oaks, CA: Sage Publications.

Rose, G. (2001) *Visual Methodologies: An Introduction to the Interpretation of Visual Materials*. Thousand Oaks, CA: Sage.

Young, K. (2000) Gesture and the phenomenology of emotion in narrative. *Semiotica* 131(1/2): 79–112.

Index